Man's Dominion

Man's

The Story of

drawings by John Pimlott

Dominion

Conservation in America

By Frank Graham, Jr.

Published by M. Evans and Company, Inc. New York,
and distributed in association with
J. B. Lippincott Company, Philadelphia and New York

Thanks are due to the Boone and Crockett Club for permission to quote
from the George Bird Grinnell letter which appeared in CRUSADE FOR WILDLIFE
by James B. Trefethen, published by Stackpole Books in 1961.

32985

Contents

FOREWORD   vii

PREFACE   xi

Part 1   In Search of Guy Bradley

   1   *The Land*   3
   2   *Ship's Log*   8
   3   *The Age of Extermination*   14
   4   *A Sense of Loss*   29
   5   *Beginnings*   33
   6   *The Feather Trade*   45
   7   *To Oyster Key*   54

Part 2   The President and the Forester

   8   *Straws in the Wind*   65
   9   *Yellowstone*   76
  10   *The Lines are Drawn*   86

11   *The Road to the White House*   100
12   *The Presidency*   105
13   *The Second Term*   123

Part 3   The Fight for the Land

14   *Ballinger*   139
15   *Hetch Hetchy*   151
16   *Steve Mather and the National Parks*   168

Part 4   The Fight for Wildlife

17   *Hornaday*   179
18   *Milestones*   189
19   *War*   200
20   *Dead Ducks and Brickbats*   207

Part 5   God's Plenty, and What Became of It

21   *A Little Black Bag*   227
22   *TVA*   240
23   *Geological Suicide*   252
24   *Of Muskrats and Birdwatchers*   268

Part 6   The Spirit and the Flesh

25   *The Spirit*   289
26   *The Flesh*   310
     A NOTE ON THE SOURCES   319
     INDEX   325

Foreword

By Elvis J. Stahr, President
The National Audubon Society

Earth Day, 1970, symbolized the opening of the "Environmental Decade." Increasingly aware of the planet's degradation, man hereafter would dutifully address himself to the difficult task of restoring some semblance of environmental health. Brave words were spoken, some faltering steps were taken. Relieved editorial writers welcomed the arrival of the "new conservation."

But the very adjective "new" implies the existence of conservation as a more or less workable concept prior to the recent general awakening. The public, indeed, had been vaguely aware of such a movement. But I think that replies to the question of what it was all about might have ranged from the notion that conservation had something to do with saving "dickey-birds" from the claws of marauding cats, to the similarly vague notion that it was concerned solely with fattening ducks as fodder for sportsmen's shotguns. It is no wonder that, in their comparative obscurity, long-time conservationists often felt as if they were a part of an underground (and somewhat subversive) movement.

Yesterday's conservationists generally came to their calling from a specialized point of view. Personal survival was not an issue. Mankind's future, even that of life itself, did not seem to be at stake. In the past, men became conservationists to save a threatened natural resource. Perhaps it was a resource of great commercial value, actual or potential, such as petroleum deposits, a prime hydroelectric site, or the nation's shrinking woodlands. More often the resource was a thing of less tangible value—a lovely canyon, a swift trout stream, a wilderness tract, even a species of wild

vii

creature. Beginning with a single specialized interest, these men and women came to appreciate the beauty and the value of other parts of the natural world.

It has been said that there are bound to be conflicts between the "new conservationists" (many of them concerned almost exclusively with the impact *on the human animal* of air pollution, pesticides, and runaway junkheaps) and the breed whose allegiance is to the older conservation organizations. And no doubt this is true. But part of the value of Frank Graham's book is that he makes plain the divisions (and the reasons for them) that existed in the past among conservationists. The fiercest struggles have not always broken out between the conserver and the exploiter; there has been a great deal of intramural squabbling and figurative headbreaking within the movement itself.

It is a function of history to shed light on the past, and thus render the present more intelligible. This, I think, Frank Graham has done in *Man's Dominion.* He shows us men of good will in action, men whose vision was sometimes obscured by their own passions or special interests, but who came to see what seemed special to them at first, later appeared in its true light as just a single strand in the immensely complex natural world. Revelations such as this brought the fragmented movement together in times of past crises, and will do so again in the years ahead.

And the story, as Frank Graham tells it, is all of a piece. For instance, the arguments that split men of good will during the Hetch Hetchy controversy before World War I reappeared recently in the controversy over whether to flood thousands of wilderness acres in northern Maine in order to build the Dickey-Lincoln Dam. The issue of private power versus public power obscures conservation questions and impels men who ordinarily fight shoulder to shoulder to turn on each other with a vengeance.

Frank Graham begins his story in the Everglades of the 1880's. At the National Audubon Society we are acutely conscious that battles once considered over and won keep bobbing up repeatedly in brand new guises. On assuming the leadership of the Society in late 1968 I received a prompt baptism of fire in the struggle to prevent the construction of a mammoth commercial jetport at the gateway to the Everglades. I called together the leaders of five other conservation organizations, and we decided to band into a coalition and invite others to join us in a coordinated, intense campaign. If we had not won, the Everglades as we know it would have been doomed—and with it those magnificent "plume birds" that are the central figures in Frank Graham's opening chapters. I must add that the future of the Everglades is still not secure, for major problems of water supply, both quantitative and qualitative, remain. Indeed, some of those who didn't want the superjetport to be anywhere else still harbor hopes of winning in the end, I'm told. But these problems are soluble and the "Everglades Coalition" of some two dozen conservation and allied organizations is continuing in being in order to try to force wise and effective solutions. The chances of full success are infinitely greater, I think, because of the nationwide concern generated—and exploited—by the Coalition's jetport fight.

Man's Dominion provides the colorful and occasionally violent background for the grim mission all of us have embarked on in the "Environmental Decade."

Preface

This book tells the story of the conservation movement from the middle 1880s (when a few troubled men and women began to organize against the unrestricted exploitation of America's wild lands and creatures) until the passage of the Wilderness Act in 1964. A final chapter comments on the "new conservation."

I am writing for the non-specialist reader who, in hopes of guidance or merely to satisfy curiosity, wants to know the origins of today's conservation battles. I have told the story where possible through the words and deeds of the crusaders themselves, leaving the documents for the specialists. For those who want to probe deeper into specific areas I have included a section of "References," where I list the books and other sources that I relied on most heavily.

A history of conservation necessarily deals with more than the crusade against exploiters. There must be room for that appropriately bitter struggle within the movement itself between the "users" and the "savers." It will be apparent to the reader where my sympathies lie, as my story goes into some detail on the men and women who believed there is a value, beyond dollars and cents, that we can put on the natural world. Thus the utilitarians may condemn me for skimping on the triumphs of dam-builders and petroleum geologists. In general I have left it to the reader to supply any moral he does not find baldly stated in the events themselves.

I would like to thank the dedicated librarians who were so helpful to me while I was writing this book, especially Robert C. Woodward of the Bangor Public Library, Bangor, Maine, and J. Elizabeth Yee of the U. S. Department of the Interior Library, Washington, D.C. Special thanks go also to Mrs. Annette Stanwood of Milbridge, Maine, who typed the entire manuscript. Finally, I want to acknowledge the immeasurable contribution, from moral support to hard labor, that my wife, Ada, made toward the completion of this book.

FRANK GRAHAM, JR.

Part One

In Search of Guy Bradley

The Land

Some travelers insist that the broad watery canvas of the Everglades is best apprehended from the air: compact bayheads of subtropical trees rise from their settings in the sawgrass prairie like dark exotic jewels. Blanched streaks mark the paths gouged across the prairie's underlying muck by speeding airboats. At times the sweep of sawgrass masks the wide shallow river that is the Everglades' substance, but inevitably the flow reveals itself again in glistening ribbons winding among the mangrove jungles where land grades imperceptibly into sea. Beyond land's end a galaxy of tiny islands stretches southeastward toward the Florida Keys. A land so flat and featureless, some say, must be seen not as a profile but as a pattern.

But this land's uniqueness is not geologic. America is the continent of geologic marvels, of course—mountains, canyons, geysers, waterfalls, rock-ribbed coasts, sand dunes, badlands, caverns, glaciers, and all of the other phenomena created by nature working through wind and water and volcanic upheaval. We have set them aside as national treasures to be preserved and wondered at (or sometimes as curious gimcracks to be gawked at and plundered).

The Everglades comprises a different kind of wonder—life itself. From the air one sees a complex pattern of foliage and water, but

3

it is only on penetrating the stuff of the pattern that one confronts the most incredibly various array of life on this continent. Plants of temperate and subtropic zones meet and mingle. Here among the foliage and muck the animal kingdom displays itself in every shading of beauty and ferocity. Graceful wading birds, all elegant plumage and elongation, share the watery places with drabber ducks and sandpipers. Bald eagles perch in dying trees. In varying numbers there are deer, otters, manatees (or sea cows), black bears (that staple of our National Parks), tarpon, butterflies, bobcats, panthers, alligators, crocodiles, rattlesnakes, and (most ferocious of all) swarms of mosquitoes.

The Everglades, it seems to me, is the right place to begin an account of the conservation movement in America. For one thing, I count myself among those who believe that this is the jewel in the crown of our national park system. For another, the excess of slaughter that was carried out in this wild tip of the Florida peninsula at the turn of the century touched something vital in America's conscience. The leveling of our forests, the decimation of the buffalo herds, and the fraudulent land grabs all played a part in turning the public's attitude around. But no aspect of the plunder made such a vivid impression on so many people as the crimes of the Florida plume hunters.

Because the Everglades' essence is biological rather than geological it is the most fragile of our parks. Here the defects in man's dominion over his planet, and the creatures he shares it with, are dramatized and magnified. It is one thing to rob the Everglades of its most breathtaking spectacle—the flights of its "plume birds." It is quite another to strike at the base of all its life by diverting for one scheme or another (cropland drainage, jetports, etc.) that flow of water which moves south with almost glacial imperceptibility from Lake Okeechobee. Even the systematic slaughter of its alligators for their valuable hides sets in motion ripples of unsuspected destination. "The ugly wildlife manager," as one scientist has called the alligator, left to its own devices, provides sustenance for other creatures during the long dry seasons.

"The seasonal cycle of rising and falling water is the dominant fact in the lives of all the animals of the Everglades," writes park biologist William B. Robertson, Jr. "In this ecological drama the alligator often plays a role as the natural hydraulic engineer, much as the beaver does on mountain streams. Big alligators frequently

John Pimlott

dig ponds at low places in the Glades and return to these private retreats each dry season, deepening and enlarging the pond as the years pass. Such ponds, called 'gator holes, provide places where marsh snails, frogs, and fish can survive the dry months to repopulate the Glades when summer rains come and the water rises again."

Poachers, slipping into the park by night, have taken an enormous toll of the big reptiles. Increasingly the 'gator holes, deprived of their tutelary spirits, have dried up. With them have disappeared the small life of the ponds, and finally the larger birds and animals that came there to feed on them. Alligators are not simply an attraction in the Everglades; they keep the whole marvelous machine in working order.

Men have always appeared in moments of gravest crisis to speak up for the Everglades and its creatures. At some point the destroyers (poachers, road builders, chambers of commerce, real estate operators, the U. S. Army Corps of Engineers) have had to contend with these brave men. The name of one of their number keeps recurring in accounts of the conservation movement. He lies buried at the tip of that harsh and lovely land, killed by the destroyers, yet also a symbol of an enduring struggle.

Guy Bradley, the Audubon warden, generally comes alive for us only at the moment of his death. But I wondered if there might be an earlier glimpse of him that would set the stage for the great drama of the conservation movement, a glimpse that would fix him among the horizons and life of the land where he died. On a visit to the library at Everglades National Park headquarters I came upon the young Guy Bradley unexpectedly. I found him, as one might detect the dim face of a friend in an old group photograph, moving a little wanly with gun and boat through the opening pages of an obscure ship's log. Aside from his colds and stomach upsets and other adolescent ills, he plays no greater part in this early story than the birds and animals he hunted, but perhaps in the wild setting of nineteenth-century southern Florida that is as it should be.

At any rate Bradley left no written record of himself, and it is on the log of his boyhood chum, Charles Pierce, that we must depend.*

---

*Charles William Pierce, "The Cruise of the *Bonton*," in *Tequesta,* the Journal of the Historical Association of Southern Florida, No. XXII, 1962.

Ship's Log

"After a late getup this morning, and a later breakfast, we went back to the rookery for more plumes. Guy was feeling so much better he also took a hand in the shooting. I was sitting in the bushes waiting for the birds to come, when one settled in the bush not more than ten feet above me, it stretched its neck to get a better look at me, I shot at the neck and cut it clean off, the head fell in the mud at my feet. Louie killed eleven birds, Guy killed eight, and I killed nineteen. It took us all the rest of the day to prepare the skins and dry them. We would like to stay here until we have killed all the birds, but I have promised to be back at Wagner's at the end of five days."

So wrote Charles William Pierce in the log of a unique cruise to the wildest places of southern Florida in a 28-foot sloop, the *Bonton,* during the spring and summer of 1885. It was the sort of adventure that gilds the daydreams of adolescent boys. Indeed, Huck Finn would have found it a satisfying sequel to his own mythical voyage down the great Mississippi.

For this was a boy's adventure, literally the fulfillment of Pierce's old daydream, and yet inevitably it was played out with enthusiasm in the spirit of the most destructive time in American history.

Pierce was then twenty years old. His father, a former Maine seaman and whaler, recently had been appointed keeper of the Biscayne House of Refuge for shipwrecked sailors at Miami. Pierce's dream was presented to him in the form of the *Bonton* by an uncle, who, busied elsewhere, had designated him its caretaker.

At this time a Frenchman named Chevalier roamed the coasts of southern Florida, collecting bird skins for both "science" and the millinery trade. His chief targets were the "plume birds:" the herons, egrets, and other birds whose plumes were widely used in the manufacture of women's hats. He and his assistants had established an earlier base at Boca Ciega Bay near Tampa, where it took them, one traveler to the area said, "five breeding seasons to break up, by killing and frightening the birds away, this once incomparable breeding resort" of plume birds.

Chevalier' or "the old Frenchman," as Florida natives called him, apparently had lived in this country long enough to appreciate the advantages of acquiring a monopoly. Rival hunters who tried to avail themselves of the flourishing supply of herons and other birds were ordered off the rookery. It is possible that Chevalier's reputation as an "eccentric" arose from his inability to handle the English language with the colloquial expertise of the local Crackers.

When he had cleaned out the rookery at Boca Ciega Bay, Chevalier moved to Florida's Atlantic coast, where he stayed for a while with a man named Wagner on the Miami River. An injury, and not a scarcity of birds, had kept him out of the field during the winter of 1884–85. Chevalier had managed to shoot himself through the right hand, blowing away part of the hand and two fingers. Now he was learning to shoot again, propping the gun on his right elbow to fire. One day he met the elder Pierce in Miami and inquired about chartering a boat to take him on another plume-hunting expedition. Pierce mentioned his son's *Bonton,* and the deal was settled.

Charles Pierce, observant and curious, kept a log of the expedition. Although his excitement shines through the recitation of the names and numbers of the birds they killed, the log's interest is scientific and historical, rather than literary. (Pierce, like many of his neighbors, never received formal schooling but was taught at home by his mother.) His observations of birds and their nesting places reinforce those of contemporary naturalists. His account of Chevalier and his activities fills an important gap in Florida's ornithological history. Finally, his fortunate inclusion of Guy Bradley in the hunting party ironically presents conservationists with an early glimpse of the man who, twenty years later, gave his life to protect the rookeries.

Guy and Louie Bradley had been Pierce's friends when he was their neighbor in Lake Worth. When they joined Pierce on the *Bonton* in the early spring of 1885, Guy was only sixteen years old, Louie not yet twenty.

"I do not expect to get home before the last of summer," Pierce wrote. "Mr. Chevalier is a naturalist and we are going on a bird-collecting trip. Pelican skins are the main object of the trip, plumes next, also cormorant skins, in fact all kinds of birds. Mr. Chevalier has a market for all of them in Paris. He gets fifty cents for the pelican skins, twenty-five cents for sea swallows or the least tern, $10 for great white heron, and $25 for flamingo skins. Great white herons are scarce, and flamingos more so. If it was not for that we would soon make the old man rich."

Before picking up Chevalier at his temporary home on the Miami River, Pierce and the Bradleys set out on a short trip of their own into the Everglades. Leaving the *Bonton* behind, they nosed their small boats through channels occasionally choked by floating islands of rotting lily roots. They made their way by following old Indian burns that marked a path through the endless wastes of sawgrass. And everywhere they saw rookeries or gathering places of the great wading birds whose plumes were prized in millinery shops around the world.

"About noon we come to a fine nesting place, or in other words, a series of nesting places," Pierce wrote. "There were four or five islands well filled with birds and nests, in fact more birds than we had yet seen this year. We poled up to the nearest island, and as usual all the birds flew away. We hid in the bushes waiting for them to return, but they would not come. They appeared to know we stood there ready to shoot them. I suggested that Guy take the boats away about a quarter of a mile, saying, 'I do not believe the birds can count, and will think we have left the island, and will then return to their nests.'

"Sure enough, as soon as Guy was a good distance away with the boats, here they came back, and what was strange, they did not appear to be frightened but very little by the noise of the guns. When we shot they would fly away a short distance and immediately return. Louie killed seven and I killed nine."

After the killing there was the less heady chore of skinning the birds. For Pierce and the Bradleys this was a procedure demanding more skill than the simple slit down the birds' back used by many plume hunters to peel off the feathers on the back and tail. "The old Frenchman," who sold some of the skins as scientific specimens, set high standards.

"The way Mr. Chevalier wanted us to do was this," Pierce wrote. "Commence about halfway up the neck and skin down to the tail, taking all the skin off the body, and out to the first joint of the wing, then rub the skin with corn meal and stretch them with small sticks until dry. The skins would dry in a few minutes, but it took much longer to prepare them than our way, which was to skin the back where the plume was only, and let it lie in the sun without stretching until dry. In fact our old way was after the Indians' manner of scalping a man to a certain extent."

Pierce recalled an evening when, just as they were finishing supper, two ibises flew over their camp, their long necks and arched bills pointed like graceful prows toward the setting sun.

"They were out of reach of our guns," he wrote, "so all we could do was to admire their beauty and watch them go."

It was a vision that was to remain with at least one of the boys. As we trace the destruction that engulfed America's wildness we will rediscover Guy Bradley, now a man, his destiny locked into the violent drama that the bird protection movement became, pitting his backwoods' skills and new commitment against the "old Frenchman's" successors in the Everglades. Bradley's skills and commitment would lead him at last to a tiny island in Florida Bay where a plume hunter's bullet was to end his life. As his lifeblood drained away his eyes must have gazed on just such a sky, with long-necked birds beating silently across it toward another horizon.

The Age of Extermination

The latter half of the nineteenth century has been called by modern naturalists "The Age of Extermination." The new technology and the relentless westward march of civilization converged in space and time to step up the old hit-and-run raids on the continent's natural resources into systematic plunder. In a sense this was the inevitable culmination of the early settlers' fear (in some cases their heedless ignorance) of the great untamed continent. The New England Pilgrims saw themselves as "Souldiers of Christ" advancing upon the "barren Wilderness," which harbored little but "Heathenism, Idolatry and Devil-worship." Some years later, and a few hundred miles to the south, men like George Washington and Thomas Jefferson cautioned their compatriots against the destructive land practices that left many of the great tobacco estates of Virginia in ruins.

"Nothing in my opinion would contribute more to the welfare of these states than the proper management of our lands," Washington wrote of the new nation. "And nothing in the state of Virginia seems to be less understood."

The woodsman, the hunter, and the farmer treated the earth and everything in it as if they were inexhaustible. Every living creature (often including the red-skinned race of his own species) was fair game to the gunner. Before the end of the eighteenth century one popular game bird, the heath hen, had dwindled to such an extent that calls arose for its protection. New York State passed a law in 1791 that established a closed season on the bird. In his *American Ornithology* Alexander Wilson recalled an odd circumstance connected with the law's passage:

"The bill was entitled 'An Act for the preservation of Heath-Hen, and other game.' The honest Chairman of the Assembly—no sportsman, I suppose—read the title, 'An Act for the preservation of the *Heathen,* and other game!' which seemed to astonish the northern members, who could not see the propriety of preserving *Indians,* or any other heathen."

But it was the heath hen, and not the Indians, that totally disappeared. Despite some abortive attempts to protect it, this once abundant subspecies of the prairie chicken was extirpated from the mainland before 1870, and drifted to extinction on Martha's Vineyard in the present century. Meanwhile, only occasional voices were raised on behalf of all the hard-pressed wild creatures of the new nation. One of the voices belonged to Wilson, a remarkable Scotsman who immigrated to this country as a peddler and weaver and became the "Father of American Ornithology." Despite his utter lack of formal training in science, he set himself a formidable goal.

"I am most earnestly bent on pursuing my plan of making a Collection of all the Birds of this part of N. America," he wrote to a friend in 1804. "Now I don't want you to throw cold water as Shakespeare says on this notion, Quixotic as it may appear. I have been so long accustomed to the building of Airy Castles and brain Windmills that it has become one of my comforts of life, a rough Bone that amuses me when sated with the dull drudgery of Life."

Wilson, of course, took his share of birds in the field. But he was not what later came to be called "a game hog." He indited a verse to the spunky kingbird, and relished the account of a "humane person" (thought by some to be himself) who stopped the slaughter of robins for food around Boston by writing an anonymous paragraph for a newspaper which suggested that these birds fed on poisonous berries. It was probably not a coincidence that, in 1818, Massachusetts passed a law protecting the robin and the horned lark during a closed season.

Wilson's scheme turned out not to be "Quixotic." Though he died before his great work was completed, the paintings and text in his *American Ornithology* were surpassed only by those of John James Audubon. Audubon, in fact, plagiarized several of Wilson's paintings in compiling his own work. The two men seemed as far apart as any two could be (indeed, they failed to hit it off very well during their two brief encounters). Yet Wilson, born in humble circumstances in a far northern country, and Audubon, born aristocratically though a bastard, on the tropical island of Haiti, both cast their lot with the young United States and contributed much to an understanding of its bird life. They could not modify the increasing slaughter, unfortunately, and Audubon himself sometimes took part in it. His writings reverberate as often with the crack of rifles as with the songs of birds. Describing a visit to the Florida Keys, Audubon wrote:

"The yawl for a while was urged at a great rate, but as we approached a point, the oars were taken in, and the pilot alone sculling desired us to make ready, for in a few minutes we should have 'rare sport.' As we advanced, the more slowly did we move, and the most profound silence was maintained, until suddenly coming almost in contact with a thick shrubbery of mangroves, we beheld, right before us, a multitude of pelicans. A discharge of artillery seldom produced more effect; the dead, the dying, and the wounded, fell from the trees upon the water, while those unscathed flew screaming through the air in terror and dismay. 'There,' said he, 'did not I tell you so; is it not rare sport?'"

And again:

"Over those enormous mud-flats, a foot or two of water is quite sufficient to drive all the birds ashore, even the tallest Heron or Flamingo, and the tide seems to flow at once over the whole expanse. Each of us, provided with a gun, posted himself behind a bush, and no sooner had the water forced the winged creatures to approach the shore than the work of destruction commenced. When it at length ceased, the collected mass of birds of different kinds looked not unlike a small haycock."

Yet elsewhere Audubon condemned the senseless waste of wildlife, defending in his *Ornithological Biography* even the hated crow. In 1833, during his trip to Labrador, he was able to write:

"We talked of the country where we were, of the beings best fitted to live and prosper here, not only of our species, but of all species, and also of the enormous destruction of everything here, except the rocks; the aborigines themselves melting away before the encroachments of the white man, who looks without pity upon the decrease of the devoted Indian, from whom he rifles home, food, clothing, and life. For as the Deer, the Caribou, and all other game is killed for the dollar which its skin brings in, the Indian must search in vain over the deserted country for that on which he is accustomed to feed, till, worn out by sorrow, despair, and want, he either goes far from his early haunts to others, which in time will be similarly invaded, or he lies on the rocky seashore and dies. We are often told rum kills the Indian; I think not; it is oftener the want of food, the loss of hope as he loses sight of all that was once abundant, before the white man intruded on his land and killed off the wild quadrupeds and birds with which he has fed and clothed himself since his creation. Nature herself seems perishing."

Audubon's growing misgivings extended to the mammals of his adopted country as well. He reinforced his own descriptions by recalling the words spoken by Daniel Boone during their meeting some years before.

"But ah! Sir, what a wonderful difference thirty years makes in a country," the old frontiersman had said to him. "Why, at the time when I was caught by the Indians, you would not have walked out in any direction for more than a mile without shooting a buck or a bear. There were then thousands of buffaloes on the hills in Kentucky; the land looked as if it never would become poor; and to hunt in those days was a pleasure indeed. But when I was left to myself on the banks of Green River [about 1810] . . . a few *signs* only of deer were to be seen, and, as to deer itself, I saw none."

Whim, not purpose, decided what lived, what died. The beaver, which was on its way out early in the nineteenth century, clung to precarious existence when beaver hats for men went out of style about 1840. At the same time baleen, or whalebone, became an item in great demand for the hoops and stays of women's fashions, and added another incentive to the chase of the declining baleen whales. The sea otters, as the century progressed, were slaughtered for their impermeable hides from the Aleutians to Southern California, while only dwindling rafts of these delightful animals escaped in remote coves. By 1880 the alligator industry was booming; a contemporary magazine reported that dealers were paying seventy-five cents for hides, and additional sums for alligator oil. Three men in Louisiana killed 9000 alligators in the winter of 1879–80.

The bison, or American buffalo, has come to symbolize the fate that overtook much of America's big game at that period. The bison's population originally was numbered at anywhere between ten million and one hundred million animals. Horace Greeley, writing about his trip to the Far West in 1859, recalled the two great lines of migration that intersected near the forks of the River Platte in early summer. One was the endless procession of settlers moving into the "yet unmade garden of the world"; while the other was the bison, migrating north toward the spring grass "in countless legions." The collision brought disaster to the bison.

"Thousands of the noblest natives of the Plains bite the dust," Greeley wrote, "most of them shot in sheer wantonness by hunters already gorged and overladen with buffalo meat, whose only poor excuse for this wanton butchery is a passion for slaughter. Where food is the object—and the hides are good for nothing in spring and early summer—cows or calves are marked out for destruction; thus increasing the proportion, already far too great, of surviving males, and dooming the race to earlier extinction. Sometimes, advantage is taken of the blind, bisonic instinct of following, and a whole herd driven pell-mell down a precipitous brook bank, to the certain destruction of scores, whose carcasses are left to rot where they fell. Nowhere is the blind, senseless human appetite for carnage, for destruction, more strikingly, more lamentably evinced than in the rapidly proceeding extermination of the buffalo."

Any visitor to the West might observe the destruction, or its telltale signs. The herds, already cut off from one another by the advancing railroad tracks, were harassed by tourists, who fired at them for sport from the windows of passing trains. Elsewhere market hunters gunned down the great beasts for their tongues alone. Along the tracks of the Santa Fe Railroad the bleaching bones of buffaloes could be seen in a vast pile, twelve feet high and a half-mile long; during the 1870s and 1880s the railroads shipped 300,000 tons of bones, representing 31,000,000 buffalo, from Kansas to fertilizer plants in the East.

The slaughter was not completely mindless. The great herds were victims of the white man's war on the Indians, for the military mind knew that to deprive the Indians of buffalo meat and hides would be to bring them to their knees. "Let them kill, skin and sell until the buffalo is exterminated," said General Phil Sheridan, "as it is the only way to bring about lasting peace and allow civilization to advance." Ranchers who coveted the range for its herds of cattle, and railroad men who looked for additional business in the shipment of hides, encouraged the assault on the buffalo. Professional hunters like Buffalo Bill Cody took advantage of the recent technological advances in the production of arms; General George A. Custer, in a letter to the manufacturers of a new Remington .50-caliber sporting rifle, attested to the weapon's efficiency by listing the numbers of different animals he had killed with it. Then he added:

"The number of animals killed is not so remarkable as the distance at which the shots were executed. The average distance at which the forty-one antelopes were killed was 250 yards by actual measurement. I rarely obtained a shot at an antelope under 150 yards, while the range extended from that distance up to 630 yards. With the expedition were professional hunters employed by the Government to obtain game for the troops . . . I was the only person who used one of your Rifles, which, as may properly be stated, there were pitted against it breechloading rifles of almost every description . . . With your Rifle I killed far more game than any other single party, professional or amateur, while the shots made with your Rifle were at longer range and more difficult shots than were those made by any other rifles in the command."

The new technology, manifested by more efficient killing instruments, took its toll among most of America's big game. Bears, antelope, and bighorn sheep were wiped out over huge areas of their former range. The great herds of wapiti, or American elk, once the most widespread hoofed mammal on the continent, were slaughtered almost to extinction, at first for food and "fun," and finally so that the members of a celebrated benevolent order might adorn their watch chains with genuine elks' teeth.

The story is a part of our history. Yet, while the disappearance of the buffalo and other big game mammals brought on a national nostalgia for something fine in the primitive past, it remained a distant event for most Americans east of the Mississippi where, of course, the great bulk of the population still lived. The fate of familiar birds, on the other hand, was an event of immediate concern. Game birds or song birds, and sometimes both, were prominent diversions in daily life. The decline of many species was not solely the result of indiscriminate shooting. Forests were felled, swamps were drained, habitats were wiped out: some birds merely fell victim to progress.

But tangible evidence of slaughter could be found almost everywhere. Many Victorian parlors boasted a scattering of stuffed birds and some parlors were so set about with glass cases displaying their feathered bric-a-brac in more or less lifelike attitudes that they resembled small museums. Taxidermy flourished. (Families even had their household pets stuffed and mounted.) Outside, small boys learned the pleasures of the chase by killing song birds in the garden with whatever weapon they could lay their hands on, or practiced "science" by finding and smashing sets of freshly laid eggs.

"Two ten-year-old lads in that quiet and moral hamlet, Bridgehampton, Long Island, confessed this autumn that with pea shooters they killed during the season fifty robins and other birds which frequent the gardens, orchards and cemeteries," the ornithologist J. A. Allen wrote in 1886. "Such boys exist all over the United States and war on birds as things made to be killed . . . The pea shooter gives no sound and can be carried in the vest pocket; but so destructive is it in the hands of a skillful child that the legislatures of some of the Western states were obliged to pass laws making the sale of the thing a misdemeanor and punishing the use or possession of it."

Perhaps the greatest menace to birds of all sizes arose from the tastiness of their flesh and their eggs. Even birds which do not present themselves to modern man as likely items for the table often were eaten in the past. Tongues of flamingos were a luxury dish in the ancient world, and the depraved Roman emperor, Heliogabalus, fancied the brains of both flamingos and parrots (he had the rest of the carcasses flung to his lions). Birds of large size and spectacular form have furnished many an American with a meal too; herons, whooping cranes ("They are also at times killed as game, their flesh being well flavored," a naturalist wrote in 1834), and young whistling swans ("It is like shooting an angel," commented another naturalist) all went into the pot at one time or another.

Egging flourished as a popular means of augmenting the larder during the nineteenth and twentieth centuries. Residents of coastal

towns in Texas used to take a brief holiday from their regular jobs each spring and collect the eggs of sea birds on nearby islands and remote beaches. This business was carried out in two steps. On the first day, the eggers rowed out to the islands and smashed all of the eggs they were able to find. A few days later, assured that the eggs they found would be freshly laid, they returned to collect them, store them in barrels, and take them back to the mainland. Eggs of all species were collected, except for "those of the pelican, which are too fishy for any stomach." Most of the eggs that survived the trip to the mainland found their way to local markets, where they were priced according to size.

No bird was safe from the market gunner. In the South robins were hunted relentlessly, well into this century, for inclusion in pies and stews. The residents of one small town in central Tennessee, close to a cedar forest where robins came to feed on berries during the winter, were said to have grossed about $500 a year selling the birds to nearby markets at five cents a dozen; a swift calculation places the annual toll at 120,000 robins. "They are easily caught at night in the roost in young cedars," one of the hunters said. "We go to the roost with a torch and kill them with sticks. Others climb the trees and catch the robins as they fly in."

Visitors to southern shops told of seeing robins hung up for sale in strings, "like onions." The omnipresence of bobolinks, or "rice-birds," in the shops satisfied a double purpose; these birds' reputation as a table delicacy may have been enhanced by their equally widespread notoriety as destructive pests in Southern rice fields. Meadowlarks, blackbirds, sparrows, thrushes, warblers, vireos, and even woodpeckers could be found hanging beside robins and bobolinks in the stalls.

"This daily exhibition in southern markets," wrote J. A. Allen, "indicates an immense destruction of northern breeding song birds which resort to the southern states for a winter home."

But the steady attrition of birds for the market was not solely a Southern practice. Through Illinois, Wisconsin, Michigan, Indiana, and other Midwestern states hunters remorselessly pursued the pinnated grouse, or "prairie chicken." In 1873 Chicago markets bought 600,000 prairie chickens at $3.25 a dozen. Frank M. Chapman, the ornithologist, recalled as a boy in the 1870s the glut of prairie chickens in the butcher shops ("my first ornithological collection, indeed, being composed largely of wings of Prairie Hens, obtained with the cook's cooperation"). By the end of the century he had to travel to the sand hills of Nebraska to find them in any numbers.

One of the groups of birds most susceptible to the hunters' guns were the shorebirds, which include the plovers and sandpipers. Their habit of crowding together on rocks and beaches at high tide made them easy marks; a gunner was able to bag dozens of the smaller birds with a single blast. A lighthouse keeper, describing the hunting of small sandpipers or "sandpeeps," on an island off the coast of Maine, said: "They form in flocks and sit on the shore. Gunners come here and slaughter them awfully, for it is no trick to fire into a big flock of them and wound a large number. After the gunners have been here, my children bring in many wounded ones, some with broken wings or legs shot off, or eyes shot out, in all shapes. The gunners don't get half they shoot down."

Many shorebirds are almost human in their reluctance to abandon the fallen members of their flock. It is indeed like shooting fish in a barrel; the gunner maneuvers his boat to within point-blank range of the tame birds which cover the rocks like a dense blanket of seaweed; as he fires into them, the birds rise in a cloud, many of them fluttering back at once to die on the rocks, others struggling a few yards before plummeting into the water; the survivors, instead of continuing their flight, return to circle over the dead and dying with sharp cries apparently meant as warnings; the gunner has time to reload and send another volley into the hovering remnant.

A fearful toll was taken among these birds. Of the lesser yellow-legs, a pretty brownish sandpiper whose name points out its chief distinguishing feature, Ralph S. Palmer writes in *Maine Birds:* "This bird has not yet recovered from the heavy shooting which lasted five decades. Data from shooting journals of Scarborough hunters show that this species was much hunted in August. From 1842 to 1845 [Caleb G.] Loring shot 4093 . . . In the early 1880s, the Parker House and other Boston hotels paid gunners 50 cents per bird for Lesser Yellow-legs."

The golden plover is another bird which has not completely recovered along the Atlantic coast, while its frequent companion on migration, the eskimo curlew, fared even worse. This plump, long-billed shorebird was called the "doughbird" because of its dough-like sponginess to the touch. Gunners reported that its breast often burst open when it hit the ground after being shot. Eskimo curlews migrated in flocks of thousands, and they were shot the same way. Today the bird is very nearly extinct.

There are few incidents in the accumulating tragedy of man's relationship with his fellow creatures that cause biologists as much dismay as the destruction of the passenger pigeon. The "wild pigeon," as it was popularly known, was the most numerous bird of all time. This native American species was a graceful, long-tailed bird, somewhat resembling in color the common pigeon, or "rock dove," that is such a pest in our cities and farmland. The passenger pigeon's population was at least three billion birds, and one ornithologist has estimated that it made up 25 to 40 per cent of the total bird population of the United States.

The size of its flocks seems incredible to anyone who did not watch their passage across the sky. Early naturalists compared the flocks to shoals of herring. It is in these eyewitness accounts, repeated over and over, that we get confirmation of the awesome formations. The noise of the birds rose like a tornado, their dung rang like hail in the forest, their close-packed forms darkened the sun. People sometimes panicked and horses bolted as a flock roared overhead. Audubon has given us a picture of one of their tumultuous roosts.

"The dung lay several inches deep, covering the whole extent of the roosting-place, like a bed of snow," he wrote. "Many trees two feet in diameter, I observed, were broken off at no great distance from the ground; and the branches of many of the largest and tallest had given way, as if the forest had been swept by a tornado. Everything proved to me that the number of birds resorting to this part of the forest must be immense beyond conception . . . Suddenly there burst forth a general cry of 'Here they come!' The noise which they made, though yet distant, reminded me of a hard gale at sea, passing through the rigging of a close-reefed vessel. As the birds arrived and passed over me, I felt a current of air that surprised me . . . The Pigeons, arriving by thousands, alighted everywhere, one above another, until solid masses as large as hogsheads were formed on the branches all around. Here and there the perches gave way under the weight with a crash, and, falling to the ground, destroyed hundreds of the birds beneath, forcing down the dense groups with which every stick was loaded. It was a scene of uproar and confusion. I found it quite useless to speak, or even to shout to those persons who were nearest to me. Even the reports of the guns were seldom heard, and I was made aware of the firing only by seeing the shooters reloading."

Such enormous flocks formed a powerful environmental force of their own. The weight of their numbers broke down branches and whole trees, and their dung killed the roots of plants. Because of their fondness for grain, a visitation of pigeons was sometimes compared to that of grasshoppers. When flocks visited the neighborhood, boys often were stationed in the fields to frighten them away with guns, tin pans, and cowbells.

Fortunately for the early settlers, the wild pigeons preferred beechnuts, acorns, and other nuts in the forest to grain. Moreover, they seldom remained long in one place. The great "pigeon cities" where they built their nests in the forests—some nesting sites were estimated to be forty miles long and two miles wide—were used but once, and then abandoned for years. Early in the nineteenth century, awed travelers along the Allegheny River in Pennsylvania reported seeing at least twenty of these "cities," each containing an estimated one million birds. (Everyone always spoke in terms of "millions" when describing the wild pigeons.) The establishment of a nesting site created a great stir among the residents nearby. One Pennsylvania farmer described a "city" in these terms:

"All the trees were loaded with nests, so that branches broke down, trees came crashing to earth and nests of eggs and young birds were destroyed. Wild beasts of prey devoured the young and fought over them through the night, making a hideous uproar, and owls and hawks attacked the old birds upon the roosts above the nests.

"The farmers brought their hogs to the grounds and built log pens to keep them in, feeding them upon the young birds, or they turned them loose each morning to gather up whatever could be found. Whole families came with barrels and salt; the young birds, from ten ounces to twenty ounces weight, were dressed, salted, and packed in barrels and carted away to markets and for storing until needed."

To the superstitious, the arrival of the passenger pigeon was looked forward to with dread, since many of the colonists and pioneers believed that sickness was sure to follow. Longfellow, in *Evangeline,* wove the superstition into his tale:

"Then it came to pass that a pestilence fell on the city,
Presaged by wondrous signs, and mostly by flocks of wild pigeons,
Darkening the sun in their flight, with naught in their craws but an acorn."

But to later generations the pigeon represented only a windfall of food, oil, and feathers. The pigeon's suicidal gregariousness made it child's play to kill. Small boys assaulted the close-packed flocks with sticks and killed dozens in a few minutes. The act of squabbing—knocking young birds out of the nest with long poles—reminded observers of shaking apples out of a tree. Boys fired into the low-flying flocks with arrows. Their elders sometimes killed over a hundred pigeons with one blast of their shotguns. Even city people retired to the rooftops to fire away at the flocks.

Railroad and express company officials alerted the professional hunters to the whereabouts of the largest gatherings. The pigeons were slaughtered, packed, and shipped to the cities in great numbers; 300,000 pigeons found their way to the market in New York in 1855. Those that were not sold to the game dealers or fed to the hogs were melted down to make an oil used as soap-stock.

Most unpardonable of all was the annual netting of thousands of birds to be used in trapshooting contests. Wild pigeons were lured to the nets by stool pigeons—birds netted earlier and tied to perches as decoys. The captured birds were packed into tiny crates, often without food and water, and shipped to the site of the next big tournament. Many died en route; the others, cramped in their cages for days, could hardly fly when they were released, and usually proved an easy mark for even the most incompetent gunner.

At the end of the Civil War, Americans still considered the passenger pigeon a fantastically abundant species. But it had already begun its irreversible decline. The great flocks were decimated wherever they alighted. Occasionally someone sounded a cautionary note, but few gunners paid attention. Beginning in 1862, several states passed laws to prohibit killing the pigeons during their nesting season. In 1876, Ohio prohibited killing the birds at their roosts as well. But the laws generally went unobserved, and almost never were enforced.

Many species of wildlife were able to withstand intensive hunting. But the wild pigeon, gregarious and unwary, did not adjust to the enemy. It could not survive the tremendous toll at its nesting grounds where ordinarily it might recoup its losses (no species could), and at those times it was most vulnerable. The stripping of the vast American forests, where the pigeon found its favorite food of beechnuts and acorns, helped to seal its doom. Finally, the passenger pigeon carried within its being the seeds of its destruction, a notion best expressed by ecologist Aldo Leopold.

"The pigeon was a biological storm," Leopold wrote in *A Sand County Almanac.* "He was the lightning that played between two opposing potentials of intolerable intensity; the fat of the land and the oxygen of the air. Yearly the feathered tempest roared up, down, and across the continent, sucking up the laden fruits of forest and prairie, burning them in a traveling blast of life. Like any other chain reaction, the pigeon could survive no dimunition of his own furious intensity. When the pigeoners subtracted from his numbers, and the pioneers chopped gaps in the continuity of his fuel, his flame guttered out with hardly a sputter or even a wisp of smoke."

The wild pigeon disappeared from the American forest. A few lingered on in captivity. Martha, the last of her species, died in the Cincinnati Zoo in 1914, surrounded, so a pretty story goes, by hushed ornithologists. In truth, she was found dead on the floor of her cage one September afternoon by a keeper.

For years afterward, men who had been boys when the countless birds blotted out the sun recalled the sight as they would a momentous historical event. Others described a glimpse of a single remnant pigeon threading its way through the forest. Like Audubon, they had seen the bird pass "Like a thought, and on trying to see it again, the eye searches in vain; the bird is gone."

4

A Sense of Loss

There is a school of conservation historians that contends the beginning of reform sprang from a dedicated bureaucracy. This premise is based on a narrow concept of what conservation is, and even then, if we take a hard look at bureaucratic achievement in this field, it becomes apparent that bureaucratic initiative in large matters is rare and generally overstated; inertia is the rule. When relief appeared for America's hard-pressed wild birds it came (just as it has during so many other environmental crises) from private individuals working through organizations of their own.

On August 1, 1883, the following letter was sent to a number of prominent ornithologists;

Dear Sir:

You are cordially invited to attend a convention of American ornithologists, to be held in New York City, beginning on September 26, 1883, for the purpose of founding an American Ornithologist Union, upon a basis similar to that of the British Ornithologist Union. The place of meeting will be announced hereafter.

The object of the Union will be the promotion of social and scientific intercourse between American ornithologists and their co-operation in whatever may tend to the advancement of ornithology in North America.

The letter was signed by J. A. Allen, William Brewster, and Elliott Coues. It was hardly a coincidence that all three men were closely identified with New England, Allen and Brewster writing from Cambridge, Massachusetts, and Coues (though writing from Washington, D.C.) being a native of Portsmouth, New Hampshire. The birds of farm and garden were an integral part of a New Englander's memory and cultural heritage. Thoreau marveled at the scarlet tanager, flying "through the green foliage as if it would ignite the leaves." Longfellow sang of the bluebird, "balanced on some topmost spray, flooding with melody the neighborhood." And, from her home in Amherst, Emily Dickinson watched the hummingbird and the bobolink, and noted to a friend that "the wind blows gay today and the jays bark like blue terriers."

Now, in the 1880s, New Englanders noticed a trend that had set in over most of the United States. The familiar birds were not as abundant as they had been only a few years before; some were scarce, a few had vanished. Men with long experience in the field compared notes with their colleagues and confirmed their suspicions. Allen, Brewster, and Coues knew, better than most, the true state of affairs. Allen, with his impressive whiskers and immense learning, was the most prestigious mammalogist in the United States. Coues, a former Army surgeon and later a leader in the theosophist movement (from which he was ousted for his heretical tendencies), had written important books on bird life for the federal government. Brewster was the greatest field ornithologist of his time. His influence on the conservation movement became so decisive that, two decades later, another prominent conservationist could say that from Brewster's work "has come all of the non-game protection work in this country, and the marked improvement in game conditions."

Like nearly all of the other men who played vital roles in this movement, Brewster was as familiar with guns as were any of the professional hunters of the day. He was born into a comfortable, pre-Revolutionary War house on Brattle Street in Cambridge. This was Longfellow's street; there the poet's "tapestried mind" spun out its verses, or contemplated "the cry of the herons winging their way" over James Russell Lowell's house in the Elmwood thickets nearby. In the Brewster front yard tall elms rose just as they did everywhere along that magic street. Behind the house a bower of white and purple lilacs, an "old-fashioned" flower garden, and fruit trees and bushes provided food and shelter for the thirty-some species of birds that Brewster saw there regularly in summer. Inside, the young Brewster was surrounded by the varied collection of books one expected to find in a cultured Cambridge home, Audubon's *Ornithological Biography* prominent among them. He learned to love the woods around Cambridge, where he went hunting with his father and collected eggs with all the enthusiasm other boys of his age showed for that pastime.

Brewster grew to manhood in those surroundings, tall, lean, and handsome, remarkably intense and admired by his friends as an excellent conversationalist. That passion for birds which many lose with their youth never deserted him, and it became his ambition to be the foremost authority on birds in New England. His position as Curator of the Museum of Comparative Zoology at Harvard provided him with an ideal base from which to function as a scientific arbiter. Though he published little during his lifetime, he was an indefatigable observer and correspondent; in his notebooks and journals, meticulously maintained, he created the scholarly bedrock from which later ornithologists stepped up into print.

Through long hours in the field, Brewster acquired a skill at identifying birds that was quite extraordinary in a day when optical aids and guidebooks were nearly non-existent. His ability to detect, even in old age, call notes and the nests of birds bordered on witchcraft. He made of the garden of his Cambridge home what has been called one of America's earliest bird refuges. Not even the marauding Cambridge cats were able to violate Brewster's sanctuary.

"They literally swarm in the neighborhood," Brewster wrote of the cats. "After making a number of unsuccessful experiments I finally contrived a fence over which they cannot possibly clamber. It is of wire netting surmounted by heavy twine fish seine which is fastened at the bottom to the wire and looped at the top to the end of long, flexible garden stakes. When the cat gets a little above the wire her weight causes the tops of the stakes to bend over toward her and she presently finds herself hanging back downward beneath a strip of loose swaying fabric which affords her no means of farther upward progress. If the seine be tarred and kept under cover during the winter it will last a dozen or more years."

Like other naturalists and sportsmen of his day, Brewster sometimes rivaled cats in his depredations. He took part as a young man in trapshooting contests in which passenger pigeons, netted in the wild for the purpose, were the living targets. Thousands of these birds, then within a few decades of their total extinction, were destroyed during each trapshooting contest.

And yet, at a time when primitive optical aids made shotguns the only certain instrument of identification, Brewster could not be described as trigger-happy. When puzzled about what sort of food an adult flicker was feeding its young one day, he remained unenlightened, concluding, "I could not bring myself to kill one of the latter and settle the point in that way."

It seemed a matter of only local significance when, in 1873, Brewster and some of his colleagues founded the Nuttall Ornithological Club. (The club was named after Thomas Nuttall, an English collector of birds and plants who had served for ten years as the Curator of the Botanic Garden at Harvard and written his famous *Manual of the Ornithology of the United States and Canada* while living in Cambridge. Nuttall was so singleminded a collector that he was dubbed "Old Curious" by his shipmates when he sailed aboard the *Alert* with Richard Henry Dana in 1836. On another expedition to the West Coast, when Indians threatened to attack his party, the gun with which he had been digging up plants was found at the critical moment to be useless because it was clogged to the muzzle with dirt and gravel.) Brewster became the Nuttall Club's first president. He established its headquarters in his home on Brattle Street and built in the garden a fireproof museum for his large collection of birdskins.

Soon many of the country's outstanding naturalists (including the youthful Theodore Roosevelt) joined the Nuttall Club. It was from this base that Brewster, Allen, and Coues, alarmed by the abrupt decrease in bird life they had become aware of through their travels and correspondence, sent out in 1883 the call to create a truly national organization. The first meeting of the American Ornithologists' Union was held at the American Museum of Natural History. Its results generally have been understated by historians, though they were the wellspring from which flowed a large part of the modern conservation movement.

5

Beginnings

By one of those queer tricks of fate the ornithologists of the new union stepped briskly off on their high-minded pursuits and almost immediately found themselves mired in an ignominious controversy. Bird destruction was not at its root. The controversy had arisen as city parks and streets became transformed into what one observer called "avian ghettos crammed with greedy, filthy, bickering clouds of a single alien species."

The objectionable alien was the English sparrow. Only very distantly related to the three dozen or so species of attractive little native sparrows, it is an aggressive, prolific, and adaptable bird imported from Europe by well-meaning Americans in 1850. Its sponsors had been influenced by the English sparrow's reputation for eating destructive insects.

"This bird actually does consume the geometrid caterpillar to some extent as well as certain other insect pests," a government publication said later. "Unfortunately, its sins in other directions are so multitudinous that great areas thereof are left uncovered by the blanket of its virtues."

Among the English sparrow's sins were a fondness for the farmer's grains and fruits, and a hankering for the traditional nesting places of native species. One of its chief victims was the popular bluebird. On returning from the South in the spring, the bluebird invariably found its nesting holes and boxes appropriated by the hardy sparrows, which did not migrate for the winter. Soon what Thoreau had called "the plaintive, spring-restoring peep of the bluebird" was absent from many localities.

A principal reason for the English sparrow's astounding success in populated areas was its penchant for picking grain and other seeds from the droppings of the omnipresent horse. Gutters, stables, and barnyards teemed with sparrows foraging among the droppings. As the birds increased to pest proportions and the public outcry grew there broke out what came to be known as the "sparrow war." The English sparrows had their defenders, just as the domestic pigeons of our parks and streets do today. These people provided food, and even shelter, for the sparrow. But aligned against the alien birds were some of the era's most influential ornithologists, who deplored their ability to drive out so many other species and thus rob the landscape of its diversity.

In 1878, the Nuttall Ornithological Club took up the matter. Among the anti-sparrow contingent was a twenty-year-old Harvard student by the name of Theodore Roosevelt, who had joined the club only the year before. Roosevelt (he had considered for a time becoming a professional naturalist) read a paper in which he recounted his observations of the English sparrow while touring Egypt with his family several years earlier. He said that he had observed flocks of hundreds of these birds feeding on grain; those he had shot contained only grain in their crops. He claimed that in the United States he had seen mobs of English sparrows "assault" other small birds, and actually kill a sapsucker. A sparrow enthusiast retorted that Roosevelt was "sophomoric."

The sparrow war continued for many years. The American Ornithologists' Union (AOU), as one of its first matters of business, appointed a committee to study the bird's economic and ornithological effects. When the AOU, as we shall see, turned many of its projects over to a government agency, that agency continued the war, asking the public to destroy the sparrow, its nests and its eggs "on sight," and giving further encouragement by describing its flesh as "palatable and nutritious." In Boston, the city sent men into the Common with ladders and poles to destroy sparrows' nests. A

great outcry from humanitarian groups caused the project to be abandoned. The war faded away only when the horseless carriage appeared on the scene and both horse and sparrow went into something of a decline.

The AOU's other concerns were of a more positive nature. Committees were created to deal with the distribution of each species, and its migration patterns, within the United States. The committee members made contact with interested students, naturalists, sportsmen, and lighthouse keepers all over the country, sending out questionnaires and asking for certain information. The response was formidable. So much interest had been aroused by the new organization and its quest for information that the AOU realized it was not equipped to handle the work.

The AOU turned to the government, where it found a receptive ear. There was a growing interest in Washington at the time in birds and their relationship to agriculture. A convenient precedent had been set in 1871 when the government had established the post of Commissioner of Fish and Fisheries. Spencer F. Baird, a naturalist employed by the Smithsonian Institution, served as Commissioner. One of his first duties was to solicit such institutions as Johns Hopkins, Princeton, and Williams to act as subscribers in establishing a Marine Biological Laboratory at Woods Hole, Massachusetts. A British scientist, contrasting the project's success with that of incipient investigations in England, said that in America "the questions are put to nature and not to fishermen."

Now, in 1885, some of the AOU's most prestigious members went to their friends in Congress. What was wanted was a niche in one of the government departments where necessary studies of birds and their economic importance could be carried on with government funds. The Department of Agriculture was the obvious place for such studies. Created in 1862, this department had busied itself chiefly with the purchase and distribution of seeds and plants. By the 1880s its duties had multiplied (it would become a member of the executive branch in 1889) and one of its components was a Division of Entomology. Senator Warren Miller of New York was persuaded to lead a move in Congress which added $5000 to the agricultural appropriation and set up a section on economic ornithology within the Division of Entomology. In 1886 an independent Division of Economic Ornithology and Mammalogy was created within the Department of Agriculture. Dr. C. Hart Merriam, a member of the AOU, was named the division's first chief, apparently through the intervention of his father's influential friends in Washington.

Merriam, a graduate of Columbia's College of Physicians and Surgeons, had practiced medicine for a time in the Adirondacks. But natural history grew from a distraction to a passion with him, and he abandoned the study of human beings for that of birds. When the AOU was established, Merriam was elected the organization's secretary and chairman of its Committee on Bird Migration.

There was a great deal to be done in the field of economic ornithology when Merriam took charge of the division. What a modern ecologist has called "the Mother Goose Syndrome" ruled man's approach to the animal kingdom, just as it often does today. Some species were "noble" or "friendly." The monument to the California gull in Salt Lake City stands as a tribute to those birds who happened on the scene just as swarms of "black and baleful crickets" were about to consume one of the Mormon settlers' first harvests; by consuming the crickets instead, the gulls earned for themselves in the feathered pantheon a niche that is hard for modern observers to honor. Conversely, other creatures were "villains," a designation which sometimes served as a passport to oblivion for whole animal populations. Farmers, Merriam knew, needed to be educated in the facts of animal life. For the most part, they were killing carnivores, not realizing it was the herbivores that were most harmful to agriculture. In doing so, the farmers removed a vital natural check on the herbivores, permitting their numbers to increase even further.

An especially flagrant example of this confusion had occurred in 1885 when Pennsylvania passed a "scalp act." Under the act, the state paid a bounty for each hawk, owl, weasel, or mink killed in the attempt to control predators. E. H. Forbush, a noted ornithologist, pointed out that bounty laws invariably put a premium on dishonesty.

"Under the so-called scalp act of 1885 in Pennsylvania," Forbush wrote, "upwards of two thousand dollars were realized for a buffalo hide and a mule skin in one county, by a party of hunters. These hides were cut up and 'fixed' to resemble the scalps or ears of predatory mammals. Whether the magistrates also were 'fixed' is not recorded. A red fox was slain in one of the mountainous districts and its pelt cut into sixty-one parts, for which the hunter received sixty-one dollars. Bounties were paid on the heads of domestic fowls, grouse, cuckoos, or even English sparrows, which were supposed to have been palmed off on the authorities as the heads of hawks and owls. Birds and mammals were killed in other states and shipped into Pennsylvania, and large amounts of money was thus fraudulently obtained."

In a report issued by the Department of Agriculture, Merriam went to great pains to explain why the scalp act did not make economic sense. There were an estimated 5000 chickens killed each year by hawks and owls in Pennsylvania, he said. Chickens, at the time, were worth about twenty-five cents apiece. This brought a total loss to farmers of $1250. Yet the state paid out on 125,000 hawks and owls bounties that totaled $90,000. Merriam went further to estimate the numbers of harmful insects and rodents eaten by the hawks, and calculated that this service alone was worth nearly $4,000,000 to Pennsylvania's agriculture.

"In other words, the state has thrown away $2105 for every dollar saved!" he wrote. "And this does not represent fairly the full loss, for the slaughter of such a vast number of predaceous birds and mammals is almost certain to be followed by a correspondingly enormous increase in the numbers of mice and insects formerly held in check by them."

Under Merriam the Division of Economic Ornithology began studies of the food habits of various birds in order to show farmers how often they unwittingly killed useful species. Ironically, one of the division's chief duties was the identification of skulls and other animal parts sent there by local officials hoping to verify them for bounty payments. Merriam was considerably more interested in those studies of migration and geographical distribution of species that had claimed his attention immediately after the AOU's creation. He abandoned the word "Economic" in his own title, and soon his agency identified itself simply as the Division of Ornithology and Mammalogy.

As Merriam spent an increasingly greater part of his time working on "biological surveys," he made important contributions to biology. One was the concept of "life zones," which he formulated from his studies in Grand Canyon. Living things in the canyon arranged themselves in sharply delineated zones from its floor all

the way up to its rim. Merriam saw that this arrangement corresponded with the life zones that occur on the continent itself,
beginning with tropical species in Key West and grading northward
through intermediate zones to the Arctic species. Animals and
plants normally restricted to the North may also occur at high
elevations in the South. He concluded that life zones are a matter
of climate, varying with altitude as markedly as they do with
latitude.

Merriam's biological investigations altered the concept of his
division. In 1890 Secretary of Agriculture Jeremiah M. Rusk observed that the division "is in effect a biological survey, and should
be so named, for its principal occupation is the preparation of
large-scale maps of North America, showing the boundaries of the
faunas and floras, or life areas."

A year later Congress made the division's shift in emphasis official
and renamed it the Division of the Biological Survey. In this guise
(and today as the Bureau of Sport Fisheries and Wildlife) its
programs have contributed much to wildlife preservation. It never
quite freed itself of its origins, however, and we shall see these
origins emerge in a more unpleasant light during the present
century.

Meanwhile William Brewster and other ornithologists wrestled
with the destructive pressures on bird life. One of the members
of the AOU most concerned was George Bird Grinnell, the editor
of the famous sporting publication *Forest and Stream Weekly*. A
slender, scholarly man, Grinnell had traveled widely in the West,
exploring the Black Hills with General Custer and taking part in
the hunts and ceremonies of his friends, the Pawnee Indians. He
was an authority on the buffalo and its decline. In the pages of
Forest and Stream he campaigned for sound game laws and urged
restraint on his readers when they were in the field. Nothing
angered him more than the market gunners, who blanketed the
nation's fields and woodlands with their deadly barrage.

"The game supply which makes possible the general indulgence
in field sports is of incalculable advantage to individuals and the
nation," Grinnell wrote in *Forest and Stream*. "But a game supply
which makes possible the traffic in game as a luxury has no such
importance. If this be granted, public policy demands that the
traffic in game be abolished."

He was to be a leader in the campaign that finally outlawed
market hunting. Meanwhile, though a renowned big-game hunter

and explorer, he was distressed by the senseless destruction of small birds. In February 1886 Grinnell wrote an editorial suggesting an "Audubon Society" which would be dedicated to the preservation of wild birds and their eggs. The suggestion met with enthusiastic response, and that summer the society, named after America's greatest painter of birds, was incorporated. Oliver Wendell Holmes, John Greenleaf Whittier, and the Reverend Henry Ward Beecher joined the Audubon Society. So did thousands of other men, women, and children who sent in their dollars and pennies, and signed pledges to observe the society's purposes. Within two years the Audubon Society boasted nearly 50,000 members.

But the society's strength, paradoxically, was sapped by its rapid growth. Grinnell and his staff at *Forest and Stream* were unable to handle the added duties thrust on them so unexpectedly by the new society. In self-defense, Grinnell stopped mentioning the society in his publication's pages and so, for want of a strong central organization, it faded away in 1889. Like so many of the birds it was created to protect, the Audubon Society appeared to have become extinct.

Meanwhile, the AOU was keeping its finger in the dike. Its Committee on the Protection of North American Birds issued a bulletin in 1886 making explicit the unremitting destruction of those birds. At the end of the bulletin appeared one of the most important documents in the history of conservation. This was a carefully considered yet concisely written "Model Law" on which the AOU hoped that each of the states would base protective legislation of its own.

In the past there had always been bitter legislative battles over game protection bills; the market hunters and their business support rejected any bill that might deprive them of the water fowl, shorebirds, grouse, and other birds on which their living depended. The ornithologists, therefore, tried to sweep around the flanks of the Model Law's potential opponents by specifically omitting the "game birds"—water fowl, shorebirds, grouse, pheasants, quail, turkeys, rails, and coots—from its protective umbrella. All the other native American birds were to be rigidly protected. (A later section excluded the English sparrow from the law's mercy.) Another vital section of the law prohibited the destruction of the eggs and nests of any *native* bird, the English sparrow, of course, not satisfying the definition's requirements.

Opposition to the Model Law arose quickly in several unexpected corners. Many taxidermists protested, claiming that the restrictions would drive them out of business. William Brewster replied that the Model Law was not aimed at honest taxidermists and collectors. He pointed out that the law made provision for permits to collect birds for scientific and other legitimate purposes. Brewster contended that the law was aimed at "certain obnoxious persons, who had rendered themselves so by their wholesale slaughter of birds for gain, and who were not taxidermists in any true sense."

There were ornithologists, A. K. Fisher and others, who also opposed the Model Law on the grounds that it was designed to restrict scientific collectors. "I don't protect birds," one ornithologist said, "I kill them." And it was true that in the fever to collect new and rare specimens, scientists sometimes contributed to the eclipse of a species. Consider the case of the Bachman's warbler, a very rare little bird originally described in 1833 by Audubon from only two specimens. He named the bird after John Bachman, a minister and naturalist who lived in Charleston, South Carolina, and who later became the father-in-law of Audubon's sons, John and Victor. No Bachman's warbler was seen again until 1886, when a plume hunter shot seven of them near Lake Pontchartrain, Louisiana. Then, in 1890, no less a personage than William Brewster, with his colleague, Frank M. Chapman, collected forty-six Bachman's warblers along Florida's Suwannee River. Another ornithologist collected fifty more in the same area in 1891. A modern ornithologist, writing in 1967, said: "The species has never been reported in such numbers anywhere again, and it has not been seen in Florida since 1909." No wonder!

No one has better stated the conflict of interests here than the humorist Will Cuppy in his book, *The Great Bustard and Other People:*

"Ornithologists as a class, so far as I have been able to observe them, generally from a safe distance, do seem to suffer from a touch of split personality when faced with a dwindling species of bird. They appear to be torn between a sincere desire to bring that bird back to par, at any cost to themselves and to certain well-to-do persons whose names they keep in a little black book, and an uncontrollable urge or compulsion to skin a few more specimens and put them in a showcase at the earliest possible moment . . . Right here I might offer a word of advice to the Ivory-billed Woodpecker, now the rarest bird on the North American continent and one that is going to come in for more and more attention. Keep away from bird lovers, fellows, or you'll be standing on a little wooden pedestal with a label containing your full name in Latin: *Campephilus principalis*. People will be filing past admiring your glossy blue-black feathers, your white stripes and patches, your nasal plumes in front of lores, your bright red crest, and your beady yellow eyes. You'll be in the limelight, but you won't know it. I don't want to alarm you, fellows, but there are only about twenty of you alive as I write these lines, and there are more than two hundred of you in American museums and in collections owned by Ivory-billed Woodpecker enthusiasts. Get it?"

A similar inexplicable urge seemed to dominate the öologist, or egg-collector, now happily a declining species himself. Ludlow Griscom, the noted ornithologist, once described his visit to an amateur egg-collector around the turn of the century. This man possessed one of the largest collections in the United States.

"To my surprise," Griscom wrote, "I found that he had 235 sets of eggs of the robin. There was every possible type of variation shown in this series. There were sets of three eggs, four eggs, five eggs, and six eggs. There were small eggs, medium-sized eggs, and large eggs, and there were pale blue eggs, medium-colored blue eggs, and dark blue eggs; but, when every possible allowance for all these variations had been made, there were still 150 sets or so of just robins' eggs. When I asked him why there were so many, he said: 'That proves that the robin is the commonest nesting bird in this part of the country!'"

Unfortunately, the AOU had opposition other than that furnished from within its ranks. New York and Pennsylvania passed legislation based on the Model Law, but it was quickly repealed or emasculated under counterpressures exerted by interests that profited from market hunting: the railroads, food shops, restaurants, and hotels. There was even a challenge to the state's jurisdiction in regulating the hunting of game. In October 1889 a man named Geer was taken into police court in New London, Connecticut, charged with having in his possession, with the intent of shipping it out of the state, "certain woodcock, ruffed grouse, and quail." This was in violation of a Connecticut law, passed in 1888. Geer claimed that the birds had been shot legally in season and that he had the right to ship them out of the state. The judge fined him and Geer appealed.

The appeal, "Geer v. Connecticut," was heard by the Supreme

Court in 1896. The Court was asked to decide the question: Did the State have "the power to regulate the killing of game within her borders so as to confine its use to the limits of the State and forbid its transmission outside of the State?" The Court noted that the common law of England "based property in game upon the principle of common ownership, and therefore treated it as subject to governmental authority." This right was vested in the King, as well as in colonial governments, and thus it passed to the states after Independence. In its landmark decision, the Court ruled that game was indeed the property of the state.

And slowly the states were awakening to their responsibility. In 1894 Michigan passed a law prohibiting the sale of woodcock, grouse, and quail at any time. Indiana authorized officers of other states to seize in Indiana game illegally killed or shipped from their own states. Wisconsin and Colorado ordered that all packages of game shipped there from outside the state be plainly marked with the contents and the name and address of the shipper. Editorials in publications such as *Forest and Stream*, and personal observations by sportsmen and scientists, were beginning to exert an influence on the state legislatures.

One important segment of the population had not yet been touched by the appeals for restraint. America's women, encouraged by the millinery industry, were allowing some of the world's most beautiful birds to slip inevitably toward oblivion.

6

The Feather Trade

Men adapted the plumes of birds for their own use long before they solved the birds' secret of flight. Indian chieftains, medieval crusaders, and Renaissance dandies adorned their heads or head-gear with plumes of differing shapes and colors. The occelated pattern of the peacock's feather has stimulated man's acquisitive-ness for uncounted centuries. The Mayas prized the quetzal for the long green plumes that, like the source of a peacock's pride, are not true tail feathers at all, but upper tail coverts. The Mayas did not kill quetzals for their plumes; fortunately for this splendid tropical species, it belongs to an order of birds called trogons, from whose thin tender skins (described by one ornithologist as the "flimsiest imaginable excuse for an epidermis") the feathers tear away at a touch. The Mayas, practicing the concept of sustained yield, simply relieved the quetzals of their long plumes and turned them loose to grow another set.

Ladies, of course, could not be expected to abandon such adornments to their men. Madame de Pompadour added, among other ornaments, the feathers of exotic birds to her innovative coiffure. Shipments of bird skins made their way to French ports from all over the world, ultimately to embellish the natural charms of grand ladies. One such shipment from French Guiana, seized by a British warship, was found to contain a species new to science; George Edwards, the British ornithologist, perhaps with ironic gallantry, named this gorgeous little reddish-lavender bird the Pompadour cotinga, after the lady for whom its plumage had been intended.

In the final quarter of the nineteenth century the desire to adorn oneself with feathers swept the United States and Western Europe like some contagious disease. The milliners,* well-organized and supported by their friends in government, encouraged the fashion among women while staving off every attempt to mitigate the slaughter. Plumes, and even whole birds, adorned the hair, hats, and dresses of women. Small numbers of ostriches (whose plumes may be clipped without harm to the birds) were imported to "ostrich ranches" in the western United States from Africa in the 1880s. But this source did not rival that of other birds killed in the wild. Bulky bales of plumes flowed unendingly into New York City, which was the national center of the millinery trade.

The result of this craving for flamboyant plumes was a daily fashion parade, on the streets and in the ballrooms, depressing to humanitarians and ornithologists alike. The top of a lady's hat became transformed into a grisly *nature mort,* chiffon, lace, and taffeta ribbons mingled with plumes, wings, and indeed the entire bodies of birds (the grotesqueness heightened if the specimen happened to be any of the long-billed shorebirds). William Dutcher of the AOU's Committee on the Protection of North American Birds, reprinted an item from a New York newspaper in 1886: "Mrs. _____ had her gown of unrelieved black looped up with black birds; and a winged creature so dusky that it could have been intended for nothing but a crow, reposed among the curls and braids of her hair." To which Dutcher added the comment: "It is said where ignorance is bliss, 'tis folly to be wise. Perhaps if the lady in question could have seen the crow during its lifetime perched upon and feeding on the decaying carcass of a horse, she might have objected to the association."

Another contemporary newspaper observed that "Miss _____ looked extremely well in white, with a whole nest of sparkling, scintillating birds in her hair, which it would have puzzled an

Milliner is an English corruption of *Milaner,* after the inhabitants of the Italian city from which ladies' finery was long exported to England.

ornithologist to classify." In fact, only an ornithologist of formidable learning was able to appreciate the variety of which *les fantasies* were composed. Frank M. Chapman, during two strolls through the "uptown" shopping districts of Manhattan in 1896, counted, with a birdwatcher's incomparable zeal, 700 hats, 542 of which were decorated with feathers. (Most of the unadorned hats belonged to "ladies in mourning or elderly ladies.") Chapman recognized forty different species of birds, including Wilson's warblers, pileated woodpeckers, Acadian owls, bluebirds, pine grosbeaks, and a northern shrike, or "butcherbird."

The American Ornithologists' Union estimated in 1886 that five million North American birds were killed annually "for fashion." The feathers most in demand were those of the two white egrets (sometimes called herons)—the American, or common, egret and the snowy egret. Of these, the most highly prized were the so-called aigrettes, or long plumes, that grow only in the breeding season from between the shoulders and extend to or beyond the tail of the snowy egret. When these plumes are in good condition they are gracefully recurved at the tips. The plumes of the larger common egret extend beyond the tail, but are not recurved. As public disapproval of plume hunting mounted, the milliners dragged a couple of red herrings across the trail, claiming (1) that the herons were not killed, but only "plucked" for their plumes, and (2) that, in any case, the plumes were "manufactured."

Both stories were false. "Scalps," of "flats," were cut in strips from the backs of the dead herons, just as Charles Pierce described the procedure in "The Cruise of the *Bonton.*" The scalps, as shipped to the dealers in New York, contained not only the plumes but also the broad feathers that were the birds' scapulars. William Dutcher of the AOU countered the other distortion.

"Dealers often state that aigrettes are manufactured," Dutcher wrote, "but this is not so; man has never yet been able to imitate successfully these beautiful plumes; all that are offered for sale have been torn from the backs of the smaller White Herons. Even the stiff plumes, or 'stubs,' are not manufactured but are the plumes of the larger species of White Herons. Heron's plumes are often sold as 'Ospreys'; that is simply another trade name used to disguise the fact that they are Heron's plumes. The Osprey [or fish hawk] . . . produces no plumes of any kind."

The milliners' agents, especially in the South, employed hundreds of gunners on a piecework basis to collect the skins they required. Prices varied considerably over the years, and according to the dictates of supply and demand. Terns, graceful white and gray relatives of the gulls, were always in demand as ornaments for women's hats, and prices for their skins ranged from 25 cents to 40 cents; the dealers paid about 15 cents just for a pair of wings. By the turn of the century the prices paid for egret plumes had risen to $32 an ounce (four herons contributed an ounce), or twice the price of gold.

One of the most curious case histories among the plume birds belongs to the roseate spoonbill. Called the "pink curlew" by gunners, this bird has fitted itself for feeding along muddy bottoms in shallows by developing a remarkable pair of spatulate shaped mandibles, tipped with sensitive nerves. But while it earned its living with its unique bill, the roseate spoonbill also invited extermination with its sumptuous plumage of white, pink, and carmine. Horace A. Kline, a collector, described its irresistible attraction: "As he passed within 30 yards a charge of No. 6 [shot] caused him to reel in the air; but catching his balance, he started to move on when a charge from the second barrel brought him to the earth. I shall never forget how we admired him as he lay dead. His bright rose colored wings, delicate pink head and back, snowy white head and wondrous bill. Many a time ladies in looking over my birds have exclaimed, 'Oh, how lovely you have got that pink bird colored'."

Ironically, those marvelous colors tended to fade rather quickly, and after a while the milliners lost interest in the spoonbill; its plumes seemed best fitted for use as fans. This apparent stroke of good fortune helped it very little, for the spoonbill's nesting patterns were easily disturbed. And here we come to the central fact of plume bird destruction; the birds were chiefly killed during the breeding season when their plumes were at their showiest, and therefore most valuable. (The egrets' superb "nuptial plumes"—its long, graceful feathers that attract prospective mates—fell out after the breeding season; but by that time they were too worn to be useful to the milliners.) This was also the time of the year when plume birds, being colonial nesters, came together in the great rookeries, and thus simplified the hunters' task. When the hunters opened fire on egrets nesting in the mangroves and other trees of swamp and shore, the birds were reluctant to abandon their young which lay huddled in the nests. They remained in the area, to fall victim by the hundreds to repeated fusillades. Their carcasses were skinned and tossed aside to rot in the blazing subtropical sun. With the adult birds killed or driven away, the young were left in the nests to starve, which they did in great numbers, thus depriving the once-great flocks of an opportunity to restore themselves to their former numbers.

The spoonbills, though sometimes spared by the gunners in their anxiety to kill all of the more valuable egrets, were driven from the rookery. Their extreme shyness prevented their return, and thus produced on their young's survival an effect identical with that had the adults been killed. W. E. D. Scott of the AOU, who visited the Florida rookeries on several occasions, wrote of his findings in 1889; "As late as the season of 1880 in March I found the birds in great numbers . . . All this is changed. I have spent the past four winters and two summers in Florida. My old hunting grounds have all been carefully traversed, some of them many times, and the Roseate Spoonbill is almost as great a stranger to me as to my fellow workers who live the year round in Massachusetts."

The roseate spoonbill's numbers dipped to a remnant population early in the twentieth century, when one ornithologist estimated that there were no more than "twenty or twenty-five nests in all of the United States." It has never completely recovered. Nor has the reddish egret, whose Florida population presently numbers about two hundred birds, mostly confined to Everglades National Park. The flamingo, once a regular visitor (but probably not a breeder) in Florida, is now seen only as a captive bird at places such as roadside zoos and Hialeah Race Track. That the snowy egret survived at all, and finally re-established healthy populations, may have been due almost entirely to a large private refuge created in Louisiana in 1892 by E. A. McIlhenny of the Tabasco family.

As the century drew to a close the Audubon movement revived in the United States. Massachusetts was the scene, and William Brewster a prime mover, of the organized drive that was to play a decisive part in future conservation battles. Brewster founded the first permanent state organization of its kind, the Massachusetts Audubon Society for the Protection of Birds, in 1896. Apparently this movement's time had come, and it flourished on the local level. A similar organization was founded in Pennsylvania later that year.

Rhode Island and New York each added a state Audubon Society the following year, and in 1900 even Florida, that stronghold of the plume hunter, created an Audubon Society of its own.

These societies hoped ultimately to protect song birds and other beneficial species while restricting the indiscriminate slaughter of game birds. The most immediate struggle, however, promised to be with the millinery industry. The societies' prospects were dreary. In 1899 a New York City newspaper carried an account of a meeting of the New York State Audubon Society held in the American Museum of Natural History. "About 150 persons were present," the report noted, "most of them women, and fully three-fourths of the women wore birds, or parts of birds, in their hats."

To bind the various state Audubon Societies in a loose federation, a National Committee of Audubon Societies was organized in 1901. William Dutcher was chosen Chairman of the Audubon Committee. He was one of those inspired amateurs—well-read, seriously interested in natural history—who fought the battles which the professionals in government often were unwilling or unable to undertake. A native of New Jersey, Dutcher had built a successful life insurance business in New York City. For some years he had been convinced that aggressive local organizations, campaigning for strong protection laws and then assuring their enforcement, were absolutly necessary if America's bird life was not to suffer even greater losses. From his committee chairmanship with the AOU Dutcher encouraged the revival of Audubon Societies all over the country.

One of his most successful ventures was in North Carolina. There he discovered a young college instructor, T. Gilbert Pearson, who had a flair for teaching and a zeal for protecting the remnants of the state's wildlife. Dutcher persuaded him to form an Audubon Society in North Carolina and work for the passage of the AOU's Model Law. Pearson, overcoming local lethargy and hostility, followed instructions to the letter. Then he went a step further. Aware that sound game laws could not be enforced without a staff of honest wardens, Pearson persuaded the legislature to impose a tax on non-resident hunters; the funds raised in this manner were turned over to the Audubon Society, which in turn hired a staff of game wardens.

The new law was not universally popular in North Carolina. Many citizens attacked the non-resident hunting license on the grounds that it was a violation of old-fashioned "southern hospitality." Others were outraged because the Audubon wardens arrested violators without reference to their race or social position. In Burlington, "one of the most wealthy and influential citizens" was arrested for killing dozens of chimney swifts, a holocaust he consummated by setting fire to his chimney with straw after covering it with a screen, and thus roasting the trapped swifts. One of the culprit's neighbors expressed indignation over his arrest in a letter to the Raleigh *News and Observer:* "If the Honorable T. Gilbert Pearson and his legion of women and children backers think that they can compel intelligent people to put up with a nuisance like this, he is mistaken."

There was a more determined effort in the state to control the slaughter of quail (unless, of course the killing was done in the name of sport). Pearson and one of his wardens received a tip that a market hunter was shipping quail out of the state in crates ostensibly packed with eggs. They located the contraband at the railroad station in Greensboro. Two newspaper reporters, learning that the quail had been seized, asked the warden how he had guessed that the egg crates had contained quail.

"There was no guess work about it," the warden replied. "That dog of mine pointed the box for us."

Then he leaned over and patted the head of a small, short-haired black dog which generally tagged along with him on his enforcement work. The story was duly printed, North Carolinians marveled at the dog's uncanny pointing ability, and smuggling dropped off in the Greensboro region.

There seemed to be no such local sympathy for the preservation of plume birds, which presented neither a challenge for the sportsman nor an attraction for the gourmet. A plume hunter Pearson spoke to defended the unceasing barrage that had nearly eliminated the terns from that part of the North Carolina coast.

"Pore folks have as good a right to live as city people," the gunner said. "The good Lord put us here and the Good Book says, 'man shall have dominion over all creatures.' They're our'n to use."

In 1905 the thirty-five state Audubon Societies (plus one in the District of Columbia) decided to incorporate in New York State as the National Association of Audubon Societies. The new Board of Directors elected Dutcher president and Pearson secretary of the association. Dutcher stated its objectives.

"The object of this organization is to be a barrier between wild birds and animals and a very large unthinking class, and a smaller but more harmful class of selfish people," he wrote. "The unthinking, or, in plain English, the ignorant class, we hope to reach through educational channels, while the selfish people we shall control through the enforcement of wise laws, reservations or bird refuges, and the warden system."

Pearson became the association's fire fighter, rushing to state capitals, to conventions of all sorts, and even to Congress, as trouble flared. The association continually fought to smother legislation it considered obnoxious, as it did in New Jersey when an assemblyman introduced a bill to declare the mourning dove a game bird, with an open season from August 15 to October 1. The assemblyman had explained that many of his constituents were glassblowers, "and this was their vacation period and they wanted something to shoot." The association supported the opposition that killed the bill.

On the plume hunting front the association encouraged the use of ostrich feathers ("taking plumes from an ostrich is no more painful to the bird than shearing is to a sheep," Dutcher wrote), discouraged the purchase of wild birds' plumes by women, and employed wardens to enforce whatever laws existed against killing birds on their nests. No wonder that the millinery industry fought the Audubon groups with the ferocity the chemical industry in our own time reserved for Rachel Carson. A millinery buyer in Boston expressed his colleagues' sentiments in the pages of a trade publication: "Birds do not meet with much favor, on account of the strong prejudice aroused by the Audubon Society, which is especially active in this state."

There remained muted yet nonetheless powerful opposition to the bird protectionists among professional ornithologists themselves. The suspicion lingered that the Audubon Societies hoped to prohibit even scientific collecting. The AOU dropped Dutcher, Pearson, and other "protectionists" from its Committee on Bird Protection, and abandoned the drive for a Model Law in all states to the Audubon Societies.

"The explanation given at the time," Pearson wrote, "was that the newly formed Audubon Association alone was sufficient to look out for bird protection, but many of us believe that this was not the real motive of the action. Dr. A. K. Fisher was appointed to succeed Dutcher as Chairman of the union's Bird Protection Committee and retained this position for eighteen years. During this period the committee seldom functioned, very rarely even making any report to the union. Nearly every active ornithologist at that time was engaged in collecting birds, and the use of the opera-glass in making identifications was in little vogue. Most 'sight records' were looked upon as questionable evidence . . . Fisher was frankly hostile and said that if the association did not actually advocate the stopping of scientific collecting it at least was to blame for what was taking place, because it was arousing interest all over the country in birds, which reacted against collectors."

The Audubon Societies tried to jam a foot in the door through legislation. An earlier attempt had been turned back after Senator George F. Hoar of Massachusetts (who was one of the authors of the Sherman Anti-Trust Act) introduced a bill in Congress in 1898 intended to prohibit the importation, sale, or shipment of millinery plumes in the United States. Hoar had aroused wide sympathy for his bird-protection legislation by circulating a petition, supposed to have been signed by a number of wild birds, asking men and women to spare their lives. *The Millinery Trade Review* called on all members of the trade to crush "this most iniquitous and childish measure." When the AOU, keeping its distance from Audubon groups, refused to support Hoar's bill, it was defeated.

But the various state Audubon Societies gathered behind another bill, introduced by Representative John F. Lacey of Iowa. This legislation contained the further allure of extending the war on the English sparrow. Its main features prohibited the importation of foreign creatures (such as the English sparrow) without government permit, as well as the interstate traffic in birds and animals killed in violation of state laws, including the original AOU "Model Law." Lacey's bill, which became law in 1900, invoked the "commerce clause" of the constitution to control these interstate shipments. Freight agents soon began to ask searching questions about suspicious packages because the railroads and consignees both were liable under the law.

The Lacey Act was not the final answer. It did not apply in cases where states had no protective legislation of their own, and only five states had passed the effective Model Law. But the Audubon Societies now held a club with which they could occasionally reap some satisfaction, and within five years the number of states passing the Model Law would climb to thirty-three. By then the National Association had turned vigorously to rooting out the most inexcusable and destructive force—that of the plume hunters in southern Florida.

7

To Oyster Key

The Everglades, at the turn of the century, was a wild and inhospi-
table region. "Pa-hay-okee," the Indians called it: "Grassy Water."
And in truth it is a broad river of grass, the water seeping southward
along a front nearly seventy miles wide from Okeechobee, the vast,
shallow lake in central Florida. But the ripple on the river's surface
is not of water but of grass; or rather, of a sedge called sawgrass.
Spears of sawgrass, their knifelike edges grating on each other in
the wind to create a fierce, exciting music all their own, rise from
the creeping river as a prairie that looks to the traveler as broad
as Asia. Here and there bayheads of tangled trees and vines rise
on slight elevations of the land like tiny islands from the grassy
river.

On the rim of the Everglades, separating it from the sea, yet part
of both land and sea, grow thickets of mangroves. These small trees,
standing tiptoe as it were on arched and labyrinthine roots, hold
back the surging seawater from overwhelming the sweet flow that
moves inexorably toward it from Okeechobee. Just as the Nile lays
down the fertile strip that gives life to Egypt, so this immense and
intricate world of brackish water at the tip of Florida produces a
unique community of trees and sedges, reptiles and fishes, mammals
and birds.

And mosquitoes. More than the oppressive heat, more than the flesh-tearing sawgrass, certainly more than the alligators and panthers, the mosquitoes discouraged white men in the Everglades while land-hungry settlers invaded almost every other part of the expanding nation. The Civil War overcame even this formidable barrier. Deserters from both sides made their way into the sanctuary of the Everglades, embracing all its natural terrors, rather than the man-made terrors of war. Other settlers, impelled by the economic and social disasters that were the aftermath of war, followed the deserters into the region.

"It wasn't a force of numbers, however, that spelled doom to wildlife so much as the pioneer aspect of these settlers," Robert Porter Allen wrote in *The Roseate Spoonbill*. "Everyone carried a gun, an ax and a determination to wrest a living from the wilderness. And most of them did, whether they grew tomatoes on land cleared with their own hands or shot plume birds."

The plume hunters were a mixed bag of humanity. Some were ignorant and desperate men. Others, like Chevalier, "the old Frenchman," were wandering adventurers whose motivation was partly trade and partly science. And finally there were men like J. H. Batty, who had owned a taxidermist's shop in New York City for many years, only to give it up for the adventurous life of shooting plume birds in the Everglades. Before the end of the century, however, Batty underwent a change of heart and resolved to earn an honest living by collecting birds and mammals selectively for the American Museum of Natural History. When he was killed by the accidental discharge of his own gun while collecting in Mexico, a fellow ornithologist eulogized him as "a man of the most kindly nature, trustful, and thoroughly conscientious in his work."

By the beginning of the present century ornithologists were mingling with plume hunters in the Everglades. They came to record what they could of the surviving egrets, ibises, and spoonbills before these lovely and interesting birds vanished forever. The ornithologists were tough men, willing to brave impossible conditions to complete the sorry record. Among them was the Reverend Herbert K. Job, naturalist and wildlife photographer, who arrived at what was then the terminus of the Florida East Coast Railroad at Miami in April 1903.

Job was met there in a sloop by a guide who was to lead him into that "morass which even yet remains a blank upon the map."

His guide was Guy Bradley, the boy who had sailed with Charles
Pierce on the *Bonton* into the Everglades eighteen years before. Now
a man in his middle thirties, strong, deeply tanned, with thinning
curly hair and a mustache, Bradley was something more than a
backwoods bumpkin. His father, a postal employee in Chicago, had
brought his family to Lake Worth about 1870, when Guy was still
a baby. For a time the elder Bradley carried the mail on foot from
Lake Worth to Miami, before the railroad was extended there, and
later served as Superintendent of Schools in Dade County. Mrs.
Bradley, an educated woman, taught Guy and his older brother,
Louis, the violin. When they were growing up they sometimes
earned five dollars a night playing in a string band at a Palm Beach
hotel.

There were development schemes for southern Florida even in
those days; promoters envisioned draining the Everglades to plant
vegetables and fruit trees, and building a railroad from Cape Sable,
at the tip, to Key West. As a part of one of these schemes, free
land was offered to families that would settle in the little isolated
community of Flamingo near Cape Sable. The elder Bradley moved
his family there and became the local postmaster. Guy, a man by
this time, married and fathered two sons of his own. It was then
that the course of his life merged with the incipient bird protection
movement in America.

As early as 1877, Florida had passed a law to prevent the wanton
destruction of the nests, eggs, and young of plume birds. Two years
later, under pressure from the "feather merchants" and their gunners, the act was repealed, though aliens were forbidden to kill the
birds. Chevalier was probably in violation of this law, but for a
long time he was not in violation of any other. In 1891 a new law
was passed, forbidding the killing of birds (herons, egrets, ibises,
etc.) for the purpose of trafficking in plumes.

There was no possible means of enforcing this law in the great
wastes of the Everglades or on the remote islands off the coast.
Then, in 1897, the legislature authorized the governor to appoint
game wardens for each county, their salary to be paid by the county
commissioners. This, too, was inadequate protection for birds in
isolated regions. At last, when the Florida legislature was persuaded
to pass the Model Law in 1901, the Audubon Societies stepped
in and hired extra wardens to patrol the most critical areas. Bradley,
highly recommended by members of the Florida Audubon Society
as fearless and dependable, became an Audubon warden.

Job and Bradley proceeded by sloop to Flamingo by way of the Keys, where Job drank coconut milk and observed that potatoes, planted in crevices in the coral rock, were dug with crowbars instead of shovels. Flamingo proved more of a nightmare than a curiosity. This settlement of crude cottages and palmetto shacks existed under a state of siege, especially during the summer rainy season, by mosquitoes and hordes of horseflies that the inhabitants referred to sardonically as "sharpshooters." Tall palmetto leaves stood by every door so that visitors could brush the insects off their clothes and bodies before entering a cottage. Smudge pots of black mangrove sent up an endless cloud to drive the mosquitoes away. Women wheeled baby carriages under which they had tied small smudge pots, "so the carriages moved along enveloped in smoke and an outlying cloud of 'skeets and flies." Domestic animals were kept in stables, and wrapped in burlap before being led out to work.

Job described the countryside: "Back from the strip of timber on the shore is a moderate area of marshy prairie which is flooded in the summer rainy season. Aside from this all the Cape Sable peninsula is a wild tangled pathless swampy jungle of red and black mangrove, buttonwood, and other trees extending back a number of miles to the open sawgrass marshes of the Everglades. In the embraces of this mangrove swamp lie a series of shallow lakes with muddy bottoms, connected together by various channels through the mangrove thickets and more or less overflowed by the sea, when stormy winds pile the water up into the shallow bays . . . Poor forlorn country! Though the soil is suitable for the raising of tropical fruits, the lack of fresh water and the terrible insect scourge make it simply torture to stay here."

It was into this forlorn country that Job plunged with his cameras and photographic plates in search of the plume birds. "We struck inland with our guide, Bradley, the game warden of Monroe County," Job wrote, "to visit a lake that lay several miles through the mangrove swamp. There was no boat in the lonely lake, but Bradley proposed to carry a canvas canoe. This we found hidden in the confines of the swamp. It weighed over fifty pounds, and as we pushed on hour after hour through the maze of mangrove roots and tropical jungle, following a trail so blind that we often lost it, I was amazed at the strength of the hardy pioneer who carried it—a man of only moderate weight and size. We took only an occasional rest, during one of which Bradley climbed to the nest of a Red-shouldered Hawk in a slender tree. He brought the young hawk down to me to photograph and returned it to its home."

Job followed Bradley through the "forbidding and awful wilderness," the guide slashing a path for them with his hatchet. When the sawgrass became impassable, Bradley touched a match to it, and the two men waited until the fury of the heat had subsided before continuing through the burn. Job tumbled into "deceitful" mud holes with his cameras and fell ill after succumbing to the temptation to drink the brackish water in the swamp. But at last he reached his heart's desire.

"I shall never forget the sight that greeted me as I emerged from the tangle," Job wrote, "and came to the edge of one of the impassable muddy bayous, about thirty feet wide bordered by thickets of mangrove. The trees were fairly alive with splendid great birds and their young (half-grown). The most abundant was the White Ibis, a fine creature snow white with black wing tips and brilliant red legs and bills, both long, the latter decurved. They are locally called 'White Curlews,' and are esteemed as one of the best and most abundant food birds of the region. The young are a dark gray color with white on the rump and were now at the stage when, though unable to fly, they had left the nests. The woods were fairly alive with them. Droves of them raced over the ground under the mangroves or climbed among the branches in all directions . . .

"Across the bayou we could hear, though not see, the large, graceful, snow-white American egrets and their young. As with the Peacocks, beauty of form and plumage is not matched with sweetness of song, and this lovely dream of a bird speaks in harshest rattling grunts. Much the same is true of the elegant Snowy Heron of plumage as its name implies. But what almost paralyzed me with excitement was the sight of half a dozen or so of large rosy pink birds quietly perched on the trees just opposite us across the border—the Roseate Spoonbill on its nesting ground! What a spectacle, the dark green mangroves' foliage dotted with ibises of dazzling whiteness, 'Pink Curlews,' and blue tinted [Louisiana] herons. Here I felt I had reached the high water mark of spectacular sights in the bird world."

The ultimate object of Job's journey was Cuthbert Lake, a name that reverberates as hauntingly in the history of plume hunting as that of Little Big Horn in a history of the Indian wars. Job has left us the best account of the rookery's discovery:

"About fifteen years ago it was known to the plume hunters that somewhere in the great mangrove swamp near the southern extremity of Florida was a very large rookery or breeding colony of herons, egrets and other water birds. Heretofore all efforts to locate it had proved unavailing—a fact which will surprise no one who has been even to the portals of that terrible wilderness. At length an individual named Cuthbert, with a hardihood worthy of a better cause, made a business of tracing out this mysterious rookery. Starting from the southern end of the west coast, probably somewhere on Whitewater Bay, he watched the flight of birds, formed an exact conclusion as to the direction of their course and plunged into the bewildering maze of the mangrove swamp.

"Carrying a meager outfit and a light canoe, he slept among the mangrove roots where night overtook him. From time to time he climbed a tree and verified his course by that of the birds. Now and then he utilized one of the muddy brackish lakes and secured a few moments' rest, as he paddled across, from the noise of the innumerable hordes of mosquitoes that made the life of man almost intolerable.

"How many days he was thus engaged is not known, but at length, forcing his canoe through a narrow overgrown channel from one of these lakes which seemed to lead to some other body of water, he came out into a round, open lake a mile-and-a-half across. Out in the middle he saw a small island of about two acres densely overgrown with mangrove trees, whose dark foliage was almost hidden under a canopy of snow-white birds—ibises, herons, egrets, and others of darker plumage. Making a closer investigation he found that the island was crowded by innumerable thousands of several kinds of birds, some of them the species whose plumage would bring the biggest prices. There they were, the nesting season at its height, brooding their eggs and feeding their young . . . The snap of his tiny Flobert rifle, inaudible a few rods away, attracted the attention of no wandering alligator-hunter.

"Weeks went by and matters were very different on the island. No bird now winged its way to the solicitude, save hordes of Turkey Vultures and Fish Crows. In the thousands of nests were swarms of flies around the decaying bodies of young birds that had starved to death. On the ground were reeking piles of the bodies of their natural protectors, each with strips of skin and plumage torn from its back. The rookery was as the local term has it, 'shot out!' The buzzards were gorged and happy, and so was the brutal Cuthbert with the $1800 from the wholesale milliners—so the story goes."

Bradley had located the Cuthbert Rookery in the course of his duties as an Audubon warden. The colony had somewhat recovered and Job, upon his arrival there after an arduous trip, found the sign warning away plume hunters that his guide had erected a few months before. Job estimated 3000 pairs of various wading birds were nesting there at the time. He photographed as many of the birds as he could reach, struggling through the tangled mangroves and mashing, quite by accident, quantities of mosquitoes between the films in packing his plates away. He even found the time to reflect on the superiority of his way of treating birds to that of Audubon, when "he and John Bachman visited an egret rookery and killed forty-six of the birds. He quaintly comments in his great book that 'many more of them might have been killed, but we became tired of shooting them.' No wonder! But those were un-enlightened times, and there was no camera hunting."

Guy Bradley made other trips to Cuthbert Lake, keeping watch over the rookery, but plume hunters kept watch over Bradley too. Often they observed his movements and went in to ply their destructive trade after he had gone away. In 1904 Bradley contracted to escort Frank M. Chapman to Cuthbert Lake, but brought bad news instead to their meeting place. The plume hunters had recently "shot it out," killing or driving away all of the nesting birds.

"You could've walked right around the rookery on those birds' bodies—between four and five hundred of them," Bradley said.

Then he mentioned something to Chapman that he had told him on earlier occasions. He expected an attempt to be made on his life.

There was good reason for Bradley's anxiety. He had made enemies among the gunners, especially a Flamingo man named Walter Smith, whose son he had arrested several times for killing birds. Smith had told his neighbors that if Bradley ever again tried to arrest any member of his family he would kill him.

Bradley went right on about his job. "He took a personal interest in his work," William Dutcher said later, "and he was genuinely proud when he could report an increase in the birds' numbers."

On July 8, 1905, Bradley was in his cottage at Flamingo. From the cottage he could look out across the wide calm sweep of Florida Bay. Once, happening to step out on the little porch, he caught sight of a sail on the horizon. He watched curiously as the sail moved toward a small island called Oyster Key, where a few plume birds occasionally gathered. Bradley guessed the boat was a schooner that belonged to Walter Smith. He pushed his own small boat into the water and rowed the two miles under a warm sun to Oyster Key. As he neared the schooner, which now lay rocking gently at anchor, he heard shots from the key. A figure appeared on the schooner's deck and fired a rifle into the air. Bradley knew that this was a signal for the hunters on the key to return to the schooner.

Rowing harder, Bradley reached the schooner just as Smith's son and a friend were climbing aboard. Each of them carried two dead egrets.

"What do you want, Bradley?" Walter Smith called down from the deck.

"I want to arrest your son," Bradley told him.

"You need a warrant to arrest him."

"No," Bradley said. "I heard the shots and I saw him with the dead birds. I don't need a warrant if I catch him in the act."

"Well, if you want him you have to come aboard and get him."

"Put down that rifle, Smith, and I'll come aboard," Bradley said.

The Audubon warden maneuvered his small boat closer to the schooner. Smith raised his Winchester rifle and fired. The bullet hit Bradley in the chest, killing him instantly. His body drifted for twenty-four hours in the small boat before two boys, curious about the turkey vultures wheeling over East Cape Sable, rowed out to it to make the discovery.

Bradley was buried nearby, on a ridge of snow-white shells overlooking the sea. Smith was taken to the county jail at Key West. Disturbed by the authorities' indifferent investigation, the National Association of Audubon Societies engaged a lawyer, Colonel James T. Sanders of Miami, in an attempt to see that justice was carried out. Smith pleaded self-defense when he appeared before a Grand Jury in Key West, contending that Bradley had fired first. Sanders pointed out that Bradley's pistol showed no powder marks on the barrel, "neither was the cylinder under the hammer of the pistol in a correct position, showing that the pistol had not recently been discharged." Several men who had been with Smith aboard his schooner testified to the events leading up to the shooting, but told the Grand Jury that they had gone below deck before the shots were fired. The Grand Jury, noting that the state had not presented a strong case against Smith, refused to indict him. Smith's neighbors in Flamingo burned his house down.

The incident had touched the public's conscience. "A home broken up," Dutcher wrote, "children left fatherless, a woman widowed and sorrowing, a faithful and devoted warden, who was a young and sturdy man, cut off in a moment, for what? That a few more plume birds might be secured to adorn heartless women's bonnets. Heretofore the price has been the life of the birds, now is added human blood."

The Audubon Societies raised money to buy a home for the widow in Key West. The names of Brewster, Chapman, Dutcher, and other ornithologists were high on the list of contributors; Job wrote an article for *Collier's* called "Bird Protection's First Martyr," and donated the magazine's check, $225, to the fund. Elsewhere, women's clubs forswore the use of plumes and encouraged others to do the same. And to Dutcher at the association's office in New York came a note under the letterhead of the White House, written by a man whose impact on the conservation movement already had been incalculable.

Dear Mr. Dutcher:

Permit me on behalf of both Mrs. Roosevelt and myself to say how heartily we sympathize not only with the work of the Audubon Societies generally, but particularly in their efforts to stop the sale and use of the so-called "Aigrettes"—the plumes of the white herons. If anything, Mrs. Roosevelt feels more strongly than I do in the matter.

The letter was signed by Theodore Roosevelt.

Part Two

The President and
the Forester

8

Straws in the Wind

The plume hunters were only a single agent in the massive assault that continued almost unchecked on America's natural resources until the end of the nineteenth century. An appreciation of scenic beauty, or even a sense of stewardship in relation to the land, was no part of the spiritual makeup of the settlers. Rather, most seemed to agree with Cotton Mather's pugnacious contention that "What is not useful is vicious." Mather himself had leaned on an even older authority. Genesis commanded man to "have dominion over the fish of the sea, and over the fowl of the air, and over the cattle, and over all the earth . . . and replenish the earth and subdue it."

To the Divine Word the settlers of the young nation added the conviction of their own political heritage. Men had been restrained in the Old World by rights traditionally assigned only to kings and the nobility. Much of the land, and the wild creatures on it, were forbidden to the great majority of the populace. Poaching was the only means by which common men could tap those rich natural resources. Now the Old World's fetters had been thrown off, and men would take what they could get without fear of authority or concern for tomorrow. The Bible and the Constitution seemed to allow Americans to exercise their dominion over the earth and its life without regard to the prick of conscience. And so, intent on wresting a living from the land, they confronted it with plow and ax and rifle, unmindful that its health depended upon its capacity for self-renewal.

Only occasional men concerned themselves with self-renewal, and they seemed to stand apart from their fellows. John Chapman, who called himself Johnny Appleseed, was no myth. He might well have served, however, as the prototype of a flower child—small and lean, unshaven, with long dark hair and a costume more in keeping with a rock festival than with old-time rural America. He trudged his lonely way barefooted, once in a while compromising himself by slipping on a pair of primitive sandals. (It is said that his novel method of curing the cuts he incurred by walking through thorns and briers was to "sear the wound with a red-hot iron, and cure the burn.")

His cloak was an old coffee sack, through whose random holes he thrust head and arms, and his hat the pot in which he cooked his mush. Later, bothered by the setting sun into which he walked on his way west, he fashioned a pasteboard hat with a long peak. Over his back he tossed a leather sack filled with the apple seeds he obtained from a cider press in western Pennsylvania. For almost fifty years, until his death in 1847, Johnny Appleseed crisscrossed Ohio and Indiana, planting orchards of apple trees at every likely spot. His fee was simply a meal, or a night's shelter. To this improbable pioneer, the act of cutting a tree seemed "a cruelty inflicted upon a sentient being."

But Johnny Appleseed was only a pretty story to the majority of Americans who found his view of life as preposterous as a monkish cell is to an old reprobate. They preferred to burn the environmental candle at both ends. And, it seemed, with good reason.

It was the vast region west of the Alleghenies that encouraged the belief that America's resources were unlimited. The public domain, and all it contained, were reckoned a bottomless grab bag into which the settler might dip his fingers and take what he wanted. Between 1781 and 1802 the Union's original states had ceded to the federal government most of their land claims in the West. To this abundant foundation of the public domain were added the Louisiana Purchase and each succeeding region envel-

oped by the young nation as it rolled inexorably to the Pacific. (Texas was an exception, retaining its public land as a condition of its agreement to join the Union.) The federal government's reaction to finding itself a huge landowner was to try to divest itself of its holdings as quickly as possible. In this procedure it was ably assisted by the railroads, the timber barons, and the other land-skinners, not always to the ultimate advantage of the nation.

To expedite the sale of the public domain, Congress established the General Land Office in 1812 as a part of the Treasury Department. The bargains henceforth available from this source inspired so many transactions that "doing a land-office business" became a part of every successful salesman's vocabulary. In 1849 the General Land Office became the first bureau in the newly created Department of the Interior. The government also gave away land as "incentive grants" to the railroads, gifts that finally totaled 150,000,000 acres before the end of the century; the railroads, in turn, often sold part of the land to raise money to lay their tracks, or for any other reason that caught their fancy. Finally, the government threw open the gates to westward expansion with the passage of the Homestead Act which became effective on January 1, 1863, the same day as the Emancipation Proclamation. Now each aspiring landowner could gain title to 160 acres of the public domain for a nominal fee, provided he lived on the land and worked it for a period of five years. Settlers flocked to the West, many to escape the draft during the Civil War. "The occupation of wild territory," wrote William Gilpin, an early governor of Colorado, "proceeds with all the solemnity of providential ordinance."

It was not a moment too soon. Both the land and the natural resources of the East were nearly exhausted. The dense forests of Maine, where twenty yoke of oxen had been needed to pull the giant white pines to wharves from which they were shipped across the Atlantic to be fashioned into the tall masts of English sailing vessels, were reduced to shambles. Even where the settlers did not require vast tracts of forest for timber or fuel, they set fires to clear the land for farming and hunting (and sometimes for protection from the Indians). In the South many farmers burned the forests simply to uncover oak and beech mast for their hogs and to clear the land of snakes. From Maine the loggers moved on to forests around the Great Lakes and to remote pine stands in the South; and from there across the Rocky Mountains to the Pacific Coast.

But the destruction was not entirely purposeful. Ignorance often played a large part, as it did in the Great Lakes region, where sloppy and inept forestry practices laid the land open to fires that devastated millions of acres. A fire that started in the woods near Peshtigo in northeastern Wisconsin in 1871 swept two counties of its trees, soil, and lumber camps, and killed 1200 people. In 1881, 169 people died in forest fires in Michigan, while 418 died in the great Hinckley fire that ravaged Minnesota in 1894. More than half a century later naturalist Aldo Leopold was to write that "when the modern cottager builds a log cabin, he uses imitation logs sawed out of slab piles in Idaho or Oregon, and hauled to Wisconsin woods in a freight car. The proverbial coals to Newcastle seem a mild irony compared with this."

Farther west grazing rivaled the ax in reducing the forests. John Muir, who had herded sheep and knew their habits at first hand, often railed at these "hoofed locusts."

"Nearly all our forests in the West are on mountains, and cover and protect the fountains of the rivers," he wrote. "They are being more and more deeply invaded and, of course, fires are multiplied; five to ten times as much lumber is burned as is used, to say nothing of the waste of lowlands by destructive floods. As sheep advance, flowers, grass, soil, plenty, and poetry vanish."

And indeed as the settlers themselves moved westward they swept from their path wildflowers and poetry as well as trees. Aldo Leopold has pointed out that it was, ironically, the railroads which preserved the diversity of flora across the prairies; delicate species survived beside the tracks, while they were plowed under and grazed over practically everywhere else (just as in densely populated regions of Europe certain rare plants persist only on the crumbling façades of ancient walls). The public domain, and with it the wilderness, was disappearing. Congress dreamed up new bargains almost every year:

·   The Timber Culture Act of 1873 gave land to any settler who cultivated trees on forty acres.

·   The Desert Land Act of 1873 gave land at $1.25 an acre to any settler who would agree to irrigate it.

·   The Timber and Stone Act of 1878 gave 160 acres of "nonmineral" land, at $2.50 an acre, to miners and settlers so that they could gather timber and other building materials with which to build needed structures on the land they intended to mine nearby.

• The Mineral Land Act of 1886 gave free land to those who settled it and developed its mineral potential.

All of the interest lay in "development" in its crudest sense. Few Americans cared for the scientific management of the land. Contemporary encyclopedias did not even mention forestry. There was not a native-born professional forester on the continent, although the American Forestry Association was founded in 1875, chiefly by landscape gardeners and the owners of large estates, whose interest lay in the appreciation and study of individual trees rather than in the management of large forests. It was with the support of many of these people that Governor Sterling Morton of Nebraska had proclaimed the first Arbor Day in 1872. (Later some forestry people were faintly critical of Arbor Day, contending that its purpose was simply to plant a few trees, and thus it obscured plans for the scientific management of existing forests.)

Reform did not flag for want of exhortation. Two of the most fertile minds in the history of the conservation movement were contemporary with the worst abuses, and even much of the most advanced thinking in environmental matters is based upon the work of George Perkins Marsh and John Wesley Powell.

Marsh was one of the most extraordinary Americans of the century—a Vermont lawyer, businessman, and farmer; and at the same time a linguist (he knew twenty languages), a geographer, a naturalist, a congressman, and a diplomat (President Zachary Taylor appointed him Minister to Turkey, President Abraham Lincoln appointed him Minister to Italy). He counted among his friends on the continent Matthew Arnold, the Brownings, Garibaldi, and de Lesseps. His travels in Europe, Asia, and North Africa confirmed the observations he had made at home: "The earth is fast becoming an unfit home for its noblest inhabitant, and another era of equal human crime and human improvidence . . . would reduce it to such a condition of impoverished productiveness, of shattered surface, of climatic excess, as to threaten the deprivation, barbarism, and perhaps even extinction of the species."

These peculiarly modern observations were made in Marsh's epochal book, *Man and Nature,* published in 1864. He saw things broadly, detecting the momentous consequences which follow the destruction of the land's forest cover; and he saw things close up,

tracing the chain of events through the "destruction of the mos-
quito, that feeds the trout that preys on the May fly that destroys
the eggs that hatch the salmon that pampers the epicure."

Marsh pointed out a new approach to man's relationship with
the earth. Because of his potential power to change the earth so
drastically—a new geological agent, so to speak—man must assume
a moral responsibility toward it. This was the idea of stewardship
on a global scale. A *laissez-faire* policy toward the riches of the earth
is immoral, for man is obliged to pass on these things to generations
yet unborn. Marsh urged large-scale planning to develop the nation's water resources and renew its forests. Nor was the responsibility to later generations simply an economic one.

"It is desirable that some large and easily accessible region of
America should remain, as far as possible, in its primitive condition," Marsh wrote, "at once a museum for the instruction of the
student, a garden for the recreation of the lover of nature, and an
asylum where indiginous tree, and humble plant that loves the
shade, and fish and fowl and four-footed beast, may dwell and
perpetuate their kind, in the enjoyment of such imperfect protection
as the laws of a people jealous of restraint can afford them."

Marsh had launched a seed on the wind that would bear mighty
fruit before the end of the century. But for the moment the words
of *Man and Nature* were taken seriously only by a small number of
scientists; General Ulysses S. Grant was at the threshold of the
White House, and his entry touched off the most unrestrained raids
on the country's natural resources that Americans are likely to
experience. Then, in 1868, the year that Grant became President,
another man was off on an adventure whose ultimate consequences
were to help undo some of the missteps of that unfortunate administration.

John Wesley Powell was an Illinois schoolteacher who fought with
the Union Army during the Civil War and lost his right arm at
Shiloh. After the war he became a professor of geology at Illinois
Wesleyan, from where his attention wandered to the geologic
marvels of the Far West. A man "electric with energy and ideas,"
Powell obtained partial government subsidies for his exploration
of the Grand Canyon in the form of rations from U.S. Army posts.
His voyage down the wild Colorado River in 1869 became one of
the great sagas of the opening of the West; several members of the

expedition turned back because of the hardships, three others who wandered off before its close were killed by Indians, but Powell completed the trip and proved that there was no passage through the Rocky Mountains to the Pacific Coast. The fame and honors that came to Powell after his return helped him to complete his monumental surveys of the "Great American Desert."

The old wives' tale that "rain follows the plow" had convinced many starry-eyed promoters that the great arid regions of the Southwest would blossom like the rose as soon as settlers arrived in force to till the land. Some of these settlers with their Midwest farming techniques were already moving into the region when Powell began his studies under a $10,000 appropriation from Congress. He completed the survey in 1878 and submitted it to the government under the title *A Report on the Lands of the Arid Region of the United States.*

Powell's report laid bare the principal myths; he pointed out the West's climatic uniqueness in the American picture, that in much of the area the annual rainfall amounted to less than twenty inches. Ordinary farming techniques were doomed to failure. Irrigation was the only solution to the region's aridity, but there was not enough water to go around. Powell called, in specific detail, for far-reaching reforms in the way Westerners would use their land and water. Among his recommendations was the revision of the Homestead Law; 160 acres were twice what a family would be able to farm under the limited amounts of water available, he said, but too little for ranching. Powell also submitted plans for the federal government to supervise the collection and distribution of water so that it would be done equably. These plans included the construction of dams and canals by the government, and the designation of prime reservoir sites so that they could not be claimed by speculators. In effect, Powell had designed a comprehensive land-and-water use plan for all of the western United States.

Neither Congress nor Westerners themselves were ready for the plan. It undermined the Homestead Act, as well as the glowing plans some western promoters had devised for the rapid exploitation of their part of the country. Years would pass, and numberless farmers and ranchers would come to grief, before Powell's farsighted suggestions were set, piece by piece, into practice. His most immediate accomplishment was the injection of science into the government land programs of the time: Congress created the Geological Survey, from which Powell, who soon became its chief, was able to carry on important pioneer surveys of the land and water of the United States.

Powell's most vigorous supporter in government was Carl Schurz, a German immigrant who, in 1877, became Secretary of the Interior in the cabinet of President Rutherford B. Hayes. He too was doomed to frustration in putting his plans into effect. On his inspection tours of government lands Schurz found all sorts of abuses, particularly in the destruction of forests on the public domain. At one place he discovered that private interests had built an entire mill town on public land to make their exploitation easier.

In calling for a new national forest policy, Schurz proposed the creation of government forest reserves. It was still the heyday of the exploiters, however, and their spokesmen in Congress were properly shocked. House Speaker James G. Blaine, from the logging state of Maine, accused Schurz of trying to introduce "Prussian methods" into an American administration. Schurz received little encouragement from Congress other than the passage of the Timber and Stone Act of 1878, granting the forests no relief from destruction, but at least forcing the loggers to pay the government a nominal fee for timber cut on the public domain.

"Deaf was Congress, and deaf the people seemed to be," Schurz lamented.

Schurz's proposal for national forest reserves was not as revolutionary as shocked congressmen pretended. The idea to set aside public land for the people's use or enjoyment was already in the air. As early as 1849 Andrew Jackson Downing, a well-known horticulturist, had made just such a proposal for an urban setting. Downing campaigned for a large municipal park in New York City, suggesting as its site the area where Central Park stands today. Though he died in 1852 in a spectacular fire aboard a Hudson River steamboat (its boilers blew up when it tried to meet another passenger boat's challenge for a race), his ideas continued to be spread by men like William Cullen Bryant.

There was, of course, bitter opposition to the idea of such an urban park. *The Journal of Commerce* called it "a perpetual edict of desolation against two and a half square miles of this small island," and a great many promoters and real estate men have shared this opinion in the years since. But in 1856 the city acquired the land suggested by Downing. Designed by Frederick Law Olmsted and Calvert Vaux, its 840 acres became a breath of life in the heart of the teeming island and an inspiration to civic reformers all across the country.

Now the idea of a "pleasuring ground" for the people was to take on a new dimension.

9

Yellowstone

In the summer of 1870 a party of nineteen men, many of considerable attainments in government service, set out on an exploration of the "Rock Yellow River" country in what is now northwestern Wyoming and the adjacent portions of Montana and Idaho. The region was known to the outside world chiefly through what many people believed to be myths: Jim Bridger, Joe Meek, and other mountain men had told fantastic stories about a land where smoke and boiling water poured out of the earth to form a landscape of yellow rock and ghostly shapes. No one believed them. Nor did they believe a writer by the name of David E. Folsum, who tried to sell an article in 1870 about a trip he had made to the area the year before; several magazines rejected the article on the grounds that it was "unbelievable," and only with considerable difficulty did he finally manage to get it into print.

Now an official exploring party under General Henry D. Washburn, a former Union officer in the Civil War and later surveyor-general of the Territory of Montana, was on its way to certify the questionable accounts. As the party reached the Yellowstone River, it continued across a plateau of stunning vistas. Lieutenant G. C. Doane, in charge of the expedition's military escort, later described the region:

"The river breaks through this plateau in a winding and impass-able canyon and trachyte lava over 2000 feet in depth; the middle canyon of the Yellowstone, rolling over volcanic boulders in some places, and in others forming still pools of seemingly fathomless depth. At one point it dashes here and there, lashed to a white foam, upon its rocky bed; at another it subsides into a crystal mirror wherever a deep basin occurs in the channel. Numerous small cascades are seen tumbling from the lofty summits, a mere ribbon of foam in the immeasurable distance below. This huge abyss, through walls of flinty lava, has not been worn away by the waters, for no trace of fluvial agency is left upon the rocks; it is a cleft in the strata brought about by volcanic action plainly shown by that irregular structure which gives such a ragged appearance to all such igneous formations. Standing on the brink of the chasm the heavy roaring of the imprisoned river comes to the ear only in a sort of hollow, hungry growl, scarcely audible from the depths, and strongly suggestive of demons in torment below. Lofty pines on the bank of the stream 'dwindle to shrubs in dizziness of dis-tance.' Everything beneath has a weird and deceptive appearance. The water does not look like water, but like oil. Numerous fishhawks are seen busily plying their vocation, sailing high above the waters, and yet a thousand feet below the spectator. In the clefts of the rocks, hundreds of feet down, bald eagles have their eyries, from which we can see them swooping still further into the depths to rob the ospreys of their hard earned trout. It is grand, gloomy, and terrible; a solitude peopled with fantastic ideas; an empire of shadows and turmoil."

This was the awesome West that people wanted to know more about—a land of majestic creatures and majestic scenery that pays no tribute to any other continent or older civilizations; something indisputably American, that is no myth at all, but which has provided the backdrop for some of our most cherished myths and romances. As the members of the expedition sat around their campfires in the evening and talked over what they had seen, they felt that this region should not go the way so much of the West already was headed. Apparently the leader of this sort of speculation was Judge Cornelius Hedges of Helena, an Easterner by birth, a graduate of Yale and later of Harvard Law School, who had adopted this territory as his own. He believed that the country they camped in was too grand to be staked out by any of them as a private possession. It should, instead, be deeded to all of the people of the United States as a "national park."

Hedges' companions agreed with him. The idea was carried back East, particularly by Nathaniel P. Langford, a member of the party who, several years earlier, had been appointed governor of the territory by President Andrew Johnson, but who never assumed the position because the appointment was defeated by Johnson's enemies in the Senate. Langford undertook a lecture tour through the East, extolling the precious resource that the people should seize and hold for their own. A man whose fancy was especially piqued by Langford's account of the region was Jay Cooke, the financier of the Northern Pacific Railroad. If a popular attraction were established in that remote area, Cooke reasoned, the railroad would be its chief beneficiary. Cooke subsidized Langford's lecture tour, and put up additional money to lobby in Washington for an act establishing a national park.

With such powerful support, the bill to establish "a pleasuring ground for the benefit and enjoyment of the people" sped through Congress in 1872. Curiously, it was neither the region's wild grandeur nor its value as a sanctuary for the West's dwindling big game that recommended it as a national park. Yellowstone was thought of as an oddity, a place of "beautiful decorations," a geological sideshow; it was as if nature itself had something to do with theatrical tableaux and menageries. This notion was in keeping with the cast of mind that prompted cultural leaders of the time to suggest that Phineas T. Barnum be appointed director of the Smithsonian Institution. The Yellowstone bill was put before President Ulysses S. Grant for his signature. Two years later Grant was to pigeonhole a bill designed to "prevent the useless slaughter of buffaloes within the Territories of the United States"; but in this case he signed into law the act creating Yellowstone, the nation's first national park and a refuge which eventually would shelter the last remnants of the great buffalo herds. *Scribner's* magazine applauded the act, predicting that "Yankee enterprise will dot the new Park with hostelries and furrow it with lines of travel."

The act creating Yellowstone National Park had ordered "the preservation, from injury or spoliation, of all timber, mineral deposits, natural curiosities or wonders within said park and their retention in their natural condition."

Because Wyoming, in which most of the park lies, had not yet achieved statehood, Congress gave custody of Yellowstone to the Department of the Interior. Charged with the park's "preservation," Interior found it an almost impossible burden. The concept of conservation had not yet taken hold in America. The park was valued chiefly for its geysers and fantastic geological formations, and there seemed to be no reason why curiosity-seekers should have to travel all the way to Yellowstone to admire the latter. Langford, appointed as Yellowstone's first superintendent, could stop neither the hunters who invaded the park to kill the buffaloes nor the vandals who came to carry away its geological treasures. Congress had appropriated no funds for law enforcement, and very little for upkeep and fire protection. Langford was succeeded as superintendent in 1877 by Major P. W. Norris, who supplemented the appropriation by killing buffaloes to feed his men and selling the rock formations to get needed cash. Norris, according to a later report, "protected the wonders by breaking them off with an ax and crowbar and shipping them by the carload to Washington and elsewhere."

In Washington itself the sentiment often seemed to be on the side of those who would not bother selling the park piecemeal, but proposed to get rid of it all at once. In opposing the appropriations for the park's upkeep in 1883, Senator John J. Ingalls of Kansas said, "The best thing the Government could do with the Yellowstone National Park is to survey it and sell it as other public lands are sold." It is no wonder then that a considerable menace to the park's preservation soon presented itself in the form of a railroad.

In the mid-1880s the Fork Railroad Company (an affiliate of the Northern Pacific) proposed building a line through the northeastern section of the park to reach such isolated mining towns as Cooke City. The proposal, of course, would have set a dangerous precedent, opening the park to all sorts of destructive schemes. But by this time a realization of the park's true value had dawned on many Americans, and in 1886 this realization found its expression on the floor of the House of Representatives.

"Is this not the only home for the game now in the park?" one congressman asked. "Is it not the only place that has been left to them?"

A spokesman for the bill minimized the extent of the land, and the numbers of game, that would be affected by the railroad. "But Mr. Chairman," he went on, "even if it were otherwise, is it true that the rights and privileges of citizenship, the vast accumulation of property and the demands of commerce of this country are to yield to the mere caprice of a few sportsmen bent only on the protection of a few buffalo in the National Park? . . . It is wholly unattractive country. There is nothing whatsoever in it, no object of interest to the tourist and there is not one out of twenty who ever visits for purposes of observation this remote region."

But the park found one of its ablest and most resolute defenders in Congressman Samuel S. Cox of New York.

"Mr. Chairman," Cox said, "I believe this bill is wrongly entitled. It should be denominated 'A bill for the spoliation of Yellowstone Park . . . This is a measure which is inspired by corporate greed and natural selfishness against national pride and natural beauty."

The bill was defeated at the time, but for ten years the growing conservation movement in this country repeatedly had to hurl back similar proposals. In 1892, Theodore Roosevelt, then a member of the United States Civil Service Commission, wrote to George Bird Grinnell:

"I have just read your article, 'A Standing Menace,' printed in *Forest and Stream,* in reference to the attempts made to destroy the National Park in the interests of Cooke City. I heartily agree with this article. It is of the utmost importance that the park shall be kept in its present form as a great forestry preserve and a National pleasure ground, the like of which is not to be found on any continent but ours; and all public-spirited Americans should join with *Forest and Stream* in the effort to prevent the greed of a little group of speculators, careless of everything save their own selfish interests, from doing the damage they threaten to the whole people of the United States, by wrecking the Yellowstone National Park."

It was thus fitting that Grinnell struck the heaviest blow against the proposed railroad. The railroad lobby had managed to have introduced in Congress, wrapped up in a "Segregation Bill," a neat solution to the problem: simply remove the contested region from the park, and there would be no unpleasantness about pushing a railroad through park property. The bill seemed to have an excellent chance of passage early in 1893 when a telegram, exhorting Democrats in Montana to apply political pressure on House Speaker Charles F. Crisp, fell into Grinnell's hands. Grinnell printed the wire with an indignant editorial entitled "Will Speaker Crisp Be Deceived?" Crisp had no choice but to resist the pressure and the House defeated the Segregation Bill. Plans for a railroad through the park were dropped completely several years later.

Meanwhile, Grinnell and the conservationists were fighting on another front. There had appeared in the vicinity of Yellowstone a number of those ruffians, brave, resourceful, ruthless, and just a little bit stupid, who make it hard to unravel fact and fiction in the history of the old West. These men invaded the park regularly to secure buffalo heads as trophies for wealthy collectors. Since they held a monopoly on the supply (the buffalo had been nearly extirpated everywhere else in the United States) the poachers demanded and received top prices for their wares. The average price of a head by this time was $300, it sometimes rose to $500, and eventually a collector in New York City was to pay $1500 for a splendid specimen. The poachers risked very little; though the U.S. Army had taken over the task of patrolling the park for vandals and poachers, Congress had not set any penalty for the destruction of animals or park property. If apprehended, the villain could receive no greater punishment than to be relieved of his equipment and ejected from the park.

A succession of poachers slipped in from Cooke City, the center of the silver and lead mining interests, just south of the park. If they could not locate the 400-odd buffaloes remaining in the area, they took elk or beaver—other species which seemed to have retreated to Yellowstone for a last stand. One of the most notorious poachers was T. S. Van Dyck, a market hunter who supplied game to the restaurants in Cooke City. (He should not be confused with T. S. Van Dyke, the noted outdoors writer of the time.) In 1891 a detachment of soldiers came upon Van Dyck sound asleep in his camp near the east fork of the Yellowstone River. The soldiers went about their business softly, gathering up Van Dyck's guns, field glass, and even his Kodak camera. With the camera they snapped pictures of him still sleeping peacefully next to his traps and contraband. Then they awoke him, hauled him into Fort Yellowstone, and held him in the guardhouse until it was evident that there were no grounds on which to prosecute him.

But the capture of another poacher, Ed Howell, became national news and influenced national policy. Howell was a drifter in the frontier tradition, working as a sheep-shearer in Arizona for ten dollars a day during the spring, and returning north to poach in Yellowstone in the fall. As winter drew near, the Army's chances of catching a poacher in the immense frozen wilderness of the park became almost nil. Isolated outposts were maintained by the Army in the park year-round. In winter the soldiers' only contact with the outside world was by the telephones to be found in three hotels scattered throughout the park and occupied during the off-season by caretakers whose isolation surpassed that of any doughty lighthouse keeper in the North Atlantic. (The telephone lines through the park were kept in repair by an Army employee known as "Snowshoe Pete," who was the only man allowed to travel alone through the inner vastnesses of Yellowstone during the winter.) The government's defense against wary poachers such as Howell was a single civilian scout, whose formidable assignment was to patrol, usually in the company of a soldier, Yellowstone's nearly 3500 square miles.

In the winter of 1893–94, Captain George S. Anderson, the park's superintendent, learned that Howell had left Cooke City heading for the Pelican Valley region of the park. Anderson must have wanted very badly to capture Howell; it was embarrassment enough for him to know that Howell was supplying taxidermists in nearby towns with buffalo heads and hides, but now there had appeared in the park a party of journalists and photographers assigned by *Forest and Stream* to prepare a story on "Yellowstone's Winter." Anderson ordered his civilian scout, Felix Burgess, to try to pick up Howell's trail.

To Emerson Hough, the author of *The Covered Wagon* and other popular novels of frontier life, and then *Forest and Stream's* chief correspondent on the Yellowstone expedition, the outside world owed a salute for a firsthand description of the rascally Howell. This is how Hough saw him at the end of the episode:

"Howell was, we found, a most picturesquely ragged, dirty and unkempt looking citizen. His beard had been scissored off. His hair hung low on his neck, curling up like a drake's tail. His eye was blue, his complexion florid. In height he seemed about five feet, ten inches. His shoulders were broad, but sloping. His neck stooped forward. His carriage was slouchy, loose-jointed and stooping, but he seemed a powerful fellow. Thick, protruding lips and large teeth completed the unfavorable cast of an exterior by no means prepossessing. He was dressed in outer covering of dirty, greasy overalls and jumper. He had no shoes, and he had only a thin and worthless pair of socks. He wrapped his feet and legs up in gunny sacking, and put his feet when snowshoeing into a pair of meal sacks he had nailed on to the middle of his snowshoes. The whole bundle he tied with thongs. His snowshoes (skis) were a curiosity. They were 12 feet long, narrow, made of pine (or spruce), Howell himself being the builder of them. The front of one had its curve supplemented by a bit of board, wired on. All sorts of curves existed in the bottoms of the shoes. He had them heavily covered with resin to keep the snow from sticking to them.

"To cap the climax he had broken one shoe while in the park—a mishap often very serious indeed, as one must have two shoes to walk with, and elsewise cannot walk at all. With the ready resources of a perfect woodsman, Howell took his axe, went to a fir tree, hewed out a three-cornered splice about 5 feet long, nailed it fast to the bottom of his broken shoe, picked out some pieces of resin, coated the shoe well with it, and went on his way as well as ever. He said he could travel as far in a day on those shoes as any man in the party could with any other pair, and I presume this is true. Moreover, Howell pulled a toboggan behind him all the way from Cooke City with a load of 180 pounds."

Burgess, the scout, proved to be a match for Howell in courage and woodsmanship. As a younger man Burgess had been captured and tortured by Crow Indians, losing two of his toes and a part of his "great toe" during the ordeal. Now, in the company of a private named Troike, he found the tracks of the wide runners on Howell's toboggan and set off in pursuit. By calculating Howell's probable destination (a small herd of buffaloes near Pelican Valley) Burgess cut across country to gain time. At Astringent Creek in Pelican Valley he came upon the heads of six buffaloes, packed in gunny sacks and hoisted out of reach into the trees by Howell with the aid of a block and tackle he carried with him on the toboggan. ("He was fixed for business," as Burgess said later.)

Burgess, his mutilated feet swollen and painful in the intense cold, stepped up his pace. After a time he heard six shots in the distance. Burgess knew that Howell had further reduced the world's few remaining buffaloes, for it was a simple matter to approach at close range the ponderous beasts, partly mired and thus defensless in the deep snow.

"The six shots killed five buffalo," Burgess told Hough afterward at the park's Norris Station. "Howell made his killing out in a little valley, and when I saw him he was about 400 yards away from the cover of the timber. I knew I had to cross that open space before I could get him sure. I had no rifle, but only an Army revolver, .38 caliber, the new model. I wouldn't have needed to get so close with a rifle before ordering him to throw up his hands. Howell's rifle was leaning against a dead buffalo, about 15 feet away from him. His hat was sort of flapped down over his eyes, and his head was toward me. He was leaning over, skinning on the head of one of the buffalo. His dog, though I didn't know it at first, was curled up under the hindleg of the dead buffalo. The wind was so the dog didn't smell me, or that would have settled it. That was lucky, wasn't it? Howell was going to kill the dog, after I took him, because the dog didn't bark at me and warn him. I wouldn't let him kill it. That's the dog outside—a bob-tailed, curly, sort of half-shepherd. It can get along on a snowshoe trail the best of any dog I ever saw, and it had followed Howell all through the journey, and was his only companion.

"I thought I could maybe get across without Howell seeing or hearing me, for the wind was blowing very hard. So I started over from cover, going as fast as I could travel. Right square across the way I found a ditch about 10 feet wide, and you know how hard it is to make a jump with snowshoes on level ground. I had to try it, anyhow, and some way I got over. I ran up to within 15 feet of Howell, between him and his gun, before I called to him to throw up his hands, and that was the first he knew of any one but him being anywhere in the country. He kind of stopped and stood stupid like, and I told him to drop his knife."

Burgess signaled Troike, who had remained hidden in the woods, and together they brought Howell back to Norris Station. Awaiting them was the jubilant Captain Anderson and the party from *Forest and Stream*. Though Howell balked at having his picture taken, he ate a hearty breakfast of twenty-four pancakes and readily submitted to an interview by Emerson Hough.

"If I'd seen Burgess first, he'd never arrested me," Howell bragged. "I'd have got away from him. It was so windy and stormy I never heard him until he got right up against me and hollered for me to put up my hands. He was sort of blowin', and was nervous like. I see I was subjec' to the drop, so I let go my knife and came along."

Howell was soon released, by order of Secretary of the Interior Hoke Smith, while a surgeon removed the remainder of Burgess's frozen big toe. But the exploit had a far-reaching influence on the future of the remaining buffalo. On the very day it occurred, Hough was able to telephone his story of the capture to the outside world; and later his more detailed account expressed "the firm belief that half the buffalo of the Park have been killed, and that not over 200 now remain alive. Certain it is that the traceable total of buffalo killed this year in the Park is alarmingly, appallingly large. There are not many more left to kill."

The public finally was ready to demand federal legislation to protect the buffalo. This was the end for which Representative John F. Lacey of Iowa (whose "Lacey Bill" was to help to save the plume birds six years later) had been working for some years. Now, in 1894, his colleagues felt they must take a firm stand against the Yellowstone poachers. Congress passed into law, and President Grover Cleveland quickly signed, the bill that Lacey had introduced for the protection of wildlife in national parks. The so-called "Park Protection Act of 1894" provided a jail sentence of up to two years, or a fine of up to $1000, for removing mineral deposits, cutting timber, or killing game in the park. The law also made it illegal for any railroad, stagecoach line, or individual to transport game taken from the park. Finally, it provided funds to build a jail within the park to hold violators of its provisions. Fittingly, the jail's first occupant was Ed Howell, who wandered into Yellowstone in violation of Anderson's order that he was permanently barred from the park.

Poaching continued off and on for some years, but the poachers themselves were now fair game.

10

The Lines Are Drawn

Dawn of a sort was breaking over the gloomy natural resources picture in the East. One of the few great wilderness areas left there was in the Adirondack region of upstate New York. Like every other region of the United States it had been badly abused by man: loggers, heedless of tomorrow, threatened to destroy its rich forest cover, while such game animals as the white-tailed deer were relentlessly pursued with dogs ("hounding") and shot at night ("jacklighting"); often hounds drove the deer into lakes, where hunters followed the struggling, half-drowned animals in boats and shot them at point-blank range.

A convergence of powerful interests proved to be the Adirondacks' salvation. Many wealthy families (among them Theodore Roosevelt's) spent part of their vacations there, hiking and camping, or living the elegantly simple life of well-to-do "rusticators." They began to grow apprehensive over the fate of their favorite playground.

Even more important was the apprehension felt by many businessmen in New York City, already sold on forest cover's value in maintaining watersheds.* Rumors abounded that if the loggers completed the destruction of the upstate forests, the state's rivers and canals would disintegrate in a ferment of alternating floods and droughts. The resultant blow to water transportation would hand the railroads a monopoly which any astute businessman (aware of the railroads' rapacious habits) might well anticipate with a certain grimness.

There was ample evidence to support the view that the water-retention capacity of the forests had diminished; water levels in the Hudson River and the Erie Canal already were declining in the 1880s. Accordingly the New York City Chamber of Commerce supported a bill to create a "Forest Preserve" in the Adirondacks. The New York State Legislature passed the bill in 1885, setting aside 715,000 acres. In 1892 the preserve was enlarged to 3,000,000 acres (larger than any national park today), and two years later, with the continuing support of the business community, the preserve's permanence was established by the state's Constitutional Convention. This kind of interest in New York's natural resources helped to create one of the earliest state fish and game commissions (1895) and eventually led to the Adirondack Deer Law that prohibited hounding and jacklighting.

"It is interesting to note," writes James B. Trefethen in his book, *Crusade for Wildlife,* "in view of an annual deer kill well in excess of 50,000 in recent years in New York State, that a contemporary [circa 1895] estimated seasonal kill of 5000 was regarded as 'excessive'."

But it was the creation of the Forest Preserve that left the most enduring mark on conservation. Though state forest agencies had been set up earlier in Ohio, Colorado, and California, the immensity of the Adirondack area presaged the first federal reserves six years later. American forestry, here and there, was coming into its own.

By this time the federal government's interest in its forests had been confirmed by the formation of a Division of Forestry within

*A hillside covered with trees or other vegetation tends to slow, and eventually store, much of the rainwater that on bare slopes rushes all at once into nearby rivers and streams; conversely, in times of drought the stored water slowly seeps into waterways, maintaining a relatively even flow. While the value of forest cover in this respect has often been overstated, in the main it serves an extremely useful purpose in mitigating the effects of both droughts and floods.

the Department of Agriculture (in 1881). Bernard E. Fernow, a German immigrant, became the division's first chief. He was a capable and dedicated man, a little before his time in attempting to make some order out of the approach Americans took toward their forests, and certainly better fitted for his position than anyone else in the country. He had studied at the Forest Academy in Hannover, then practiced the new science of forestry in Silesia and East Prussia. After marrying an American woman he came to the United States and set himself up as the country's first "forestry consultant."

Unfortunately, the work was slow until the government cast about for a chief for its Division of Forestry. After he was appointed to the position Fernow busied himself for a time with statistics on American forests and their products, then became sidetracked into performing some experiments in rain-making. A series of tumultuous explosions over Washington resulted, and sent him back to his statistics. However, Fernow wrote an important bulletin on the value of forests in preserving water supplies, thus planting the seed which produced support later on in the thirsty West for the government's forest programs.

Salvation was just around the corner, though it would have been hard to detect from the vantage point of 1890. The audacity of the land-skinners, dramatized on the circumscribed stage of Yellowstone, was becoming increasingly apparent in all sectors of the public domain. Charles S. Sargent, director of the Arnold Arboretum at Harvard, suggested that public forests be entrusted to the Army's care, and that the science of forestry itself be taught at West Point. This suggestion was by no means a sign of panic. The perils of the frontier had brought the Army into all sorts of scientific undertakings, and many of the men who contributed most to the natural sciences and resources during the nineteenth century (from Captain Meriwether Lewis to Major John Wesley Powell) prefixed their names with military titles. The Army, which carried on weather forecasting as well as vital geological and topographical surveys, remained an important scientific arm of the government until the final (oh, so final) pacification of the Indians.

It would indeed have called for an army to save the forests from men like S. A. D. Puter, and the "Eastern capitalists" who used his special talent for larceny. Puter was a West Coast lumberman who learned early in life that the fastest road to a comfortable living

lay through a thorough knowledge of the existing governmental legislation designed to protect the public domain. There was, for instance, the Swamplands Act—a congressional grant of "swamp and overflow" lands to the states in order to encourage the drainage and settling of swampy areas. A state might obtain a patent to those parts of the public domain which it could prove to be a "watery place"; then claimants were entitled to buy the land from the state at $1.25 an acre. Generally the process was initiated by an individual, who signed a statement which somehow proved the land to be "watery." The General Land Office, looking into the sale of extensive and valuable redwood tracts in California under this statute, learned a claimant under suspicion for fraud had not falsified his declaration that he had traversed the land by boat; indeed, he had had his boat mounted on an axle and wheels, and pulled through the redwood forests by oxen.

Puter found the Timber and Stone Act of 1877 especially susceptible to craftiness. When portions of the public domain were offered for sale under the terms of this act, each individual or corporation was restricted in the amount of land it was permitted to buy. Puter, who was involved in much of the scheming in California's Humboldt County during the 1880s, later repented and exposed the way in which the scoundrels worked.

"As soon as the land was surveyed and thrown open to entry," Puter wrote, "the California Redwood Company, with offices in Eureka, began to file on the entire tract under the Timber and Stone Act. At that time, the persons desiring to avail themselves of its provisions were not required to make a personal examination of the portions they wished to file on, nor were they obliged to go to the land office to make final proof. All that was necessary in this connection was for the entryman to appear at the land office at the time of making the filing, exhibit his first papers to show that he was a citizen of the United States, or had declared his intention to become such, or, in the case of his being a bona fide citizen, to make an oath to that effect, and his entry would be allowed . . .

"Under the conditions, the company was enabled to run men into the land office by the hundreds. I have known agents of the company to take at one time as many as twenty-five men from 'Coffee Jack's' sailor boarding house in Eureka to the county courthouse, where they would take out their first papers, declare their intention to become citizens of the United States, after which they would proceed direct to the land office and make their filings; all the location papers having previously been made out. Then they would appear before Fred W. Bell, a notary public, and execute an acknowledgment of a blank deed, receive the stipulated price of $50, and return to their ships, or to the boarding house from whence they came. The description of the tract filed on was afterward inserted and the transfer of the title completed to the corporation. As fast as this land came into the market, the company gobbled it all up in this fashion."

Puter moved his base of operations to the Northwest, where he was later described by the press as "King of the Oregon Land Fraud Ring." At one point, so many claimants had filed for land that the local Land Office was obliged to suspend business for several days in order to catch up with the accumulated paper work. Speculators poured into Oregon from all over the country, in turn sending men hired for the purpose into the woods to file on timber claims.

"Thousands upon thousands of acres," Puter wrote, "which included the very cream of the timber claims in Oregon and Washington, were secured by Eastern lumbermen and capitalists, the majority of whom came from Wisconsin, Michigan, and Minnesota, and nearly all of these claims, to my certain knowledge, were fraudulently obtained. As to the special agents sent out by the government, they were picked up, each in turn, as they appeared on the scene, and with the capitalists and locators standing hand in hand, it was an easy matter, with the aid of these agents, to baffle the Government in its attempts to secure evidence."

So topheavy did the structure of corruption become at last that the government was able to obtain its evidence. Puter and many others, including a United States Senator (John H. Mitchell of Oregon), a congressman, two former United States attorneys, and several members of the state legislature, were arrested and sent to prison. Puter whiled away the time in his cell by dictating his memoirs to a former employee of the General Land Office. The memoirs eventually were published in a bulky volume entitled *Looters of the Public Domain.*

Relief when it did come has since been described as a "fluke." One of the landmark pieces of conservation legislation was slipped past the looters and their representatives in Congress through a rider hastily inserted in a public lands bill late in 1891. The man most instrumental in this master political stroke was John W. Noble, Secretary of the Interior in the cabinet of President Benjamin Harrison. Noble, encouraged by his chief forester, Fernow, approached Harrison with the idea of setting aside a part of the public domain as forest reserves.

Though there existed no presidential authority for such an act, Harrison was interested. He permitted Noble to append a rider to a bill then before Congress. It was toward the end of the session and the members of Congress were anxious to adjourn. Noble countered their objections to such a rider with a hint that Harrison might veto the entire bill unless the rider were included, and the bill went through intact. This, the General Land Law Revision Act of 1891, gave to the President the authority to create forest reserves from the public domain by proclamation. Though Congress had not provided funds for their management, Harrison almost immediately set aside fifteen reserves, totaling 13,000,000 acres, most of which were on the Pacific slope. Among them was a large tract of sequoia, a tree often cut though its brittle wood made poor lumber. (Ray Lyman Wilbur once remarked that talking about the majestic sequoia in terms of board feet was like talking about German soldiers in terms of lard.)

"We are all heartily in earnest in endeavoring to reserve forest lands for the preservation of the water supply hereafter," Noble wrote at the time. "It is made somewhat difficult by the outcry of a few wherever these reservations are attempted; but I think the country will come to understand that the great need of the future ought not to be retarded in the interests of but a small part, indeed, of the people now living. There is no interest more important, or demanding greater care."

At first many Western groups looked favorably on the reserves. Those who were interested in the use of water for irrigation and power (and those in California who feared damaging floods) understood the forests' role in the protection of watersheds. But there was as yet no plan for the management of the reserves. Westerners began to grumble about a "lockup" of their natural resources. In 1897, when President Cleveland withdrew another 21,000,000 acres from the public domain and placed them in reserves, there was a deafening outcry from the West. Westerners, mostly adherents of William Jennings Bryan and the free-silver crusade, already harbored considerable hostility toward Cleveland and the other Eastern "gold" Democrats. It is said that over 30,000 people attended a mass meeting in Deadwood, South Dakota, to protest the President's proclamation. Threats of impeachment proceedings against Cleveland arose in Congress. They were not carried out, but Western congressmen pushed through a bill rescinding the orders of both Harrison and Cleveland that created forest reserves. Fortunately it was late in the session, and Cleveland (a lame duck President) saved the reserves by killing the bill with a pocket veto.

Nevertheless, the entire concept of forest reserves faced disaster. Westerners in the new session of Congress tried once more to rescind the proclamations, but were beaten back by Easterners concerned with forest preservation. One Western congressman cried out in frustration: "Why should we be everlastingly and eternally harassed and annoyed and bedeviled by these scientific gentlemen from Harvard College?"

The new session of Congress managed to clarify the forest problem a little by passing the Forest Management Act of 1897. This act placed the reserves under the management of the General Land Office in the Department of the Interior; the Secretary was given the authority to "regulate the occupancy and use" of these reserves, as well as to sell their timber. While the act neither granted nor forbade grazing in the reserves, it reflected the pressure of mining interests by allowing them to apply for patents, as they were able to do on all the rest of the public domain. But the Forest Management Act was merely a stopgap. It was politically (and, some said, economically) unfeasible at that time to restrict entry to great tracts of the Western forests. Clearly, an exceptional man with an exceptional plan was needed for the salvation of those forests—and that man was already on the scene.

Gifford Pinchot transformed early conservation ideas into administrative action. He was, in a sense, to the manor born. His wealthy father, James M. Pinchot, sent him to Yale and afterward financed the extensive training that made him America's first native-born professional forester. (Pinchot's parents were to establish the School of Forestry at Yale, endowing it with $300,000.) Since Europe was the only place where he could learn the principles of forestry, Pinchot studied at the National School of Forestry at

Nancy, France, and toured other countries to see practical demonstrations and results of the science. Upon his return from Europe in 1892 he was hired by George W. Vanderbilt (a grandson of Commodore Cornelius Vanderbilt) to manage the forest on his estate, Biltmore,* near Asheville, North Carolina.

The challenge presented to the young forester by these 7800 acres may be gauged by a description of Biltmore that appeared sometime later in *Forest and Stream:*

"Up to the time of its purchase by Mr. Vanderbilt, this forest was owned by a number of different individuals, who treated it in the usual American farmer's way. They cut all the timber that was salable either for saw logs, fence rails or cord wood, and turned the cattle into the forest to graze, often burning the woods over for the sake of the pasturage. The evil results of such a course are sufficiently obvious, and the woodland—never in its best days very good—grew steadily worse."

Pinchot began by excluding cattle from the forested areas, then cut only those trees which shaded the younger, still-growing, ones. The forest responded quickly to this form of selective logging: Pinchot's first year of operations showed a loss of only $400, a period when much heavier losses were expected. Biltmore was soon another profitable addition to the Vanderbilt holdings, and young Pinchot's reputation was made. Already afire with the notion of public service in his new profession, he was gratified when the call came from Washington.

Hoke Smith, as Secretary of the Interior, had been asked by a number of men interested in the fate of American forests to prepare some sort of census of their present condition. Since very little information of this nature was at hand, Smith suggested that the National Academy of Sciences appoint a National Forest Commission to prepare the study. Congress, falling in step, appropriated $25,000 so that the commission's members could tour forests on the public lands. Charles S. Sargent, the Harvard professor who wanted to put the Army in charge of the forests, became the commission's chairman; Gifford Pinchot, though not a member of the National Academy of Sciences, became its secretary.

As he set off with the commission in 1896, the thirty-one-year-old Pinchot was by no means overshadowed by his elders on the

---

*"Biltmore" was a word created by the Vanderbilts from *Bildt,* the Dutch town from which the family took its name, and *more,* an obsolete English word for rolling, upland country.

tour. Tall and lean, with clear blue eyes and a sharp patrician nose, he was every inch the "promising young man." There was something of the Spartan general in his leadership. He could ride and shoot, and for all his money he smacked somehow of austerity (he became an outspoken prohibitionist). In fact, Pinchot met his match only in the West when John Muir joined the tour in an *ex officio* capacity.

Here were the two men destined to be the most influential conservationists of their time. Pinchot, who hitched his wagon to a presidential star, was to use his favored position at the White House to shape the nation's basic conservation policies for decades to come. Muir, a voice crying in the Sierra wilderness, was to end his life in bitter defeat (a defeat to which Pinchot substantially contributed), but the seeds he sowed in his books and articles were to shoulder their way to equal prominence when they were most needed.

At first the two men were friends. Every man on the tour, of course, was awed by the elemental strength of Muir's personality. They had read his articles, they knew of his lonely wanderings in the mountains and of the religious intensity with which he communicated his conviction of man's oneness with the rest of the natural world. But between Pinchot and Muir a special admiration sprang up. It seemed that these two men could pool their gifts to shape the environment of a whole continent. Pinchot later recalled (not without some nostalgia) the commission's side trip to the Grand Canyon:

"While the others drove to the woods to a 'scenic point' and back again, with John Muir I spent an unforgettable day on the rim of the prodigious chasm, letting it soak in. I remember that at first we mistook for rocks the waves of rapids in the mud-laden Colorado, a mile below us. And when we came across a tarantula he wouldn't let me kill it. He said it had as much right there as we did.

"Muir was a storyteller in a million. For weeks I had been trying to make him tell me the tale of his adventure with a dog and an Alaskan glacier, afterward printed under the title of *Stickeen*. If I could get him alone at the campfire! We had left from our lunches a hard-boiled egg and one small sandwich apiece, and water enough in our canteens. Why go back to the hotel?

"That, it developed, suited Muir as much as it did me. So we made our beds of cedar boughs in a thick stand that kept the wind away, and there he talked until midnight. It was such an evening as I never had before or since.

"That night it froze, but the fire kept us from freezing. In the early morning we sneaked back like guilty schoolboys, well knowing that we must reckon with the other members of the Commission, who probably imagined we had fallen over a cliff. They had done just that, and they told us what they thought of us with clarity and conviction."

But intracommission amity soon foundered on more serious issues. Sargent still believed the Army should be employed to keep the forest reserves inviolate; Pinchot led a dissident faction on the commission, arguing from both a professional forester's and a wise politician's standpoint that the reserves should be "managed" rather than locked up. He knew the bitterness that the presidential proclamations had spread through the West. To irritate any further the Westerners, who felt put upon by Eastern do-gooders, would be to jeopardize the whole concept of the reserves. The two factions agreed only in their report that new reserves must be created if the forests were not to face total ruin.

Pinchot, the forester, had now plunged into politics. He crusaded among congressmen, government officials, and the interested public for his ideas about forest management. Some of these ideas (clearly reflecting his training abroad) received their most concise expression a little later when Pinchot wrote his *Forestry:*

"Except China, all civilized nations care for the forest. Until recently the United States ranked nearly with China in this respect and our country still remains far behind the progressive modern nations in nearly all that relates to the protection, preservation and conservative use of the forest . . . Nearly 200 years before the discovery of America the city of Zurich began to make rules for the protection and management of the Sihlwald . . . In the canton of Bern, a decree of the year 1592 warned the people against the wasteful use of timber and directed that for every tree cut down a young one should be planted in its place. [It is curious to find this mistaken prescription for the ills of the forest already in fashion more than three centuries ago. To save the forest every old tree must be replaced by *many* young ones.] In Germany the scientific treatment of forests has reached perhaps its highest development. The forests of France have perfected a most practical and effective general system of forestry and have created the difficult art of controlling the floods of mountain torrents by planting trees . . . They developed the art of reforesting denuded mountains and were the first to plant trees on moving sand dunes along the seashore. More than 150,000 acres of these dunes which once were blown about by the wind until they overwhelmed great stretches of fertile ground and even threatened to bury whole towns are now covered with forests and provide great quantities of turpentine, timber, and charcoal."

In 1897 Cornelius N. Bliss, Secretary of the Interior under President William McKinley, appointed Pinchot a "confidential forest agent" to keep an eye on the reserves and submit recommendations to him. Pinchot toured the country again, campaigning for his forestry plans while placating the various Western interests who feared they would be locked out of the reserves. He was adept in the art of compromise. In Seattle he calmed sheepmen's fears by telling them he saw no harm in letting them graze their animals in the reserves (an opinion he later revised). Unknown to Pinchot, John Muir was in the city that day, stopping there on the way home from a trip to Alaska. Muir was stunned when he read his friend's statement in the newspaper. Still carrying the paper, he went downstairs to the hotel lobby, where he encountered Pinchot.

"Are you correctly quoted here?" Muir demanded, his eyes blazing.

Pinchot, knowing he was being overheard by several reporters nearby, could not compromise in this situation. He acknowledged that he had been correctly quoted.

"Then I want nothing more to do with you," Muir said.

At that moment more than a friendship split. The American conservation movement (as yet even unnamed!) broke in two. For Muir, the wilderness was a temple in which man needed to seek the refreshment—literally the re-creation—of body, mind, and spirit; though he recognized the value of forest products, water power, livestock and mining, all of these, he believed with all his heart and soul, took their places behind the primary purpose of the diminishing wilderness. Pinchot believed otherwise; the forests' salvation was through use, its trees to be perpetually renewed through wise management. He embraced the concept of "multiple use," but re-creation, wildlife preservation, and all the other values ultimately must fall into line behind the primary value of utility: forests are for cutting.

In 1898 "Tama Jim" Wilson, Secretary of Agriculture, appointed Pinchot chief of the Forestry Division in his department. It was a little like being appointed Admiral of the Fleet in the Swiss Navy. The forests were still under the jurisdiction of the General Land Office over in the Interior Department, an arrangement Pinchot looked upon with ill-disguised hostility. The General Land Office was a refuge for all the incompetents, congressmen's cousins, and political hacks in Washington. Pinchot bided his time. From a nucleus of ten employees in his division, he began to build a tightly knit corps of competent, utterly loyal men. As of now they could only collect statistics, offer advice, and perform other chores of a less than urgent nature. But Pinchot, talking, writing, studying, was preparing for the day when the forests would be deposited in his lap.

He did not have long to wait. In 1898, Colonel Theodore Roosevelt, the hero of San Juan Hill, returned from Cuba and the Spanish-American War to win the governorship of New York. Intensely interested in wildlife, forests, and the outdoors generally, he sought capable advice, and asked Pinchot to make suggestions that would improve the state forests. Pinchot went to Albany, and the Governor and the Forester hit it off at once.

"I laid before the governor my plan for a singleheaded New York Forest Commission instead of the spineless, many-headed commission of those days, and he approved it entirely," Pinchot wrote in *Breaking New Ground*. "TR and I did a little wrestling, at which he beat me; and some boxing, during which I had the honor of knocking the future President of the United States off his very sturdy pins."

This friendship was going to endure.

11

The Road to the White House

We tend to think of Theodore Roosevelt as a bluff, hearty fellow storming enemy breastworks on horseback, killing big game in the Bad Lands or on the African Plains, dispatching gunboats, busting trusts, walking always with a big stick. His nether side—the amateur scholar, scientist, birdwatcher, and "preservationist"—is less often brought up in books and histories. And yet, not altogether suprisingly, it is in this direction that his accomplishments are most permanent. Certainly he did not hide this part of himself from public view, since he approached even the less flamboyant pursuits in the spirit that caused Elihu Root, his Secretary of State, to comment that Roosevelt imagined he had discovered the Ten Commandments. In this respect, as in their love for the out-of-doors, Roosevelt and Pinchot were blood brothers.

Roosevelt's passion for natural history at first was merely literary. A sickly child, wracked by frequent attacks of asthma, he was considered too delicate for school, and received his education from tutors. And from books. Books on hunting and exploring and natural history fascinated him. That he had no laboratory at his disposal in his New York City home did not prevent him from early investigations.

"I remember distinctly the first day that I started my career as a zoologist," he wrote in his autobiography. "I was walking up Broadway and as I passed the market to which I used sometimes to be sent before breakfast to get strawberries I suddenly saw a dead seal laid out on a slab of wood. That seal filled me with every possible feeling of romance and adventure . . . I measured it, and I recall that, not having a tape measure, I had to do my best to get its girth with a folding pocket foot-rule—a difficult undertaking. I had vague aspirations of in some way owning and preserving that seal, but they never got beyond the purely formless stage. I think, however, I did get the seal's skull, and with two of my cousins promptly started what we ambitiously called the 'Roosevelt Museum of Natural History.'"

He was eight years old. Natural history also became a prominent subject in the diary he kept as a boy, and the meticulousness, over a long period of time, with which he made his observations and his entries was quite remarkable. It was still more remarkable when we consider the handicap under which he made those observations. Just before leaving on the trip abroad with his parents that was to take him to Egypt and the Nile, young Theodore learned while playing with other boys that he was extremely nearsighted. They could read distant signs, he could not even make out the fact that there was lettering on them. The idea of eye trouble simply had never occurred to him, or to his family! "The only things I could study were those I ran against or stumbled over," he wrote later with some chagrin. "I had no idea how beautiful the world was." Fitted out with a pair of thick eyeglasses, he set sail for the Nile, where he shot and stuffed a large number of birds and made observations on the English sparrow's habits which he later put to use during the "sparrow war" in Cambridge.

When he entered Harvard it was apparently with the intention of becoming a naturalist. But by this time Roosevelt had acquired a taste for the outdoors on his many trips with his family, and he chafed under the almost singleminded attention given to laboratory studies at Harvard. He felt field studies were badly underrated. Moreover, with his poor eyesight, he found painful the long hours spent peering into another world through the microscope; one is reminded of the half-blind James Thurber trying unsuccessfully for two semesters to make out the plant cells that all of his classmates saw at a glance at Ohio State.

After his graduation from Harvard in 1880, Roosevelt set out on a career in politics instead. He became a highly regarded member of the New York State Legislature. And then, on February 13, 1884, tragedy struck him a double blow. His beloved mother and his young wife died on the same day, leaving him with an infant daughter, Alice, and an overwhelming sense of bereavement. He left politics and the East for a new life on a ranch which he bought in the Bad Lands of North Dakota. (Today, much of the land he owned is preserved in the Theodore Roosevelt National Memorial Park.)

Perhaps this western experience preserved his sanity. He became tougher in mind and body as he managed his ranch (he ultimately failed in this operation), hunted big game, and even served briefly as a deputy sheriff. He welcomed physical hardship in a country that still had not been completely subdued by man. In formidable middle age he liked to tell his children about the excitement of those long-ago days.

"We used to hear stories about Father's long, lonely trips on the prairies when it was often hard to find water in that arid land," his daughter Ethel once wrote. "Of the delicious taste of tomato juice at such times; and how he even learned to like prune juice. Whether this was told us in a commendable effort to increase our somewhat lukewarm enthusiasm for prunes I do not know."

Roosevelt, the hunter, learned a great deal about animals in the West, and he was present during the period of the precipitate decline of such species as the buffalo, the elk, and the bighorn sheep. His early reading and study helped him to extrapolate the local decline to a national scale, and also to see it against the background of environmental devastation. The ruined forests, the eroded earth, and the parched riverbeds appeared to him as the reality of life in the modern West. When he returned to the East in 1886 it was with a new sense of the American land and its wildlife. This concept was to concern him until the day he died.

But first there were other matters to attend to. There were preparations for his marriage to Edith Carow, a childhood friend. And there was a return to politics when friends, aware of his special talents in that field, urged him to run for Mayor of New York City. Unfortunately, there was a skeleton in Roosevelt's political closet. Before leaving for the West in 1884 he had been a delegate to the Republican National Convention, where he had first strenuously opposed the nomination of James G. Blaine for President, then jumped belatedly on his bandwagon. This defection had not been forgotten by the dissident Republicans, or Mugwumps, whose animosity toward Blaine was intense and their memories long. (The conservative New York *Sun* once remarked that "the objectionable thing about the Mugwump is not his wumpishness but his muggery.") When the Mugwumps threw their support to Abram S. Hewitt, the Democratic candidate, Roosevelt ran third behind Hewitt and Henry George, the labor and socialist candidate. "This is the end of my political career," Roosevelt told a friend.

He turned to less punishing forms of public service. He set about completing his four-volume work, *The Winning of the West,* and also conceived the organization which became known as the Boone and Crockett Club. (George Bird Grinnell of *Forest and Stream* was another charter member.) Though a prospective member must have shot adult males of at least three species of American big game, the club's chief purpose was to work on behalf of wildlife survival, and its members were in the thick of many of the most crucial conservation battles in the years ahead. The Boone and Crockett Club worked strenuously for the preservation of Yellowstone, and was largely instrumental in the foundation of both the New York Zoological Park (the Bronx Zoo) and the National Zoological Park in Washington.*

In 1889 President Benjamin Harrison appointed Roosevelt to the Civil Service Commission. "TR" was in active public service once more, and his career proceeded with a sort of manifest destiny of its own. He served on the commission with distinction until 1895, when he became president of the Police Board in New York City. President McKinley appointed him Assistant Secretary of the Navy in 1897, a post he soon resigned to become a lieutenant colonel (and war hero) with the "Rough Riders" of the First Volunteer Cavalry during the Spanish-American War.

Roosevelt returned from Cuba to win election as the Governor of New York. In that position he so antagonized "Boss" Thomas C. Platt and other conservative Republicans that they determined to get him out of the way. No more desolate *cul-de-sac* could be conceived of by these political activists than the vice-presidency

---

*Ironically, one of the club's associate memberships was bestowed upon General Philip H. Sheridan, who had recommended the annihilation of the buffalo as the first step toward the "pacification" of the Indian.

of the United States. Feeling that this time his political career truly was moribund, Roosevelt passively took his place with McKinley on the Republican ticket in 1900. When the campaign began, however, he worked earnestly for the party and the subsequent Republican victory brought him to Washington in the nation's second highest office. His term in that office was brief. In early September 1901, McKinley went to Buffalo, New York, to speak at the Pan-American Exposition. There a bullet fired by the anarchist Leon Czolgosz cut him down, and he died on September 14. On the train returning from McKinley's funeral, Mark Hanna, the conservative Republican "kingmaker," expressed his bitterness.

"I told McKinley it was a mistake to nominate that wild man," he said. "I asked him if he realized what would happen if he should die. Now look—that damned cowboy is President of the United States!"

12

The Presidency

Theodore Roosevelt, at forty-three, became the youngest President to enter the White House. The "damned cowboy" went right to work weaving his passion for the out-of-doors into national policy. In his first State of the Union message he sounded the keynote, contending that "the forest and water problems are perhaps the most vital internal questions of the United States." Then he spelled out the approach his administration would take toward natural resources, and in the process established what was to be almost the sole basis of our national conservation policy for more than half a century:

"The fundamental idea of forestry is the perpetuation of forests by use. Forest protection is not an end in itself: it is a means to increase and sustain the resources of our country and the industries which depend upon them. The preservation of our forests is an imperative business necessity. We have come to see clearly that whatever destroys the forest, except to make way for agriculture, threatens our wellbeing."

This passage in the President's speech was written, of course, by Gifford Pinchot. An assassin's bullet had presented the chief of an obscure governmental bureau with an opportunity, almost unique in the country's history, to put into practice his cherished vision. Pinchot enjoyed a special relationship with the President, and all the freedom of action that went with it. In access to Roosevelt's ear and the influence that this position implies, Pinchot (Chief Forester in the Department of Agriculture) stood well above most cabinet members, especially the Secretaries of Agriculture and Interior. This minister almost without portfolio, characterized by immense energy, unshakable self-assurance, and impeccable probity, was bound to ruffle feathers in a great many places (and, in another administration, in the highest place of all). There is some justification for Harold L. Ickes' later reference to Pinchot as "Sir Galahad of the Woodlands." But Sir Galahad was in the saddle, and he knew that in most matters he would get his own way. Though it was now in his power to set much of the national policy toward resources, there was one tangible asset he wanted very much, and that was control over the forest reserves.

His grab for the reserves was not a manifestation of a bureaucrat's lust for power, but the reaction of a professional pained by the spectacle of incompetence. Though it was to be some time before the reserves were his, the goal was in sight and he lost no opportunity to vent his feelings on the matter. The General Land Office in the Department of the Interior still "managed" the reserves. In actuality there was not a single forester among the political hacks who staffed that bureau; the Land Office itself had been established not to manage the public lands but to give them away. The men who made forest policy in Washington had not the faintest idea about what was going on in the reserves. At one point an order was sent to several reserves to buy rakes with which to rake up the dead wood; no one in charge realized that the reserves in question comprised a total of 6,000,000 acres!

In contrast, Pinchot could say in truth that during his entire term, "from the day I entered the Division of Forestry under President McKinley until I was dismissed by President Taft, not one single person in the office or the field was appointed, promoted, demoted or removed to please any politician, or for any political motive whatsoever." As he built his staff of loyal professionals, Pinchot became more convinced that all public lands should be administered by the Department of Agriculture; that is to say, by its Bureau of Forestry, which had been raised from a division in 1901. He was against the very idea of national parks (he does not even mention them in his autobiography) and he tried to have

Yellowstone and the other new parks transferred to the Department of Agriculture along with the forest reserves. If Pinchot did not exactly agree with House Speaker "Uncle Joe" Cannon's dictum, "Not one cent for scenery," his approach was generally utilitarian. "The object of our forest policy is not to preserve the forests because they are beautiful . . . or because they are refuges for the wild creatures of the wilderness," he said. "The forests are to be used by man. Every other consideration comes secondary."

Though John Muir and his followers found the policy inadequate for intensely human needs, it certainly marked a major step forward. The movement to preserve something of wild America had stepped onto a new terrace of action. Roosevelt and Pinchot had gathered about them professionals in the new sciences that were enabling man to exert some control over the earth and water around him: men like Overton Price, Pinchot's assistant forester; Frederick H. Newell, a mining engineer and hydrologist; and W. J. McGee, whom contemporaries called "the scientific brains of the conservation movement in its inception." Their influence was so pervasive and their ideas so successful that even a modern historian can write: "It is from the vantage point of applied science, rather than of democratic protest, that one must understand the historic role of the conservation movement."*

These applied scientists came together regularly to talk over ideas that would have seemed visionary only a few years before. Like Roosevelt they believed that the way to reap the most good from the nation's natural resources was not to sell the public lands but to develop them under government supervision. (Pinchot did not trust the owners of private woodlands, knowing that they would overcut the forests whenever they believed it to be to their advantage.) During one of the discussions among Pinchot and his colleagues someone mentioned that the government-owned forests in India were called "conservancies," and then the talk returned to their own hopes for the forests.

"The idea was so new," Pinchot recalled later, "that it did not even have a name. Of course it had to have a name. Our little inside group discussed it a great deal. Finally Overton Price suggested that we should call it 'conservation,' and the President said 'O.K.' So we called it the conservation movement."

No matter who coined the phrase, it was Gifford Pinchot who

*Samuel P. Hays, *Conservation and the Gospel of Efficiency: The Progressive Conservation Movement, 1890–1920*. Cambridge, 1959.

made it common currency in the English language. In addition to his other talents, he was an indefatigable propagandist. Even before the management of the forest reserves was shifted to the Department of Agriculture, Pinchot used his position as Chief Forester to put into practice many of his ideas. The pulp industry was especially interested in the new approach to "sustained yield" forestry. The very nature of its operation prevented this industry from engaging in the migratory lumbering that until then had characterized the sawmill operators, who cut over vast areas of forests, and then went on to virgin forests where they set up their sawmills once more. The pulp manufacturers needed to invest heavily in water sources to remove their wastes, power sources to run their machines, and special machines themselves to carry on the complicated process of making paper. They had a great need for a perpetual supply of pulpwood nearby. In 1901 pulp manufacturers started to test-plant spruce and other softwoods used in the manufacture of paper.

Partly through the influence of Pinchot the small but growing number of professional foresters in the United States formed the Society of American Foresters in 1901. Lumbermen who had been converted to the new ideas, either by Pinchot's propaganda or because it suddenly dawned on them that they had no place else to move, threw their support to the professionals against the exploiters. For the first time in this country serious attention began to be paid to methods of controlling the fires that often devastated great areas of the woodlands: crews patrolled the woods in dry weather, slash was disposed of, fire-fighting equipment was stored in logging camps, protective associations were created among owners of extensive timberlands. The industry suddenly found new uses for low-grade lumber. At Pinchot's urging, its leaders looked into practical by-products of lumbering, such as the production of turpentine and maple sugar. And, more and more, they turned to sustained-yield forestry.

Part of Pinchot's achievement is that he brought about extensive changes within a somewhat limited framework of action. There was no great bulk of conservation legislation passed during the Roosevelt administrations. Rather the President and his Forester progressed by interpreting broadly the laws already in effect. This was especially true, as we shall see, in the controversial area of grazing on public lands. A major exception to this course of action was the passage of the Reclamation Act of 1902, a piece of legislation which a later-day Secretary of the Interior, Stewart L. Udall, has called "the outstanding resource achievement of Theodore Roosevelt's first term."

John Wesley Powell's warnings about the difficulties of making a living from the arid lands of the West had long since proved to be accurate. The water shortage was chronic. Many of the most celebrated cattlemen's wars of the Old West were fought over water rights, and the man who controlled the sources of water truly controlled the region. The early enthusiasm of investors for the West had waned. Clearly only the government could provide the projects to secure an equitable supply of water throughout the western states. The Carey Act of 1894 had given the states the right to appropriate public lands for irrigation projects. But something more was needed. The leader in the Congressional struggle to "reclaim" vast areas of the West was Representative (later Senator) Francis G. Newlands of Nevada.

Newlands, a native of Mississippi, had attended Yale and Columbia before getting his law degree from Georgetown University. He set out to earn his fortune in the West, first in San Francisco, and later with considerably more speed in Nevada, where he married a daughter of the "mining king," Senator William Sharon. Newlands was quick to see the necessity for water projects if the West was to grow as he believed it should. There was, however, considerable opposition to such large-scale government projects that would, of necessity, be confined to a single region. Eastern congressmen, who feared competition for their own farmer-constituents, were opposed, or lukewarm. Even in the West many of the cattle barons fought government intervention because they believed hordes of small farmers would invade the range, just as they had when the Homestead Act became law.

But Newlands found active support within the administration. Roosevelt had seen the West's need for irrigation during his years in the Bad Lands, and he proposed federal irrigation projects in his first message to Congress. Pinchot was becoming more aware that forestry and the development of the nation's water resources inevitably were interwoven. The basis of both the Adirondack Forest Preserve and the government reserves was watershed protection. The National Irrigation Congress had supported the government's action on the reserves, and men like Frederick Newell, chief hydrologist in the Geological Survey, were close associates of the growing band of foresters in the government. The interests of forestry and irrigation were seen to be identical.

Roosevelt threw his support behind Newlands' bill. He persuaded the Republican leadership in Congress, notably "Uncle Joe" Cannon, not to fight the bill actively and it was passed in 1902. The Reclamation Act provided for the financing of large irrigation projects by the sale of public lands. The money realized would be held in a general fund and, in order to discourage the sort of congressional logrolling that always had characterized the selection of rivers and harbors projects, it would be allotted according to merit and need by the Secretary of the Interior. The act established the Reclamation Service within the Geological Survey to administer the program. (In 1907 the Reclamation Service was reorganized under Frederick Newell as a separate division within the Department of the Interior and renamed the Bureau of Reclamation.) Fittingly, the first large project completed under the terms of the act was the Truckee-Carson ditch in Senator Newlands' state, Nevada.

Despite the imposing shadow of Gifford Pinchot on so much of the conservation activity during Roosevelt's administration there were certain areas in which the Forester showed little interest and took no part. Officially, wildlife concerned him not at all; nor did the matter of the so-called Antiquities Bill, which had far-reaching effects on our present system of national parks and monuments.* But whatever initiative was lacking from Pinchot was more than made up for by the passionate interest of the President himself. Roosevelt had made it one of the objects of his administration to alter the public habit "of deciding, whenever possible, in favor of private interests against the public welfare." And as William T. Hornaday, the zoologist, later said, Roosevelt "gave the vanishing birds and animals the benefit of every doubt." About the destruction of a species he felt "as if all the works of some great writer had perished," and the destruction of America's native fauna was at its peak when he entered the White House.

The clamor against the unremitting butchery by "sportsmen" and market hunters was rising in all quarters, and nowhere had

*See page 128.

it become more insistent than among ethical sportsmen themselves. Grinnell's *Forest and Stream* was in the forefront of the reform movement. More spectacular, if not quite so effective, was G. O. Shields, the outspoken editor of *Recreation Magazine,* who coined the phrase "game-hog." Shields made it a point to collect news items and photographs from newspapers that catalogued the immense daily bags of local gunners. Then he would reprint them in his magazine alongside denunciations which were colorful at least, and sometimes nearly libelous.

After recounting the field exploits of a couple of hunters (their names were conspicuously printed) who managed to kill, with the help of their dogs, 120 quail in a single day in Tennessee, Shields commented: "I pity the dogs that were forced to associate with such miserable swine as these." Addressing himself to a Kentucky angler who had caught sixty fish in an hour, Shields wrote: "Instead of boasting of your shameful work, you should have gone and hid yourself in the Ohio River swamps until the mosquitoes could have had time to suck the bad blood out of you." And of a gunner named Gardiner, who had posed in Colorado beside a small mountain of dead game, Shields wrote: "I did write the big hog and asked him if the report were correct, but he evidently smelled something besides his own filth and declined to answer."

If the victim was literate, he might not pose so proudly beside his next whopping bag of game. In the absence of sound laws and enforcement in the various states, this was as promising an instrument of reform as any. There were other areas, however, where the federal government was able to play an important role, and Roosevelt was not reluctant to lead. He was aware of the approaching extinction of the buffalo. Because of the high price of heads and "robes," the poachers were willing to brave the penalties set by the Park Protection Act of 1894. By 1902 the buffalo had been extirpated from all parts of the United States except Yellowstone Park; and there the latest count indicated their numbers had dropped to twenty-one! A few animals survived in private collections and in the Bronx Zoo.

At this point Congress was prevailed upon to appropriate $15,000 to assemble a small number of buffaloes and establish a new herd on a "buffalo ranch" within the park. Colonel Charles J. "Buffalo" Jones, who had once been a buffalo skinner, and later had mated buffaloes with domestic cattle to produce the "cattalo," was hired to supervise the new herd. Each animal, branded on the horns and left hip with a prominent *U.S.,* was kept in the enclosure built at Jones's orders. The new herd of three bulls and eighteen cows (their number matched that of the wild herd) increased rapidly under management. By 1907, when the "ranch" was moved to the Lamar Valley, there were 106 buffaloes in the park, and 239 by 1915.

Far from Yellowstone, on a tiny island in Indian River on the east coast of Florida, a similar slaughter was leading to a similarly dramatic reversal of national policy. This was Pelican Island, whose four acres were covered before the Civil War by a thick mangrove growth, and a colony of herons, ibises, and roseate spoonbills whose numbers splashed the sky with color. An overabundance of nesting birds and a severe frost in 1886 killed the mangroves, and the plume hunters later cleaned up the birds. By the time Frank M. Chapman visited the island on his honeymoon in 1898, it was a treeless mudflat taken over by nesting brown pelicans. Chapman collected some pelicans as specimens, and with his bride, Fanny, settled down to prepare their skins. Later he was to call Pelican Island during nesting time "by far the most fascinating place it has ever been my fortune to see in the world of birds"—an estimate colored, perhaps, by his own state of mind at the time. Chapman issued a plea for the preservation of the pelican colony:

"The land is very accessible, the Florida law affords pelicans no protection, and a party of quill-hunters might easily kill practically all the inhabitants of Pelican Island within a few days. The loss would be irreparable, and it is to be especially noted, would not be confined to the vicinity, but would affect the whole east coast of Florida, there being so far as is known, no other breeding colony of pelicans on the Atlantic coast of the peninsula."

Chapman's plea aroused enough interest among friends of the Audubon Society for them to raise money and attempt to buy the island from the government. The offer became bogged down in red tape in the General Land Office, where people who wanted to chop down trees or build railroads usually found no trouble in acquiring all the land they needed. Chapman and his friends then took the matter to Roosevelt. There was no precedent for presidential action, nor for governmental action of any sort. Aside from the national parks, no federal wildlife refuge existed anywhere in the continental United States. (A state waterfowl refuge had been established near Oakland, California, in 1870, and a "national salmon reservation" had been proclaimed by President Harrison on Afognak Island in Alaska in 1892.) But precedent was no barrier to Roosevelt. He declared Pelican Island the nation's first national wildlife refuge in 1903.

For a time the American Ornithologists' Union paid the salary of a warden hired to guard the refuge.* The warden erected a large sign, announcing the birds to be "wards of the government," and warning hunters away. But when Chapman visited the island the next spring he "found to my surprise and disgust that with a uniformity of action which left no doubt as to their attitude," the birds had deserted the island. For the first time within the memory of man, not a single bird nested on Pelican Island. Chapman was perplexed, especially when he found pelicans nesting on two small islands nearby. The warden suggested that perhaps the pelicans had been made uneasy by the large sign. Chapman ordered him to replace it with several small signs, and the birds returned to the island's unrelieved silhouette the next season.

Roosevelt's allegiance to birds was not confined to official policy. He was a diligent birdwatcher and, during his years in the White House, prepared for Lucy W. Maynard's *Birds of Washington and Vicinity* a list of ninety-three species he had seen there. (Of the sparrow hawk, he noted: "A pair spent the last two winters around the White House grounds, feeding on sparrows—largely, thank Heaven, on the English sparrows.") According to his sister, Corinne, he once burst into a cabinet meeting with the announcement: "Gentlemen, do you know what has happened this morning? I just saw a chestnut-sided warbler—and this is only February!"

While this was a sighting by an experienced birdwatcher that no one was likely to challenge, his report that he had seen a passenger pigeon in 1907 was a different matter. It is generally accepted that the bird was extinct everywhere but in the Cincinnati Zoo by that time. But Roosevelt, who had hunted the very similar mourning dove, insisted that he knew the difference and that what he had seen was a passenger pigeon. "If so," Robert Cushman Murphy of the American Museum of Natural History is quoted by Paul Russell Cutright in his book, *Theodore Roosevelt, the Naturalist,* "a President of the United States may have been the last to see a passenger pigeon in the wild."

*In 1906, when Roosevelt created six more wildlife refuges, the National Association of Audubon Societies began to pay the wardens' salaries.

Nor did Roosevelt's position keep him from enjoying an arduous hike in the countryside or rock-scrambling along the steep sides of Rock Creek Park. Pinchot often accompanied him on these outings, both men carrying guns because they were likely to shake off the Secret Service men assigned to guard the President. After one of these hikes in bitter weather, when TR led his party through a swamp and then waist-deep into the Potomac itself, Pinchot returned to the elegant house on Rhode Island Avenue where he lived with his mother.

"As I ran up the stairs to my room," Pinchot recalled, "my old Irish nurse, Mary McCadden, who had been with me since I was eleven weeks old, was standing with her hand on the newel post. I rubbed my wet sleeve across it. She turned like a flash, pointed her finger at me in reproof, and exclaimed, 'You've been out with that President!'"

Roosevelt carried his enthusiasm over into the evenings, when often he could be found curled up with a good nature book. He knew most of the leading naturalists of the day, he read the accounts of their travels and research with intense interest, and he reviewed their books for magazines and newspapers. Many dedicated their books to Roosevelt; and he in turn contributed introductions to their works. In the opening pages of *Wild Wings*, Herbert K. Job's account of his adventures in photographing birds (including his trip with Guy Bradley into Cuthbert Rookery) there appears a facsimile of a letter from the President, commending Job on an earlier book. It is a revealing glimpse into the conflicting emotions of a hunter and a naturalist:

My dear Mr. Job:
As a fellow Harvard man I must thank you for your exceedingly interesting book. I have been delighted with it, and I desire to express to you my sense of the good which comes from such books as yours, and from the substitution of the camera for the gun. The older I grow the less I care to shoot anything except 'varmints.' I do not think it at all advisable that the gun should be given up, nor does it seem to me that shooting wild game under proper restrictions can be legitimately opposed by any who are willing that domestic animals shall be kept for food; but there is altogether too much shooting, and if we can only get sunk somewhat in the naturalist and lover of wild things, the next generation will see an immense change for the better in the life of our woods and waters.
    P.S. But I am still something of a hunter, although a lover of wild nature first.

One of Roosevelt's cronies was John Burroughs, that "John-O'-Birds" who was one of the most knowledgeable and popular nature writers of his time. The two corresponded often, and Roosevelt accepted much advice from him on the course of nature study and conservation. In 1903 the President, "still something of a hunter," as he had told Job, prepared for an official visit to Yellowstone Park. While he was interested in seeing the sights, he was also interested in taking a shot at a mountain lion, and inquired of the park superintendent about the prospects for such sport. Fortunately for the mountain lions, the press got wind of Roosevelt's hopes, and an outcry went up over the President of the United States trying to "butcher" animals in a national park. He finally abandoned the idea and, employing the art of public relations, invited gentle John Burroughs to accompany him on the tour. Instead of shooting carnivores, the President settled for entertaining Burroughs by catching a mouse with his bare hands.

From Yellowstone Roosevelt proceeded to Yosemite, by then a national park, where he was taken in tow by another gray eminence, John Muir. Around their campfire in the evening Muir spoke to Roosevelt of the urgency in acting to preserve the great forests of the West, and inquired why the President had not got "beyond the boyishness of killing things." Roosevelt promised to take action to save the forests, and allowed as how Muir was right about the killing. In his turn, the President was amazed that Muir took in the "bigness" of nature but could not recognize the songs of even the commonest birds. Roosevelt apparently did not warm to Muir as he had to other outdoorsmen, a development which Burroughs later explained by remarking, "Two talkers, you know, seldom get on well together."

Roosevelt's intense interest in all aspects of natural history drew him into frequent scientific disputes during his long public career, the most notorious of which was the "nature fakers" affair. Because it interested so many people, and because the leading participants on both sides exerted considerable influence on the public's manner of looking at animals, the controversy belongs to the history of conservation. It had its amusing aspects, but not to Roosevelt or its chief protagonist.

The Reverend William J. Long, a Congregationalist minister in Stamford, Connecticut, was the author of *Little Brother to the Bear*, *Secrets of the Woods*, *Wood Folk at School*, and other books of nature stories, purportedly true, that were immensely popular among young readers around the turn of the century. Unfortunately for his peace of mind, Long had no more attentive reader than the President. Roosevelt looked upon this outdoorsy man of the cloth much as some later Presidents have regarded smut-peddlers, and indeed considered him a corruptor of the nation's youth. In 1903 Roosevelt (who, in a literary sense, had a delicate stomach) nearly gagged on Long's account of a woodcock he had observed near a brook.

"At first he took soft clay in his bill from the edge of the water and seemed to be smearing it on one leg near the knee," Long wrote. "Then he fluttered away on one foot for a distance and seemed to be pulling tiny roots and fibers of grass, which he worked into the clay that he had already smeared upon his leg . . . Then he stood perfectly still for a full hour under an overhanging rock where the eye could with difficulty find him, his only motion meanwhile being an occasional rubbing and smoothing of the clay bandage with his bill, until it hardened to suit him, whereupon he fluttered away from the brook and disappeared in the thick woods.

"I had my own explanation of the incredible action—namely, that the woodcock had a broken leg, and had deliberately put it in a clay cast to hold the broken bones in place until they should knit together again."

Roosevelt expressed his misgivings to Burroughs about this and some of the other stuff he had read. He was not hostile to the animal tales of a writer like Rudyard Kipling, who advertised them as just that—tales. But real animals portrayed as "heroes" and "villains," endowed with human skills and sensitivities, set his teeth on edge.

Long wrote prefaces to his books, claiming that every incident he recorded was based on fact. But what of a woodcock that, as a distinguished Harvard professor pointed out later, "is familiar with the theories of bone formation and regeneration—in a word, with osteogenesis, which by the way, is never clearly grasped by some of our university juniors?"

This was but one of the marvelous animals which thronged the natural histories of Long and other writers of the school. There were aged and infirm caribou searching out a "cemetery" in northern Labrador where they could lay their bones beside those of their ancestors; a porcupine that liked to roll around under apple trees, spearing fruit with its quills, then amble home to shake them off into its larder; a bullfrog that sprang from the water to seize inattentive swallows on the wing; and a Baltimore oriole that fashioned, as Roosevelt complained, "a contrivance of twigs and strings whereby to attach its nest, under circumstances that would imply the mental ability and physical address of a sailor making a hammock."

Cheered on by Roosevelt, Burroughs wrote an article called "Real and Sham Natural History." In it he soundly thumped Long and Ernest Thompson Seton, another of the offending writers. Burroughs referred to Seton's popular book, *Wild Animals I Have Known,* as *Wild Animals I Alone Have Known.* Seton mended his ways and worked his way up to a John Burroughs medal in 1927 for his contributions to natural history. But Long, encouraged by his fans, kept on dishing out what they wanted to read.

It was near the end of Roosevelt's administration that he began to chafe under the burden of presidential aloofness. As he admitted to Burroughs, "I know that as President I ought not to do this: but I was having an awful time toward the end of the session and I felt I simply had to permit myself some diversion."

The President's goad was Edward B. Clark, a newspaperman to whom he often grumbled about Long and his literary blood-brothers. One day Clark asked; "Why don't you go after them?"

"I think I will," the President replied.

It was much the same sort of offhand remark that set loose Henry II's henchmen against Becket. Clark went home, wrote down his recollection of Roosevelt's sentiments, and then showed it to him the next day. Roosevelt's need for diversion got the best of him. He went to his desk and, on sheets of White House stationery, broadened the attack.

The article, entitled "Roosevelt and the Nature Fakirs," appeared under Clark's byline in *Everybody's Magazine* in June 1907. It opened with testimony from Dr. C. Hart Merriam, chief of the U. S. Biological Survey, to Roosevelt's formidable achievements as a naturalist. Then Clark turned the attack over to the President.

"I don't believe for a moment that some of these men who are writing nature stories and putting the word 'truth' prominently in their prefaces know the heart of the wild things," Roosevelt said. He went on to call their writings "the wildest exaggeration," and, "as for the matter of giving these books to children for the purpose of teaching them the facts of natural history—why, it's an outrage."

He called the descriptions of wolves in Jack London's *White Fang* "the very sublimity of absurdity."

Then Roosevelt got his target in focus. "William J. Long is perhaps the worst of these nature-writing offenders," he said. He was especially put off by Long's account of the way a wolf killed a caribou—by driving its fangs "under the stag's chest just behind the forelegs, where the heart lay." Roosevelt went into a long anatomical explanation of the contortions this would require of the wolf, and of the inadequate length of its fangs. He compared the feat to that of a dog trying to bite into a grapefruit that was encased in a keg of flour. And he concluded:

"If Mr. Long wants us to believe his story of the killing of the caribou fawn by the wolf in the way he says it was done, he must produce eyewitnesses and affidavits."

Long, at first stunned by the heat of the President's attack, recovered quickly and did as he was directed. He produced for the press the affidavit "of an educated Sioux Indian, who is fitting himself to be a teacher and missionary, and a certificate to the character of the Indian from the Reverend C. J. Ryder." *The Outlook,* a publication in which Long's story of the wolf had appeared, in turn certified the character of the Reverend Ryder.

It was now Roosevelt's turn to fret. Warming to the battle, Long took the President to task in a series of open letters to the press. "A man named Roosevelt has gone out of his way to make a violent attack upon me," Long wrote, calling it "personal and venomous in spirit, while its literary style was the poorest of the poor."

Roosevelt's own writings, in fact, left him vulnerable to the minister's counterattack, and not simply from a stylistic point of view. Those writings were filled with Roosevelt's accounts of the big game he had potted in the field. Long gleaned these incidents and, in his open letter, strung them in rapid fire succession, piling horror on horror much in the manner of an Elizabethan tragedy.

"Who is he to write, 'I don't believe that some of these nature-writers know the heart of the wild things'?" Long asked. "As to that I find after carefully reading two of his big books that every time Mr. Roosevelt gets near the heart of a wild thing he invariably puts a bullet through it."

A large part of the public sympathized with this David fending off Goliath in the White House. The sentiment was that, though Long may have romanticized his animals, he did not make them bleed. The cudgels were taken up by that part of the press that was hostile to the President in any case. The old *Life* magazine, reporting later on a French society's presentation of a medal to Roosevelt for his work as a naturalist, commented: "Scientific societies do not, as a rule, bestow medals upon just that kind of naturalist; the medal should have gone to Mr. Armour of Chicago." And the New York *Sun* reprinted a verse circulated by the British Humanitarian League which called TR a "butcher of big game . . . whose murderous feats unnumbered fools acclaim!"

The anti-Roosevelt position was stated most calmly by Lyman Abbott, the editor of *The Outlook*. "First we regret to see the President of the United States making a personal attack on any individual citizen on a question of this kind," he wrote, "for the simple reason that the private individual stands on uneven terms in any discussion with any man occupying the presidential position. It is debatable whether the President might not, in an extreme case for the protection of public morals of the whole country, publicly denounce a man who, by common consent, was believed to be debauching the morals or poisoning the minds of all the school children of the country. Mr. Long is not such an individual. Moreover our close observation and experience lead us to believe that his books have, on the whole, done much more good than harm, by interesting children of the country in the life and welfare of the animals."

Professional naturalists, who considered the President one of their own and thus were uneasy at the public relations beating he was taking, rallied to his support. They organized a symposium to examine the credibility of those who had come to be called "nature fakers." (Some of the President's enemies spread the rumor, untrue, that he had helped to organize the symposium.) In Roosevelt's defense, Burroughs spoke of "the yellow journalism of the woods," while others referred to "animal novelists" and "the Creative Memory."

One scientist suggested that the gullible Long had been the butt of hunters' yarns. And William T. Hornaday of the Bronx Zoo observed that, "Whenever Mr. Long enters the woods, the most marvelous things begin to happen. There is a four-footed wonder-worker behind every bush and a miracle every hour . . . apparently there is no imaginable intimacy with the wild beasts and birds that this gentleman has not struck up."

Both sides were glad to see the controversy fade away. Long turned his attention to writing a history of English literature. And when Jack London defended himself in a *Collier's* article (consigning TR to "the Ananias Club"), Roosevelt eased his indignation by addressing a heated, but private, note to the editor. The nature fakers had seen the last of the big stick.

13

The Second Term

"I am no longer President by accident."

With these words to his wife Theodore Roosevelt had marked his victory over Alton B. Parker, the Democratic candidate in the election of 1904, and embarked on his second (and very own) administration. What was true for Roosevelt was true also for the dedicated men around him. Gifford Pinchot, for one, was ready to make his move.

He had not been inactive by any means during Roosevelt's "accidental" first term. Using his very considerable political skills, Pinchot lobbied ceaselessly for the transfer of the forest reserves to the Department of Agriculture. Opposition was still intense. Western timber interests, finding ways to circumvent federal restrictions, were carrying away all the wood they wanted from the public lands; there seemed to be no good reason for a change. Congressmen, on their part, still fancied the ripe patronage opportunities they found within the General Land Office.

But now Pinchot, supported by the President, was winning converts. Pinchot's brand of conservation, which had been made official under Roosevelt, was coming to mean *development*, rather than *preservation*, of the nation's natural resources. Many Western timbermen and stockmen liked Pinchot's promises that the reserves, under his management, would be opened to use. Timbermen especially, alarmed by Pinchot's repeated predictions of a "timber famine," were coming around to his belief that the forests must be scientifically managed. He tried to assuage every Western fear. When Representative John F. Lacey, still the most active conservation crusader in Congress, introduced a bill that would have made game refuges of all the forest reserves, Pinchot opposed it. (The influential Boone and Crockett Club, which first favored the bill, later opposed it on the grounds that all of the big game animals in the country would retreat into their vast confines, and it was defeated.)

Pinchot won his battle in 1905. With Roosevelt stifling opposition and even Interior Secretary Ethan Allen Hitchcock giving his blessing to the transfer, Congress voted to withdraw the reserves from the General Land Office. The act renamed Pinchot's bureau the U.S. Forest Service, and turned over to it the administration of the reserves. The principle of "multiple use" was established in a letter from Secretary of Agriculture James Wilson to Pinchot (a letter written for Wilson's signature by, not suprisingly, Pinchot himself):

"In the administration of the forest reserves it must be clearly borne in mind that all land is to be devoted to its most productive use for the permanent good of the whole people and not for the temporary benefit of individuals or companies."

The reserves became "national forests," a description in keeping with Pinchot's views of their utility. His victory was complete. An inventory of the nation's standing timber dramatically proved the necessity for a sustained-yield approach to forest management: of the total 2500 billion board feet of timber, 40 billion were cut annually, to be replaced by a growth of only 10 billion. But his reforms extended far beyond technique. Like Roosevelt, Pinchot did not feel the need to approach Congress for further legislation on matters that were not explicitly prohibited in the existing law; in other words, he believed in a strong executive branch of government. To cries of anguish from west of the Mississippi, Pinchot began to establish regulations for using the national forests.

• He raised the fees for taking timber and minerals well above the absurdly low bids formerly accepted by the General Land Office, believing

that the public should get a fair return for the consumption of its natural resources.

   • He established grazing fees and permits in the forests to discourage the usual rush by stockmen to stake out the best areas for themselves in early spring—a practice that prevented the young plants and grasses from reseeding themselves. (Pinchot had come around to Muir's view of sheep as "hoofed locusts," and believed they should be "rigidly excluded" from many forested areas, especially those on steep slopes; he didn't think much better of the sheepmen themselves, accusing them of setting forest fires to increase pasturage.)

   • He set up a system of leases for water power sites within the forests in order to forestall the seizure of the best sites by private interests. Under his orders, easements were granted only for limited periods. The private power interests, claiming that the water which originated in, or flowed through, the forests belonged to the states, took the matter to the courts. The Supreme Court upheld the Forest Service in 1911.

These measures were planned as merely the first steps in a long-range program to bring land management policies in line with concepts held by Roosevelt and Pinchot. They hoped eventually to lease all of the public domain for grazing, for which they thought it was best suited, rather than sell it to settlers under the Homestead Act. But by this time opposition in the West had turned solidly against them. (Some Westerners even called for secession from the Union.) Pinchot was forced to consolidate his gains within the Forest Service.

Under Pinchot the Forest Service functioned with almost Jesuitical zeal. William B. Greeley, who later became its chief, recalled that Pinchot made his men "feel like soldiers in a patriotic cause." There was no hint of personal or political influence in the advancement of its members. Once a week Pinchot called a meeting of all the Service's personnel in Washington, including its stenographers and messengers. His home on Rhode Island Avenue was open to all of his aides. There they frequently came together in what they liked to call "The Baked Apple Club," a name derived from the refreshments of gingerbread and baked apples their host served to the party late in the evening. Visiting foresters from abroad, powerful congressmen, even the President, gathered to talk to the young foresters and further enflame them with the ideals of government service. Not the least of the personalities there was Pinchot's mother, a woman of some wealth even before her marriage and one whose energy and old-fashioned courtesy made her a leading hostess in Washington's social life. (She was no mere social butterfly, however, as she shared her son's passion for far-reaching reforms; though she loved fine things she often spoke of the great human cost at which they were produced, admitting even that her precious lace had been made in "damp, dark cellars by poor laborers, whose very lives were sacrifices for their art." It was not the kind of talk heard very often in her circle.) Stirred by the evangelical atmosphere, Gifford Pinchot's young men spread out over the country like crusaders on a holy mission.

While Pinchot was saving the forests, Roosevelt was helping to preserve other portions of the country's heritage. The vandalism that had plagued Yellowstone appeared in many different areas of natural and historic interest, especially in the Southwest. There the looting of the finest archaeological sites had been going on for years. In the 1880s a move in Congress to protect these ruins had been dismissed as too costly; a senator suggested instead that the various scientific groups proceed to loot them ahead of the general public. In the absence of any effective action, parties of looters combed Indian ruins for whatever scraps of pottery and other artifacts earlier parties had overlooked. At Cliff Palace in Mesa Verde the looters broke down walls to let in light, and burned roof beams to provide heat. Even the treasures that were carried off to be sold to museums and private collectors lost much of their historic and scientific value because they were not accompanied by records of any sort.

It was not until 1906 that Congress acted on a bill introduced by Representative Lacey and supported by the President. The Antiquities Act authorized the President to withdraw from entry certain sites that he considered to be of special natural or historic value. These areas became known as "national monuments," a confusing term in that it covers a great diversity of sites, including canyons, cliffs, caves, cactus deserts, sand dunes, battlefields and even the birthplaces of famous men. Roosevelt took full advantage of the act. Before he left the White House he set aside by proclamation 1.4 million acres as national monuments. Beyond the immediate national gain, this power enabled Roosevelt to preserve from exploitation certain priceless areas such as Grand Canyon until a dawdling Congress could get around to establishing them as national parks.

Roosevelt's impatience with Congress and his contempt for the land-skinners called forth violent opposition to many of his programs, especially in the West. Western business interests, whether timbermen, stockmen, or miners, resented the "lockup" of public lands for any purpose. Eventually opposition arose to lands set aside under the Antiquities Act, which some Westerners saw as an obstacle to the development of their particular states. The attempt to relieve the President of his authority to withdraw these lands by proclamation eventually failed. So did an attempt, mounted closer to the White House, apparently by Eastern meat dealers who kept contraband game in cold storage, to abolish the Bureau of Biological Survey. Under Dr. C. Hart Merriam the Bureau had played an active part in enforcing the Lacey Law of 1900, which prohibited the interstate shipment of game killed illegally. The Audubon Societies strongly supported the administration, and this move too was defeated.

Roosevelt's support in the West had nearly evaporated. Homesteaders and other small farmers saw his plans to establish grazing fees on public lands outside the national forests as a plot to reserve the land for wealthy cattle barons who were able to afford the fees. A number of Westerners formed the Public Domain League to lead a fight for the ceding of public lands to the states. The President also came under fire for his policy on the building of dams on navigable rivers. Under the General Dam Act of 1906, which Roosevelt had signed, Congress took upon itself the right (acting on the advice of the Army Corps of Engineers) to approve each permit to build these dams. Roosevelt, at the time, felt that it would put some order into a generally chaotic procedure. Eventually he came to feel that private power companies planning to dam navigable rivers should not be granted permits "which do not provide specifically for a charge and a definite limitation in time of the rights conferred." Throughout the final year of his administration he vetoed every bill passed by Congress to authorize specific dams. (His successor would overturn this policy.)

But the most successful move against Roosevelt's conservation policies came to the surface in 1907. The Western bloc in Congress pushed through a bill that deprived the President of his right to create new national forests from the public domain in the states of Colorado, Idaho, Montana, Oregon, Washington, and Wyoming. California was exempted from the act, chiefly because there was a great deal of support in that state to protect the watersheds for drinking water, irrigation, and flood control; Pinchot's regulations in the national forests did just that by restricting grazing and logging on the steep slopes.

The bill was passed on February 25. Roosevelt and Pinchot knew which way the political winds were blowing, and realized that if the President vetoed the bill it would eventually be passed over his veto. The timbermen ("as competent a band of land thieves as ever the sun shone on," Pinchot called them) were poised to rush into the forests and stake out their claims before Roosevelt made any last-minute withdrawals. Since the bill was scheduled to be signed early in March there was no time to be wasted on either side.

Pinchot had already sent out his "boundary men" to make surveys of the likeliest forests to be marked for withdrawal. At the Forest Service headquarters in Washington there was a great flurry of activity.

"Each of us was assigned a state or part of a state," William Greeley, Pinchot's assistant, recalled. "We studied all the reports on its public lands and pored over every old map. Whenever we found reasonable evidence of forest cover, we redrew national forest boundaries. Midnight oil was burned in most of the Forest Service offices that fortnight. Wires flashed back and forth to supervisors and rangers in the West. Stenographers dropped everything and typed proclamations. And Gifford Pinchot soon began daily trips to the White House."

Roosevelt and Pinchot relished the secrecy, and the sense of having "put one over" on the opposition. The President signed each proclamation, thirty-three in all, as it was brought to him by his Forester.

"I signed the last a couple of days before, by my signature, the bill became law," Roosevelt wrote. "And, when the friends of the special interests in the Senate . . . woke up, they discovered that sixteen million acres of timberland had been saved for the people by putting them in the national forests before the landgrabbers could get at them. The opponents of the Forest Service turned handsprings in their wrath, and dire were the threats against the Executive; but the threats could not be carried out and were really only a tribute to the efficiency of our action."

In one sense a frustrating failure, but in another a major achievement, was the work of the Inland Waterways Commission. Our waterways, then as now, were badly neglected. The projects authorized by Congress, upon the advice of the Corps of Engineers, were generally logrolling operations of the worst sort. They were distributed on the basis of political leverage, and not of need. The Corps restricted its work to projects dealing with navigation. Its officers traditionally were hostile to flood control projects, and in fact did not even recognize the importance of forest cover in preventing disastrous runoffs.

But a new concept was taking hold in the government. "Every river is a unit from its source to its mouth," Pinchot insisted. Even more influential (because of his special knowledge) in determining the administration's water policies was W. J. McGee. McGee, in an era when scientists were something of a novelty in the government, was looked upon with wonder by many of his friends. As a boy he had met Audubon on the Mississippi, and had taught himself science and mathematics. Later he had served under John Wesley Powell in the Geological Survey. Of his marriage to an intellectual woman (a marriage which did not succeed), one of McGee's friends wrote: "It is said that they would discuss at length the best scientific plan on which their baby should be fed, bathed, and even sung to sleep."

McGee campaigned for the multipurpose development of rivers. It was, he believed, the only rational approach to a resource "in which the several parts are so closely interdependent that no section can be brought under control without at least partial control of all other portions."

It was chiefly at his urging that Roosevelt established the Inland Waterways Commission in 1907. He appointed Pinchot to the commission, of course, as well as Pinchot's old colleagues, Frederick H. Newell and Herbert K. Smith. Four congressmen, including Senator Newlands, and Brigadier General Alexander MacKenzie, Chief of the Army Corps of Engineers, also took places on the commission, while McGee became its secretary.

McGee, speaking through the President, outlined the Commission's challenge: "Works designed to control our waterways have thus far usually been undertaken for a single purpose, such as the improvement of navigation, the development of power, the irrigation of arid lands, the protection of lowlands from floods, or to supply water for domestic and manufacturing purposes . . . The time has come for merging local projects and uses of the inland waters in a comprehensive plan designed for the benefit of the entire country."

McGee was certainly not blind to the importance of navigation on the inland waterways. In fact, he was a leader in the campaign to expand the Mississippi's navigational potential in order to create a gateway from the country's heartland to Central America and, through the new Panama Canal, to the west coast of South America. But he did not work with the blinders that traditionally have constricted the vision of the Corps of Engineers. He was the chief architect of the commission's report that became a monument of the conservation movement and a guide to action for which the United States is still reaching. If its faith in big dams to solve many of the problems posed by our unevenly distributed water resources has not always been justified, its detailed description of the river as an entity—as a living thing we cannot alter in one respect without affecting it in all its parts—has been overlooked to our subsequent misfortune.

"Hereafter plans for the improvement of navigation in inland waterways," the report said, "should take account of the purification of the waters, the development of power, the control of floods, the reclamation of lands by irrigation and drainage, and all other uses of the waters or benefits to be derived from their control."

The report was approved by all of the commission's members except General MacKenzie. Senator Newlands, as was to be expected, concurred enthusiastically in its various recommendations. He submitted them to Congress in the form of a bill which would establish a permanent Inland Waterways Commission, appointed by the President, to coordinate all of the projects of the diverse federal water resource agencies. In order to investigate, authorize, and supervise projects, the bill would place at the commission's disposal a fund of $50,000,000 to be replenished without annual appropriations from Congress whenever it dipped below $20,000,000.

Roosevelt's support for the bill, and his suspicion that the Corps of Engineers would try to sabotage it, may be seen in a letter he addressed to the War Department early in 1908: "Senator Newlands' bill in reference to the Waterways Commission will doubtless be sent to the War Department for a report. In the regular routine this would go to General MacKenzie. This is undesirable. The bill should not go to any of the engineers. It represents in a general sense the policy of the commission, which policy is mine, but which policy is not the one approved by General MacKenzie and the engineers. Therefore I desire that the bill be sent direct to me, and I will, after a conference with the Secretary of War, direct what answer shall be sent in reference thereto."

The Secretary of War, William Howard Taft, did not share the President's enthusiasm for the bill either; but after Roosevelt had talked to him, and Pinchot had scrutinized Taft's written comments, there was no official opposition from that quarter. The Corps of Engineers need not have worried. Congress was giving Roosevelt little satisfaction at that period of his administration, particularly in matters that would diminish its authority over appropriations or its unrestrained indulgence in logrolling. The bill was emasculated to a degree that Roosevelt ceased to push for its passage. So complete was Congress's aversion to the report that the commission's members eventually had to pay out of their own pockets for its publication. (Again the lone dissenter was General MacKenzie, whose tab was picked up by Pinchot.)

There was one immediate result of the commission's labors, however. At a time when hopes for the passage of Senator Newlands' bill still survived within the administration, it was thought that a conference of the nation's governors and other state officials, in which they could express their views on water problems, would enhance the bill's chances in Congress. When the bill died, Roosevelt and Pinchot clung to the idea of a conference.

Under Pinchot, the incomparable publicist, the conference grew to include as its subject all of the country's natural resources; and as its membership, many of the country's outstanding politicians, jurists, scientists, and educators. Pinchot apparently paid the bills for this, the most distinguished company of men yet brought together for a single event in American history. There were exceptions: Pinchot pointedly ignored John Muir, nor did he include in the list of invitations such early contributors to sound forestry as Bernard E. Fernow, Charles S. Sargent, and John W. Noble. But he worked assiduously in other directions, joining McGee, for instance, in writing the speeches to be given by many of the attending dignitaries.

In opening the conference, Roosevelt expressed his debt to his Forester. "Especial credit is due to the initiative, the energy, the devotion to duty, and the farsightedness of Gifford Pinchot, to whom we owe so much of the progress we have already made in handling this matter of the coordination and conservation of natural resources. If it had not been for him this convention neither would nor could have been called." Roosevelt went on to call conservation "part of another and greater problem . . . the problem of national efficiency, the patriotic duty of insuring the safety and continuance of the Nation."

The Conference went off with scarcely a hitch. There was one moment of consternation among the insiders, later recorded by Harry A. Slattery, one of Pinchot's circle of friends and colleagues. It occurred when Andrew Carnegie rose to read the speech that had been written for him by McGee. "The address seemed to its auditors to lack something in unity and sequence," Slattery recalled, "but the canny Scotchman never batted an eye. He went right along. It turned out he had been handed a part of his own text and a part of James J. Hill's."

Though the waterways bill was dead, the White House Conference on conservation spread the new word and its concepts. Those concepts were still somewhat limited, to be sure. Both the sponsorship of the conference and its membership would not lead one to believe otherwise, and there were only one or two fleeting references to natural beauty. Nevertheless, forty-one states were inspired to form conservation commissions of their own. Roosevelt himself appointed a National Conservation Commission (with Pinchot as the chairman of its Executive Committee) to make an inventory of the country's natural resources. Congress thought no more of this group than it did of the Inland Waterways Commission and refused to fund its studies. Roosevelt, however, ordered all government agencies to cooperate with the commission. Only under these conditions was the commission able to complete its assignment. Congress brought about its demise soon afterward, not only by starving it for funds, but also by passing the "Tawney Amendment" to the Sundry Civil Bill, which prohibited government administrative officials from giving aid to executive commissions not authorized by Congress.

The defeats that Roosevelt suffered during his last years in the White House did not dim his many achievements in preserving the land and its wildlife. By proclamation he had enlarged the extent of the national forests from 42,000,000 to 172,000,000 acres.

He had created fifty-one national wildlife refuges, including six in Alaska. And he had set aside eighteen areas of special interest, including Grand Canyon and the Petrified Forest, as national monuments. Much of this land was withdrawn in the closing weeks of the administration as Roosevelt and Pinchot worked frantically to nail down their conservation gains.

Roosevelt considered as his most important achievements the agreement that concluded the Russo-Japanese War (for which he won the Nobel Prize for Peace), the building of the Panama Canal, and the creation of a powerful United States Navy. There are many historians and politicians who disagree. As Senator Robert La Follette said of the retiring President:

"His greatest work was actually beginning a world movement for staying terrestrial waste and saving for the human race the things upon which alone a great and peaceful and progressive and happy race can be founded."

Part Three

The Fight for
the Land

14

Ballinger

A golden age had ended. No one felt this more strongly than Gifford Pinchot, who remained behind in Washington while Roosevelt set off to shoot lions in Africa. William Howard Taft, TR's Secretary of War, had been handpicked by Roosevelt as his successor. But even during the final days of the lame duck administration serious doubts began to arise about the incoming President, whom Senator Jonathan P. Dolliver, the Iowa conservationist, called "that ponderous and pleasant person, entirely surrounded by men who know exactly what they want."

As Taft took the oath of office in the sleet and snow of a bitter March day in 1909, Pinchot steeled himself for the worst. Pinchot, of course, was utterly dedicated to the Forest Service. Though his position as chief adviser to the President on conservation matters no longer would be in effect, he still hoped to exert some influence on Taft. As he saw it, Taft had been captured by big business and the reactionary wing of the Republican party. And whatever sympathy (very little, to be sure) Pinchot once had for the men who controlled the traffic in timber, coal, and other natural resources, it had dissolved into contempt during his tenure as Chief Forester. His definition of conservation, where it applied to these men, had taken on a special tinge: "Conservation was like the ring on the neck of a cormorant, like the muzzle on the jaws of a hungry dog." Of Taft himself, well, he was a gentleman, and not to be held in quite that sort of contempt. "I want to be fair," Pinchot wrote later. "Taft was a man of real intelligence, great working power, abundant physical courage, high legal attainments and immense personal charm. Weak rather than wicked, he was one of those genial men who are everything that fancy paints until a showdown comes along that demands real toughness of moral fiber."

On the other side, it was reported by Taft's military aide that the new President considered Pinchot "a socialist and a spiritualist." But for a time Pinchot had Taft's ear when he wanted it badly enough, and they even saw eye to eye on some matters. There was a great deal of resentment among homesteaders in the West toward the Bureau of Reclamation, for instance. Under the terms of the Reclamation Act of 1902, the bureau had begun to build irrigation projects for the homesteaders flocking onto the barren lands. But discontent followed when the projects were stretched thin over vast areas. Even when the impatient homesteaders finally got their projects completed they complained about the act's stiff financial terms, under which the government required them to repay the cost of the project (without interest) in ten annual installments. They and their congressmen campaigned for more lenient payment schedules and a new bureau chief. But the chief was Frederick Newell, admired as warmly in engineering circles as among conservationists. No engineer wanted to step into a situation where he would be fiercely resented by Newell's assistants, whose *esprit de corps* rivaled that of the Forest Service. Taft, aware that no competent replacement could be found, stood by Newell. He survived in the post until the Reclamation Act of 1914 extended the homesteaders' payments from ten to twenty years and returned to Congress the authority to approve individual projects.

But Pinchot emphatically did not see eye to eye with Taft on a number of other issues, most of which became policy by the directive of the new Secretary of the Interior. Pinchot always looked on that department of government with suspicion and spent a good part of his life at war with it, chiefly in grappling for control of the national forests. An exception to his hostility occurred during the last years of Roosevelt's second term, when Interior was guided

by a Secretary who owed his position, in large part, to Pinchot's recommendation. This was James R. Garfield, a son of former President James A. Garfield and a man who shared Pinchot's views about the public lands. Pinchot (and even Roosevelt) understood that Taft would retain Garfield as his own Secretary of the Interior. But Taft wanted a man whose views about free enterprise and the disposition of public lands coincided with his own. Before his inauguration he asked for Garfield's resignation. In his place Taft appointed Richard Achilles Ballinger and set in motion a train of events that led inevitably to one of the classic confrontations in the history of conservation.

Pinchot described Ballinger about as kindly as it was in him to, considering the nature of their relationship: "A stocky, square-headed little man, of no inconsiderable energy and no little executive punch. In spite of being easily influenced, he had made a fairly good mayor, as mayors go."

Pinchot was speaking of Ballinger's early career in public life, a career which began in earnest after he arrived in Seattle from Alabama. Seattle, at the turn of the century, was fertile ground for an ambitious man and Ballinger made money from his law practice, in which he represented many of the leading local business interests. In 1904 he ran for mayor on a reform ticket, won the election, and served with some distinction, as even his worst enemy suggested. He was the sort of "progressive" Republican that Roosevelt was looking for in Washington; moreover, he had been a classmate and friend of the younger Garfield at Williams College. In 1907 he agreed to serve under Garfield in the Department of the Interior as Commissioner of Public Lands.

Ballinger lasted in that position for only a year. A man who believed that the federal government should turn over, rather than lease, the rights to grazing, minerals, and water power on public lands could not serve happily under the thumbs of Roosevelt, Pinchot, and Garfield. He resigned and returned to his law practice in Seattle in 1908. Within a year he was back in Washington, this time in a position to put into effect his ideas (conditioned by the needs of his law clients in Seattle) about public land policies.

Taft did not set out to be openly hostile to Roosevelt's conservation programs. He simply did not believe in a strong approach to the presidency, a political philosophy that Roosevelt overlooked to his eventual sorrow when he recommended him as a candidate. If Congress had not specifically approved a course of action, Taft did not take the initiative, and indeed considered many of Roosevelt's actions unconstitutional. TR, for instance, vetoed dam building projects that Congress had authorized without providing for fees or time limitations on the rights to power sites; Taft reversed this policy. Under his administration the Corps of Engineers took back from Interior the authority to grant water power permits on navigable streams.

Ballinger, as Secretary of the Interior, readily surrendered this jurisdiction. Often he went far beyond Taft's notions about the government's role in the regulation of natural resources. He seemed to be as eager to give away his department's responsibilities as the proverbial playboy is to divest himself of his father's money. He was in the forefront of the unsuccessful campaign to unseat Newell at the Bureau of Reclamation. Believing that the fees charged by the federal government kept power costs high, he worked to have the rights to power sites ceded to the states. He sided, too, with the Public Domain League, recently formed by anti-Roosevelt Westerners, to force the government to cede other public lands to the states. Harry A. Slattery, Pinchot's close friend and associate for many years, later presented the conservationists' view of Ballinger's policies.

"The whole tone of Interior began once more to be 'come and get it'," he wrote. "Reclamation Service officials were told to open the water power sites which had been temporarily withdrawn by Garfield from entry, awaiting legislation to put them on a leasing basis. If Ballinger's policy in this respect had prevailed there is no doubt but that the great reclamation projects of Boulder Dam, Bonneville, Grand Coulee, and others would by now have been in the hands of either the utility companies or land companies of the West."

Ballinger did not win Taft's support on a number of these issues, but he did in the matter of the coal lands, and it was there that the battle ultimately was joined with Pinchot. The Coal Lands Act authorized the government to sell limited acreage of the public domain to miners. Under Garfield, Interior had raised the price of these lands. Despite the outcry in the West that development would be stifled on those lands (which miners could exploit then for as little as $2.50 an acre) the demand increased and the public treasury began to receive a fair price for its resources. Hays* writes that in Wyoming one valuable tract of coal land (665 acres) sold for $363,330 instead of the $13,300 it would have brought under former prices; even so, the coal under the new land prices cost the owner less than half a cent a ton. Then, before leaving office, Roosevelt had withdrawn from entry 100,000 acres of coal lands in Alaska.

These decisions did not affect what came to be called the "Cunningham claims." In 1902 a miner named Clarence Cunningham had filed claims for thirty-three tracts of land, embracing 5280 acres, near the head of the Bering River in Alaska. He had paid ten dollars an acre for the claims. When land prices were raised and most of the other available Alaskan coal lands withdrawn, the value of these rich tracts soared into the millions.

The claims had been under investigation for some time by a young employee of the General Land Office named Louis R. Glavis. Glavis, who was certainly not the usual hack for which the Land Office became notorious, did not like what he found. Backing Cunningham in the project was Myles C. Moore, a promoter of mining schemes who once had served as governor of Washington; and behind Moore was a powerful New York syndicate led by J. P. Morgan and Daniel Guggenheim. Contrary to the law, Cunningham had filed for the claims in the names of a number of dummy entrymen, and the syndicate planned to consolidate them in one great tract. Glavis suspected the claimants had committed fraud.

Great sums of money were involved, because the syndicate in New York already controlled Alaskan steamship lines, railroads, copper mines, and fisheries. The coal lands would strengthen their monopoly in Alaska. Ballinger, as Commissioner of Public Lands, processed the claims for approval despite the investigation and an assessment by one of his aides that the Cunningham claimants "were engaged in a criminal conspiracy." He suspended the order only when further information arrived from Glavis that supported earlier suspicions about the claims.

TEMPORARY DELAY CAUSED BY REPORT OF FIELD AGENT, Ballinger wired Moore in Seattle.

After his temporary return to private law practice in Seattle,

*See footnote page 109.

Ballinger agreed to represent the Cunningham claimants. At one point he asked Garfield to expedite the claims. Yet, when he returned to the Department of the Interior as its Secretary in 1909, the claims were still under investigation.

Glavis, supported by other investigators in the General Land Office, had never given up his position that the claims were fraudulent. Now, in the new political climate, it appeared to him that the claims would be approved. Getting no satisfaction from Ballinger, he turned instead to Pinchot. A large part of the coal lands in question lay within the newly created Chugach National Forest and were naturally of interest to the Chief Forester. Pinchot heard Glavis's story, examined the documents, and felt that he had stumbled upon a choice opportunity to rid himself and the administration of Ballinger. As Louis D. Brandeis said after he entered the case:

"What an amazing ethical distinction it was that Mr. Ballinger drew! When he left Government service, he thought it right to use against the Government on behalf of his private clients the knowledge and influence he had acquired while in the Government's employ; but, when he returned to the Government service, he thought it wrong to use his knowledge on behalf of the Government and against his former clients."

Pinchot arranged for Glavis to bring his case directly to Taft, who was spending the summer at Beverly, Massachusetts. The President heard Glavis's story, then sent for Ballinger. Ballinger arrived with six hundred pages of statements and documents defending his action in the case. As Pinchot later remarked, the President could scarcely have digested in five hours the material it was to take lawyer Brandeis ten days to sort out; yet Taft immediately sided with Ballinger. He authorized Ballinger "to dismiss L. R. Glavis from the service of the Government for filing a disingenuous statement, unjustly impeaching the official integrity of his superior officers."

At the same time, Taft turned in a conciliatory manner toward Pinchot. He must have looked on the Forester as Roosevelt's unofficial "ambassador" to the new administration, and had no desire to antagonize the great man, though he was still in the bush halfway around the world. Pinchot, on his part, was preparing for disaster. He knew that the conflict with Ballinger, as explosive as it remained, was only a symptom of that widening cleavage between the conservative and the progressive wings of the Republican party. He began to lay the foundation from which to carry on the conservation struggle outside the administration. His first step was to form the National Conservation Association, a private organization that would rally public support for his policies and approach Congress as a powerful lobby itself.

Pinchot was in Ballinger's hair, of course, subverting him by spreading his own doctrines among Interior employees within the Bureau of Reclamation and the General Land Office; and going over his head to the White House. In one sense, Ballinger was more in tune with modern conservation philosophy than Pinchot: though he advocated turning over much of the public domain to private interests, he wanted to create a system of national parks and was among the first to recommend officially a National Park Service. Taft, too, was becoming impatient with his Chief Forester. As President, he believed he was carrying out sound conservation policies and that Pinchot was being unreasonable. But Taft had let matters drift beyond his control. The Ballinger-Pinchot confrontation was to be the first explosion in the movement that would turn him out of the White House and loosen the powerful conservative Republican grip on the House of Representatives.

The controversy was now a national issue. Glavis, prodded by Pinchot, had taken his case to the court of last resort—the press. He told his story to the editors of *Collier's,* and that magazine published the details in a series of articles bearing such titles as "Are the Guggenheims in Charge of the Interior Department?" and "Ballinger—Shyster Lawyer?" Ballinger was furious, threatening to sue *Collier's* and adding his voice to the call for a Congressional investigation. But, he told Congress, "any investigation of the Interior Department should embrace the Forest Service, since I have reason to believe that the pernicious activity of certain of its officers has been the inspiration of these charges and involve in part the common administration of the public domain." According to Pinchot's friend, Harry A. Slattery, Ballinger carried his case to the President by suggesting that Pinchot's interest in the Alaskan coal lands was prompted by his family's holdings in timber and coal.

The machinery of government began to grind toward a sensational climax in Congress. While readily admitting that his assistants in the Forest Service had supplied *Collier's* with ammunition for their articles, Pinchot contended that he was acting to defend the national forests against exploitation. He was profoundly convinced of the justness of his cause. Skilled in public relations, he felt that he had to meet Ballinger's letter to Congress with one of his own, that it was important not only to *be* right, but to *seem* right. Acting apparently without the permission of the Secretary of Agriculture, his immediate superior, Pinchot drafted a letter in which he defended his position. The letter was read on the floor of the Senate on January 6, 1910, by his friend, Senator Dolliver.

On the following day Pinchot received at his home a letter that was not wholly unexpected. It was carried to him by a special messenger from the White House and it spelled out Pinchot's insubordination. The letter, over the President's signature, concluded: "By your own conduct you have destroyed your usefulness as a helpful subordinate of the Government, and it therefore now becomes my duty to direct the Secretary of Agriculture to remove you from your office as the Forester."

At first the coming investigation held out little hope that the incident would be judged on its merits. A joint committee of Congress was to conduct the hearings, but by tradition the House members on the committee would be appointed by the arch-conservative Speaker, "Uncle Joe" Cannon of Illinois. Unexpectedly, an amendment to the resolution establishing the committee was introduced in the House by George W. Norris, a young congressman from Nebraska. He called for the entire House to appoint the men who would represent it on the committee. Norris had brought out all the simmering rebellion in the House, which passed the amendment and dealt the Speaker a crippling blow. (Cannon was finished off later by Norris and the other insurgents, who deprived him of his authority to staff the Rules Committee with his supporters and thus control the mechanics of legislation.)

The new procedure prevented the leadership in Congress from staging a whitewash of the Cunningham affair. There were congressmen on the committee now who would ask hard questions. For four months, in forty-six different sessions, the members of the committee tried, each in his own way, to get at the truth of the matter. As the hearings proceeded it became evident that it was not Ballinger, nor Pinchot, nor the Morgan-Guggenheim interests, who were on trial, but the President himself.

Pinchot appeared in the hearing room of the Senate Building each day with his lawyer, George Wharton Pepper (later a United

States Senator from Pennsylvania). *Collier's,* anxious to put the best possible face on its articles, engaged Louis Brandeis (soon to be appointed to the Supreme Court) to represent Glavis. This choice proved to be important for Pinchot because he and his own lawyer, Pepper, disagreed on tactics. Pinchot believed that, with the committee still weighted toward the administration, the anti-Ballinger forces could not hope to win a favorable majority report and so must work toward a public relations success. Pepper, already unhappy because of Pinchot's insubordinate letter to Senator Dolliver, played it as he would in a courtroom.

"Again and again I had to supplement George's failure to connect with the larger audience by making a public statement of my own, and again and again George, horror-stricken, threatened to resign," Pinchot wrote afterward. "The trouble with George was that he had lived too much with courts and lawyers, and not enough with the world of men."

Pinchot, the administrator and publicist, outshone Ballinger, who made a colorless and evasive witness in his own behalf. The Forest Service came through unscathed, in part because the only fact it had to fear was the involvement of Pinchot's aides in the *Collier's* articles; Pinchot himself had already divulged the details (shedding crocodile tears of indignation) in his letter to Senator Dolliver. Glavis, like any righteous young man, appeared to good advantage to everyone except those who had a stake in protecting the President. Taft, in fact, was compromised by Brandeis's discovery that he had predated a document sent to the committee, apparently in order to put Ballinger in a better light. (At first Taft claimed he had rejected Glavis's charges on the basis of Attorney General George W. Wickersham's report, only to retreat when Brandeis proved the report was not written until much later.)

Because the Ballinger-Pinchot issue had escaped the confines of a conservation squabble and assumed the proportions of a major political battle, the hearings were extremely well attended. Pinchot's mother, handsome and white-haired, was in regular attendance, usually accompanied by Mrs. Brandeis. Mrs. Ballinger also was a familiar figure at the hearings. ("I had genuine sympathy for Mrs. Ballinger, and real regret," Pinchot wrote. "She was a fine woman.") The press could always be sure of friendly cooperation from Pinchot, who fretted because Pepper never deigned to explain a fine point to the reporters after addressing the committee.

Consequently the administration did not fare well except in the most conservative newspapers. A political cartoon in the Newark *Evening News* was typical; a wolf in sheep's clothing (Ballinger) has slipped into the sheepfold while the portly shepherd (Taft) dozes in the distance; the sheep (coal lands, forests, water rights, etc.) stand helplessly by as the sheep dog (Pinchot) confronts the rapacious-looking intruder. In fact, the whole affair began to take on the aspect of one of those "no-decision" prize fights of the time, when state laws prohibited a verdict to be rendered by the officials and the fighters concentrated on catching the eye of the press to win the "newspaper decision."

In this case an official verdict was destined to be inconclusive. The committee split according to political viewpoint, the majority supporting Ballinger and the minority denouncing him. Pinchot's victory came outside the hearing room when Taft, in the face of mounting public criticism, rejected the Cunningham claims, and the coal lands reverted to the public domain.

Ballinger's ruin was complete. Once burned, Taft retreated to a semblance of the old Roosevelt conservation policies and his Secretary of the Interior resigned in frustration the next year. But the roar from the African bush was ominous. News of the sacking of Pinchot had reached Roosevelt on the upper Nile. Pinchot, carrying tales of Taft's treachery, set sail for Europe under the piebald pseudonym of Gaylord Smith and intercepted Roosevelt on his homeward journey in Italy. Briefed and disillusioned, Roosevelt proceeded back to the United States and the confrontation with Taft that broke the Republican hold on the White House.

15

Hetch Hetchy

Hetch Hetchy: a curiously grating name for a valley that rivaled Yosemite in loveliness, and that John Muir himself preferred to call the Tuolumne Yosemite. Today it is just a synonym for a mistake, honestly made but irrevocable. Yet, despite the immediate and jarring political effects of the Ballinger-Pinchot controversy, Hetch Hetchy has had a more lasting impact on the conservation movement and, beyond that, on the texture of American life.

"Imagine yourself in Hetch Hetchy on a sunny day in June," Muir wrote, "standing waist-deep in grass and flowers (as I have often stood), while the great pines sway dreamily with scarcely perceptible motion. Looking northward across the Valley you see a plain, gray granite cliff rising abruptly out of the gardens and groves to a height of 1800 feet, and in front of it Tueeulala's silvery scarf burning with irised sun-fire . . . Hetch Hetchy Valley . . . is a grand landscape garden, one of Nature's rarest and most precious mountain temples. As in Yosemite, the sublime rocks of its walls seem to glow with life, whether leaning back in repose or standing erect in thoughtful attitudes, giving welcome to storms and calms alike, their brows in the sky, their feet set in the groves and gay flowery meadows, while birds, bees, and butterflies help the river and the waterfalls to stir all the air into music—things frail and fleeting and types of permanence meeting here and blending, just as they do in Yosemite, to draw her lovers into close and confiding communion with her."

This was Hetch Hetchy, and this was John Muir. Hetch Hetchy lies in the Sierra less than twenty miles north of the famous Yosemite Valley itself. When Muir first knew it the Tuolumne River flowed through the valley, and waterfalls (including the Tueeulala) brought the granite cliffs alive with "sun-illumined fabrics." It was part of the glory that called him back to the Sierra throughout his life, and it was the disaster that drained the joy, if not the passion, from the strenuous days before his death.

Who *was* John Muir? In a letter to his friend and editor, Robert Underwood Johnson, Muir called himself a "politico-trampo-geologist-bot, and ornith-natural, etc.!–!–!–!'" More prosaically he was, like most Californians until very recently, not a native. He was born in Scotland, grew up in Minnesota reading the Bible and tramping the backwoods, and set out as a young man on a trek that took him the long way round to his promised land.

"I wandered afoot and alone, from Indiana to the Gulf of Mexico, with a plant-press on my back, holding a generally southward course, like the birds when they are going from summer to winter. From the west coast of Florida I crossed the Gulf to Cuba, enjoyed the rich tropical flora there for a few months, intending to go thence to the north end of South America, make my way through the woods to the headwaters of the Amazon, and float down that grand river to the ocean. But I was unable to find a ship bound for South America—fortunately perhaps, for I had incredibly little money for so long a trip and had not yet fully recovered from a fever caught in the Florida swamps. Therefore I decided to visit California for a year or two to see its wonderful flora and famous Yosemite Valley. All the world was before me and every day was a holiday, so it did not seem important to which of the world's wildernesses I first should wander.

"Arriving by the Panama steamer, I stopped one day in San Francisco, and then inquired for the nearest way out of town. 'But where do you want to go?' asked the man to whom I had applied for this important information. 'To any place that is wild,' I said."

And Muir was on his way, by foot again, into his lifelong adventure in the Sierra. The year was 1868. When he came into Yosemite

Valley he knew that he would never stay away for long. He spent days exploring the neighboring mountains. For a time he worked in a sawmill (one that cut "only windfalls," his friend Johnson assures us) and later he served as a guide. Then he married, rented land from his father-in-law in Martinez, and became a successful farmer, raising grapes, pears, and other fruit. But his true vocation was wandering in the mountains.

"In the wilderness Muir looked like John the Baptist, as portrayed by Donatello and other of the Renaissance sculptors," Johnson once wrote. "He was spare of frame, full-bearded, hardy, keen of eye and visage, and on the march eager of movement. It was difficult for an untrained walker to keep up with him as he leaped from rock to rock as surely as a mountain goat, or skimmed along the surface of the ground—a trick of easy locomotion learned from the Indians. If he ever became tired, nobody knew it. He delighted in gentle badinage at the expense of the tenderfoot. . . . Though never lonely, he was not at all a professional recluse; he loved companions and craved good talk."

The companions he liked best were good listeners, and the talk he craved most was his own, delivered with a soft burr. He was never a bore, though; his knowledge and adventures caused even Presidents to listen with respect. Like most men who spend a great deal of time alone, he could be inconsiderate of others' feelings and contemptuous of their knowledge.

"I guess you don't think I know much about geology," the venerable John Burroughs said to him during a dispute one evening.

Muir never hesitated. "Johnny," he said, "if all you know about geology were thrown into the ocean it wouldn't make a splash bigger than a raindrop."

If he reminded Johnson of Saint John the Baptist, perhaps long familiarity with Muir's letters and articles contributed as much to the impression as the beard and the ascetic visage. Muir infused his prose with the religious echoes he detected in his wilderness temples: "The grand priest-like pines held their arms above us in blessing." Again: "Meadows grassed and lilied head-high, spangled river reaches, and currentless pools, cascades countless and untamable in form and whiteness, groves that heaven all the valley!" And again: "Climb the mountains and get their good tidings. Nature's peace will flow into you as the sunshine into the trees.

The winds will blow their freshness into you, and the storms their energy, while cares will drop off like autumn leaves."

Yet Muir's reverence for the forest was pagan rather than Christian. As Lynn White has pointed out,* Ronald Reagan was being far more Christian than Muir when he said, "When you've seen one redwood tree, you've seen them all"; and White goes on: "By destroying pagan animism, Christianity made it possible to exploit nature in a mood of indifference to the feelings of natural objects . . . For nearly two millennia Christian missionaries have been chopping down sacred groves, which are idolatrous because they assume spirit in nature." Muir discovered that spirit.

There was nothing passive about Muir's passion for the wilderness. He went to meet it with all his senses open, as he did on that memorable day when he set off in a howling storm into the forest near the Yuba River. The trees bent under the force of the wind and the rain beat at his face as he lifted it toward the sky. On an impulse he picked out a Douglas fir that towered above the surrounding forest. From the ground he could see its top a hundred feet above him, "rocking and swirling in wild ecstasy." He began his ascent.

"Being accustomed to climb trees in making botanical studies I experienced no difficulty in reaching the top of this one," he wrote, "and never before did I enjoy so noble an exhilaration of motion. The slender tops fairly flapped and swished in the passionate torrent bending indescribable combinations of vertical and horizontal curves, while I clung with muscles firm, braced like a bobolink on a reed . . . free to take the wind into my pulses and enjoy the excited forest from my superb outlook."

To his own brand of pantheism Muir welded a sound scientific method. Few scientists saw with such keen eyes. It was generally accepted by geologists of the day that Yosemite Valley had been created by a cataclysmic convulsion that had pulled the valley's bottom deep into the earth. "The bottom never fell out of anything God made," Muir retorted, and began careful studies that led finally to the acceptance of his theory that glaciers had scoured out the valley during the Ice Age.

His impassioned outcry against the destruction of the mountain forests by sheep and timbermen also was based on sound scientific

* Sierra Club Bulletin, October 1967.

principles. Nor was his a voice crying alone in the wilderness. Many Westerners supported Muir's crusade for forest protection. The idea was beginning to take hold that sheep, by eating undergrowth, retarded the forest's growth and set the stage for widespread erosion and water famines. Perhaps competitive cattlemen were the source of the popular view that sheepherders were men of dull sense and vicious moral habits. Whatever the cause, sheep were despised by many Westerners, a sentiment summed up by one who remarked that he "could not see a sheep without wishing to kick it."

Muir's views were first given a national audience by Robert Underwood Johnson in *The Century Magazine*. This was a publication whose high-minded tone was set by Johnson's predecessor as editor-in-chief, Richard Watson Gilder. On one occasion Gilder was affronted by an Englishman's description of America as "a nation of prudes." Gilder replied that, "It may be that this accusation is well-founded. If so, we can only say that this is the price we pay for being, on the whole, the decentest nation on the face of the globe." Johnson, a poet and an early conservationist, carried on the attempt to make *The Century* a leader in the religious, political, social, and artistic opinion of the day. On a trip to Yosemite in 1889 he was charmed by Muir into working for the reservation of the area as a national park.

It can be said with a great deal of justification that the national park idea had its inception at Yosemite and not at Yellowstone. Yosemite Valley, with its imposing granite cliffs and tumbling waterfalls, had been admired by all the early visitors to the area, including Horace Greeley, who called it "the most unique and majestic of nature's marvels." Senator John Conness and other Californians sponsored a bill in Congress during the Civil War to remove the valley and the nearby Mariposa Grove of Big Trees from the public domain and cede it to the state. The bill swept through Congress and was signed by President Abraham Lincoln on June 30, 1864. Frederick Law Olmsted, the landscape architect who designed Central Park in New York City, was appointed one of the eight commissioners whose duty it was to manage the new park. By the governor's proclamation, trespassing, settlement, and logging were forbidden in the valley. Olmsted set about drawing up a plan that has become a cornerstone of modern national park policy. It read, in part:

"The main duty with which the Commissioners should be

charged should be to give every advantage practicable to the mass of the people to benefit by that which is peculiar to this ground and which has caused Congress to treat it differently from other parts of the public domain. This peculiarity consists wholly in its natural scenery. The first point to be kept in mind then is the preservation and maintenance as exactly as is possible of the natural scenery; the restriction, that is to say, within the narrowest limits consistent with the necessary accommodations of visitors, of all artificial constructions and the prevention of all constructions markedly inharmonious with the scenery or which would unnecessarily obscure, distort, or detract from the dignity of the scenery."

But the state legislature was not impressed—at least not enough to appropriate the funds Olmsted needed to carry out his plans in detail. In the course of time Olmsted wandered back to New York, and Yosemite Valley and its environs fell on hard days. Yosemite's lovely meadows were plowed under, fenced, and planted to hay to provide for the horses ridden by tourists into the park. Outside the park's confines sheep ravaged the land and loggers decimated the giant trees (two of the largest sequoias ever known were cut down simply to exhibit sections of them at world's fairs).

"It took more than three thousand years to make some of the trees in these Western woods," Muir once wrote, "trees that are still standing in perfect strength and beauty, waving and singing in the mighty forests of the Sierra. Through all the wonderful, eventful centuries since Christ's time—and long before that—God had cared for these trees, saved them from drought, disease, avalanches, and a thousand straining, leveling tempests and floods; but he cannot save them from fools."

And Muir added: "Only Uncle Sam can do that." He had come to realize that it is not enough simply to love the wilderness; one has to leave the forests and fight for them in the legislative bodies of man. Muir wrote about the wonders of the Sierra for *The Century,* while Johnson did some "spiritual lobbying" in Washington. With the help of Interior Secretary John W. Noble in President Harrison's administration the great area around Yosemite Valley was made into a splendid national park, comprising 1200 square miles, in 1890. (Yosemite Valley itself, standing in the center of this reservation and covering less than one-half of one percent of its total area, remained in the state's hands.) At the same time the administration created two other national parks from the remnant groves of magnificent trees, Sequoia and General Grant (the latter now a part of Kings Canyon National Park).

Muir went right on extolling his beloved mountains. Articles and books began to flow out of him; he never wrote with a typewriter, but fashioned quill pens, often from the eagle feathers he came across during his wanderings in the mountains. To guard against the lumbermen's repeated attempts to pry open the new parks for their own use, Muir organized with some of his friends the Sierra Club in 1892. The club's announced purpose was to "explore, enjoy, and protect the nation's scenic resources," a program Muir led as its president for twenty-four years, and which it carries on to this day. He found a less sturdy reed to lean on in Gifford Pinchot. For a while Muir believed that the preservation of the forests lay in the very reserves advocated by the young forester; but he had second thoughts when Pinchot, in his attempts to win support for all his programs in the West, advocated opening up the reserves to lumbering, mining, and (worst of all!) grazing.

In the early years of the century Muir, believing that the struggle for the land around Yosemite Valley had already been won, concentrated his attention on the unique valley itself. It had deteriorated badly under the management of the state and the exploitation of the concessionnaires. Muir campaigned vigorously in California for the recession of the valley to the federal government and its inclusion in the national park. When President Roosevelt visited the West in 1903 Muir preached the gospel of the Sierra to him. Roosevelt returned to Washington, converted to Muir's way of thinking. Meanwhile, in the West, Muir had gained another, almost equally important, ally in Edward H. Harriman, president of the Union Pacific Railroad. Muir had accompanied the Harriman expedition to Alaska in 1899 and was on excellent terms with the financier. Moreover, the railroads, intent on tourism, generally were favorable to national parks and played an important role in the creation of several of them. In 1905 Muir and his young friend in the Sierra Club, William E. Colby (who served as the club's secretary for forty-four years), joined Harriman in persuading the state legislature to vote for recession.

"William Herrin, the Railroad's chief counsel in California, called Colby to his San Francisco office and the strategy was laid," writes Holway R. Jones in *John Muir and the Sierra Club*. "Colby was to continue the distribution of Sierra Club material in favor of recession; Herrin would alert 'his men' in the Legislature. Herrin made it clear, however, that the Railroad could not openly attack the antirecession forces, but that when the showdown vote came, he felt there would be a sufficient number of votes to swing the bill."

The railroad produced the votes and California had made the first move toward recession. The following year, 1906, Congress accepted the recession and Yosemite Valley took its rightful place at the heart of Yosemite National Park. Johnson wrote to inquire if the news had caught up with the wandering Muir. "Yes, my dear Johnson," came the reply, "sound the loud timbrel and let every Yosemite tree and stream rejoice! You may be sure I knew when the big bill passed."

There existed another piece of legislation concerning Yosemite, however, the proper significance of which Muir was not yet aware. Five years earlier Congress had passed the Right of Way Act of 1901, at the urging of California congressmen. As John Ise has said in his study of the National Parks, "The act was in most respects perfectly tailored for looters of the parks, for it authorized the Secretary [of the Interior] to grant rights of way through government reservations of all kinds" for water conduits, as well as dams and reservoirs, that were "in the public interest." In due time the motivation for such legislation came to the surface: the city of San Francisco was looking for a solution to its water problems, and had marked out for its purposes Hetch Hetchy Valley. The stumbling block in the city's plans was that Hetch Hetchy was a part of Yosemite National Park.

This remote mountain valley, which Muir called a "wonderfully exact counterpart of the great Yosemite, not only in its crystal river and sublime rocks and waterfalls, but in the gardens, groves, and meadows of its flowery, park-like floor," also had certain characteristics that appealed to the city's engineers. The water carried through the valley by its "crystal river" was sweet and pure. Its "flowery, park-like floor" was flat, suggesting an ideal bottom for a reservoir. And its "sublime rocks" formed steep cliffs narrowing at one end into a slit that would be convenient and relatively cheap to dam. The floor of the valley was about three and a half miles long and it lay 150 miles from San Francisco.

In 1900 the city's officials made a study of Hetch Hetchy as a possible source of water supplies and electricity, an unauthorized

invasion of the national park for which they were later criticized
by Secretary of the Interior Ethan A. Hitchcock. But San Francisco,
plagued by fires, was under pressure from many of its citizens to
find a water source other than that of a private company, the Spring
Valley Water Company, whose service had been unsatisfactory.
Mayor James D. Phelan set in motion various legislative and
engineering wheels toward that end. The first plans to bring in
Hetch Hetchy water were drawn up by the city engineer, Marsden
Manson, who, ironically, was a member of the Sierra Club. The
club, the city, and the nation were to be split on the question posed
by the grab for Hetch Hetchy. As Stewart L. Udall has said,
"Drawing a line between the workshop and the temple was, and still
is today, the most sensitive assignment for conservation planners."

When the city applied for permission to build a reservoir in
Hetch Hetchy it was turned down by Secretary Hitchcock on the
grounds that the request was not in the public interest. But Hitchcock was not always in tune with the views of Gifford Pinchot, who
determined the administration's natural resource policies. As
Robert Underwood Johnson wrote later of Pinchot: "He felt it more
important to get the support of the Pacific slope and other Western
sentiment for his general conservation policies than that the recreational, hygienic, and aesthetic uses of the national parks be
preserved. He therefore contributed his great influence to the
commercialization of the Valley and but for him I believe the
scheme would never have succeeded."

This estimate is borne out by the events that followed Hitchcock's
resignation in 1906. James R. Garfield, Pinchot's close friend,
succeeded him as Secretary of the Interior. Certainly the great San
Francisco earthquake and fire of 1905 gave strength to the campaign to dam Hetch Hetchy, although Marsden Manson had
admitted there were many other sites in the Sierra from which the
city could draw its water. Lake Eleanor, near the northern end of
Hetch Hetchy, already was under consideration, though Manson
and others wanted both sources. In 1906 Pinchot wrote to Manson:
"I cannot, of course, attempt to forecast the action of the new
Secretary of the Interior on the San Francisco watershed position,
but my advice to you is to assume that his attitude will be favorable,
and to make the necessary preparations to set the case before him.
I had supposed from an item in the paper that the city had definitely
given up the Lake Eleanor plan and had purchased one of the other

systems. If the possibility of a supply from the Sierras is still open, you should, I think, by all means go ahead with the idea of getting it."

Perhaps Pinchot would not admit to knowing Garfield's mind, but Manson now could proceed with confidence. Egged on by Pinchot, San Francisco renewed its application to build a reservoir in Hetch Hetchy and the new Secretary of the Interior felt the application was now, indeed, in the public interest. By this time Muir and his colleagues in the Sierra Club were very much alive to the threat posed by Pinchot's attitude. Muir passed over his old friend's head and went directly to the President in a note that played on the camaraderie of their meeting in the West. Roosevelt, who took Pinchot's advice on conservation matters, was nevertheless torn between political reality and his "preservationist" leanings. "It does seem to me unnecessary to decide about the Hetch Hetchy Valley at present," he wrote to Garfield. But, in the absence of a firm stand by the President, Garfield granted San Francisco's request for a reservoir and a right of way in Yosemite National Park, though he stipulated that Lake Eleanor be fully developed as a water source before the city could turn to Hetch Hetchy.

"Never mind, dear Colby," wrote Muir, the indefatigable correspondent, "the present flourishing triumphant growth of the wealthy wicked, the Phelans, Pinchots and their hirelings, will not thrive forever . . . We may lose this particular fight but truth and right must prevail at last. Anyhow we must be true to ourselves."

At this point the city was dealt a pair of stunning blows that set back its plans for several years. The counterattack launched by Muir and his allies on both coasts won favor among members of Congress, and a bill to approve the exchange of Hetch Hetchy for some nearby land of lesser quality failed to get out of committee. On top of this rebuke, Taft became President and replaced Garfield with Ballinger. Among the issues on which Ballinger and Pinchot disagreed was Hetch Hetchy. If Ballinger did not especially care about the remainder of the public domain, he was sold on the advantages of national parks as pleasuring grounds for the people, and he rescinded the Hetch Hetchy permit granted to San Francisco by Garfield. Taft, whom Muir met and charmed in 1909, also was sympathetic to the preservationists' plea in this case, and the issue seemed to be dead.

But it was by no means dead in San Francisco. The longer the battle went on the hotter it grew, and old friendships were shattered. ("This playing at politics saps the very foundations of righteousness," Muir grumbled.) That the struggle was not simply one between exploiters and conservationists could be seen in the nature of the men who aligned themselves with the city—men such as Pinchot, Senator George W. Norris, and Representative William Kent, whose opposition to the exploiters in other struggles was well known. Kent, for instance, was an outdoorsman and a friend of Muir. He had saved nearly three hundred acres of choice redwoods by buying the land on which they stood and turning it over to the federal government in 1908. Accepted by President Roosevelt, the land was set aside under the Antiquities Act and named the Muir Woods National Monument. Yet Kent's support, as chairman of the Public Lands Committee, for San Francisco's claims alienated him from Muir. Like Norris and Pinchot, Kent saw Hetch Hetchy as a device to squeeze out the rapacious private power interests; the point, he felt, was not the invasion of a national park, but a matter of corporate greed against public power.

This aspect of the Hetch Hetchy controversy made the preservationists' position in San Francisco very uncomfortable. They were villified as "tools" of the Spring Valley Water Company. The bitterness against them rose. Manson spoke of the preservationists as a group of "short-haired women and long-haired men," a poorly veiled sexual slur that frustrated patriots have resorted to a good many times since then. The city's officers, in fact, were genuinely frustrated and puzzled, especially after the U.S. Army Corps of Engineers completed a report showing at least four other excellent potential sites for a reservoir, but marking Hetch Hetchy as the least expensive. Wasn't the object to find water at the lowest cost? And, anyway, why would the reservoir necessarily destroy Hetch Hetchy as a scenic attraction within the park. This argument was best stated by Mayor Phelan:

"There can be no question but that the beauty of the scene, with a dam easily concealed by grasses and rivers, will be enhanced by the effect of the lake reflecting all above it and beneath it and will in itself be a great and attractive natural object."

The struggle went on beneath the surface. Pinchot, though out of office, exerted more influence on the federal government than he had since the triumphal years when he had stood at Roosevelt's elbow. After Taft had fired him, he worked within the National

Conservation Association, a private organization with himself as president and Harry Slattery, his long-time assistant, as its executive secretary. In Slattery's words the NCA became "the organized voice of the conservation movement in America." From this position Pinchot fired at both Congress and the public frequent volleys of propaganda in support of his own utilitarian brand of conservation.

Now in Washington Pinchot worked so assiduously on behalf of his San Francisco friends for the Hetch Hetchy dam that several leading conservationists resigned in protest from his association. In San Francisco member warred with member within the Sierra Club. Muir, nearing the end of his long life, redoubled his efforts against those he referred to as the "money-changers in the temple." In 1912 he thundered: "Dam Hetchy Hetchy! As well dam for water tanks the people's cathedrals and churches, for no holier temple has ever been consecrated by the heart of man." That year he cast his vote for Taft instead of for Roosevelt. But the money-changers were closing in on the old man, and when the Republican split ensured Woodrow Wilson's victory in the presidential election, the end was in sight. Wilson chose as his Secretary of the Interior Franklin K. Lane—a former San Francisco city attorney and an ardent supporter of the Hetch Hetchy scheme.

Lane approved the city's application for the reservoir. The last step was congressional approval of the plan in the form of the Raker Bill, introduced by Representative John E. Raker of California on September 3, 1913. The bill was passed overwhelmingly by the House of Representatives. The preservationists' last hope lay in the Senate, and Muir wrote to Johnson: "We're bound to win, enemy badly frightened, up and smite 'em!" And indeed there was some uneasiness in the San Francisco camp, as expressed by William Kent, who sent a cautionary wire to Pinchot that there were continued efforts to defeat the bill, ENGINEERED BY MISINFORMED NATURE LOVERS AND POWER INTERESTS WHO ARE WORKING THROUGH THE WOMEN'S CLUBS.

In more specific terms, Kent carried the battle against his old friend, spreading the word among fellow congressmen that Muir had wandered so long in the wilderness he had never developed a "social sense." To one congressman he wrote: "I hope you will not take my friend, Muir, seriously, for he is a man entirely without social sense. With him it is me and God and the rock where God put it, and that is the end of the story. I know him well and as far as this proposition is concerned, he is mistaken."

The preservationists received little consolation in the Senate hearing room. Johnson claimed they were abused like "criminals in the box" and that the committee report distorted his testimony. One of his most persistent inquisitors was Senator Norris:

NORRIS: Mr. Johnson, I want to ask you a few questions. Just at the close of your remarks you made the statement that this bill was anti-conservation.

JOHNSON: Not at all.

NORRIS: What is the object of the argument that you have been making? I realize that men may disagree as to even the meaning of conservation, but I had always supposed that the utilization, for instance, of water power was one of the fundamental principles of conservation. Why are not the people who are in favor of the building of this dam and the use of this water power and the rest of the water itself entitled just as much to the designation of conservationist as those who are opposed to that and who desire to keep the park undisturbed?

JOHNSON: I will tell you, sir. You must go back to the object for which the park was made; the purpose for which it was created. I read you the report of the Committee on Public Lands in regard to that, and I say to you gentlemen that there should be a distinction drawn between the forest reserves and the national parks. The forest reserves were made for the purpose—

NORRIS: I am not talking about the forest reserves. I am talking about this particular bill. While I concede there is a chance for argument perhaps on both sides of it I am trying to get your idea as to what conservation is.

JOHNSON: Conservation is maintaining the natural resources of the government for the use of the people; for the highest use that each one may properly have. I do not think that the best use of Niagara would be the running of electric works.

NORRIS: Possibly so; but that question is not involved here today.

JOHNSON: The Almighty put it there to be looked at.

NORRIS: There is not a reclamation project in the country, Mr. Johnson, which has ever been undertaken by the government but that it destroys some of the beauty of nature somewhere.

JOHNSON: The point I make, Senator, is not that we shall not do it; but that we should consider the character that the reservation was made for.

NORRIS: What would be a reasonable construction of that?

JOHNSON: I say you are paying a colossal price for San Francisco's water.

It was a classic confrontation between men who call themselves conservationists, and it has been repeated over and over right down to our own time. The sentiment in Washington that year was, as it has been all too often, opposed to preservation. William Kent came over from the House of Representatives to testify that he wanted Hetch Hetchy's water to make the people "forever free from any danger of being held up in the interest of private profit." And John Raker appeared in the Senate hearing room to assure the committee of the "unanimous" belief among the experts that Hetch Hetchy would be more beautiful as a reservoir than as a wild valley. The Senate approved the bill, and the destruction of Hetch Hetchy was begun.

John Muir died the next year. He did not live to see the waters creep up those cliffs over which the streams once had fallen like silver scarves.

In the light of claim and counterclaim it might be worth a moment of our time to review the later history of Hetch Hetchy. World War I slowed construction in the valley. The dam was completed in 1925 but other parts of the reservoir, vital to its use, were left undone for several additional years. Also left undone were the fine roads and other facilities that San Francisco had promised would be provided to lure tourists to the man-made lake. When the pipes were opened at last in the 1930s the city had no means of distributing the water and sold it to the Pacific Gas and Electric Company—the very result that Pinchot, Norris, and Kent had thought to avoid by the destruction of the valley.

And what of the scenic lake that Phelan, Raker, and the other promoters had promised would make grateful travelers forget the trees and meadows of the old valley? Contrast Phelan's bright projection with the litter of stumps and barren rocks ceaselessly covered and laid bare again as the reservoir rises and falls according to the city's water needs. While nearby Yosemite is visited almost to destruction, few tourists bother to stop at Hetch Hetchy. One of them, Robert K. Cutter, described the reality of Hetch Hetchy in the *Sierra Club Bulletin:*

"Before it was flooded, the flowing water and the valley vegetation cooled it and the trees gave shade and relief from the heat reflected from the granite walls. Now, with the grass and trees all gone, there is nothing but a narrow body of monotonous water with an ugly shore line (typical of all reservoirs where the water level shifts) surrounded by stark stone walls. It is hot and uninviting. The falls, as seen through trees from the floor of the valley, were beautiful, but now, with the setting gone, they are about as interesting as the spillway over the dam."

In retrospect the Hetch Hetchy Dam was a dreadful mistake. The overcrowded park desperately needs the diversion of another superb attraction. The alternate sites for a dam have gone unused. To save a few dollars a priceless valley has been obliterated for all time. But the conservation movement came out of the struggle purified and strengthened, better prepared for similar confrontations in the years ahead, and in an unprecedented position to press for a major prize in 1916.

Steve Mather
and the National Parks

In 1915 the national parks were in trouble, a fact of which Franklin K. Lane was reminded once more as he read through his mail one morning at the Department of the Interior. He had grown used to letters complaining about some defect in management or some flagrant example of exploitation. But something in one of the letters that morning caught his attention. The letter, a comprehensive and accurate report of negligence on the part of park management, was signed by Stephen Tyng Mather. According to Mather's biographer, Robert T. Shankland, Lane sent off an immediate reply:

"Dear Steve," it read. "If you don't like the way the national parks are being run come on down to Washington and run them yourself."

Lane had known him for a long time. Mather had been an indifferent reporter on the old New York *Sun,* but found his true calling as a businessman and promoter in Chicago. An outdoorsman who was fascinated by the legends of the Old West, he took a special interest in Borax because of its "twenty-mule team" associations, and made a great deal of money in promoting and marketing it. Through the early years of the twentieth century Mather alternated between periods of hard work and mental breakdowns. To recuperate from these setbacks he hiked and climbed in the Western mountains. He had been a member of the Sierra Club for a number of years, and had met and talked with John Muir on one of his trips. He loved Yosemite and the other national parks he had visited. Now, independently wealthy, Mather could do and go where he wanted. Where he wanted to go after receiving Lane's letter was to Washington. He answered the summons and soon was established in a small office near that of the Secretary of the Interior, assigned to making some sense out of the disorganized national parks.

Until then, the director of each park reported directly to the Secretary of the Interior. All were beset with problems that could be solved neither in Washington, where the Secretary did not have time to deal with them, nor on the scene, where the director did not have sufficient authority. Even the creation of new parks was retarded by the lack of national sponsorship. Parks came into existence when local support was well organized and local opposition was not. The result was that prime areas, such as the coastal redwoods in California, were excluded as national parks because of the opposition of powerful timber interests, while lesser areas were set aside.

One of the most notorious parks established under this haphazard system was Platt National Park in Oklahoma. Each Western state wanted a national park as a tourist attraction (as long as the land was not contested by powerful interests). Despite its drawbacks, Oklahoma's congressional delegation fought for Platt, an area of sulphur and other cold mineral springs, because of the federal funds it brought annually to the state. For one thing, the area did not meet the high scenic standards generally required of national parks. And, for another, Platt was afflicted by a pollution problem; its springs were located below the town of Sulphur, which contaminated them by the regular overflow of its sewage system. Whenever it came time for Congress to appropriate funds for the park's upkeep, cries of derision could be heard from the floor. Many congressmen and government officials suggested that Platt be given back to the Indians, or at least to the state of Oklahoma. But other congressmen contemplated fund requests of their own, and Platt survived the annual ordeal.

Finally, there was a great deal of hostility in Congress to the very concept of national parks. Some Eastern congressmen, perhaps resentful because there were no national parks in the East at that time, objected to providing funds for a program confined to another part of the country. Meanwhile, a number of Western congressmen reflected the opinion of their more powerful constituents that national parks only served to "lock up" natural resources that could be put to better use. This view was rather baldly expressed during the Hetch Hetchy controversy by Representative Martin Dies of Texas. (So firmly had Gifford Pinchot tied his name to conservation that Dies, apparently confused, lumped him with the preservationists in this dispute.)

"I am not for reservations and parks," Dies said. "I would have the great timber and mineral and coal resources of this country opened to the people and I only want to say, Mr. Chairman, that your Pinchot and your conservationists are theorists who are not in my humble judgment making a propaganda in the interest of the American people. Let California have it and let Alaska open her coal mines. God Almighty has located the resources of this country in such a form so that his children will not use them in disproportion, and your Pinchots will not be able to controvert and circumvent the laws of God Almighty."

Into this troubled arena strode Steve Mather in 1915 with all the confidence of a man who has already made his fortune and now wants to make a contribution to the common wealth. The first thing he had to see about was an appropriation to run his embryonic department. Old hands at Interior advised him to ask Congress for one-third more than he actually needed.

"I'm a businessman," Mather replied, according to Shankland. "We won't ask for a penny more than we can justify, and we'll spend it exactly the way we tell them we will!"

Even the skeptical old hands were shocked by the few pennies Congress tossed Mather's way, and in future years he came to adapt his budgetary strategy to that of government traditions.

Mather turned one immediate problem facing the parks to his (and their) advantage. With Europe in the grip of war, many Americans who used to vacation abroad now were forced to look inward toward their own country's resources, and suddenly they became aware of splendors that they had imagined were confined to the Alps. It was a fresh experience for thousands of people. The response of the first settler in Bryce Canyon, that fairyland of erosion-sculpted red sandstone, had been, "It's a hell of a place to look for a cow." Now tourists spoke of the West's glories—Yosemite and Yellowstone, Sequoia and Glacier—in tones they once had affected only for Alpine chasms and Tyrolean lakes. These enchanted thousands put new pressure on the parks' staffs and facilities. Mather, an indefatigable publicist, turned to the nation's newspapers and magazines, persuading them to stop treating the parks as "if they were all in Outer Mongolia."

Most of the contacts he made himself. Soon leading newspapers in the large cities ran editorials extolling the parks' wonders. *The Saturday Evening Post* and the *National Geographic* seemed never to have enough articles to print about the parks. Through his friends in the business world Mather met railroad officials and convinced them that this was the time to take advantage of the interest in the parks that they had helped to create. The railroads became enthusiastic publicists for the national parks and, at Mather's suggestion, provided special tours for Eastern sightseers.

Mather made a charming salesman for the parks' virtues. Out-going and ruggedly handsome, with shining blue eyes and a shock of prematurely white hair, he sold himself as a first step toward selling the parks. Like all great promoters, he put himself across to his audience as vividly as he did the product he came to promote. The reporter for *Woman's Magazine,* who interviewed him about the national parks, rushed back to her typewriter all agog with the man himself: "To describe Mr. Mather, one must roll all the matinee idols and Gibson models into one, and then put the red blood of a real man into him; he has the kindest blue eyes, as clear and frank as a child's, but the mouth and chin of a man who had fought his way in life."

Over one thousand articles about the national parks appeared in a three-year period, an outpouring of hosannas that Mather designed to influence reluctant congressmen as well as to lure tourists to the parks. Subsidies for the parks' upkeep proportionately increased. When Mather was unable to wheedle an appropriation from Congress for a pet project, he dug into his own pocket for the funds. Such was the case when he hired Robert Sterling Yard, a prominent newspaperman, as publicity director for the parks. No sum had been provided by Congress for publicity. Mather arranged for Yard to be hired by the Bureau of Reclamation as a part-time employee at $30 a month, just to bring him into the government, then paid Yard's salary and expenses with personal checks. Congress scented a dangerous precedent in Mather's introduction of free enterprise to government service. Eventually it passed a bill prohibiting such practices (without offering to provide a further appropriation for the purpose) and Yard left government service to organize (with Mather's financial help) the National Parks Association. Working hand in hand with Mather, the new private organization had much to do with later additions to the park system.

From the very beginning of his assignment, Mather realized that the specter of Hetch Hetchy hung over all of the national parks. If Yosemite could be invaded successfully, he knew that other cities and private interests would come forward with "beneficent" projects of their own. Even Ballinger had seen the necessity for creating a National Park Service that would gather all the parks under a single efficient blanket, making easier the task of fighting off major raids on its lands as well as dealing with the myriads of minor problems that plagued the system.

A bill to create a National Park Service had been introduced in Congress in 1911. It was overshadowed by the Hetch Hetchy fight for several years, and there were the usual objections: prime natural resources would be "locked up" forever, and *use* must take precedence over *scenery*. But after Hetch Hetchy the opposition began to dwindle. Perhaps pangs of conscience played a part; or was it just a coincidence that the congressional leaders in the fight for a reservoir in Hetch Hetchy—Lane, Kent, and Raker—now took the lead in pressing for a National Park Service? In any case, Gifford Pinchot was not among the leaders in this campaign. He disliked the idea of national parks, believed they should be put to use as national forests, and saw a National Park Service as a rival for the funds and prestige he thought rightfully belonged to the organization he once had led and whose interests he would work for until the day he died—the Forest Service.

Among the leaders of the national parks' cause was Frederick Law Olmsted, Jr. Olmsted, a landscape architect like his father, was chiefly responsible for the wording of the bill designed to create the service. It spelled out the policy that would guide the management of the parks (a policy formulated many years before by the elder Olmsted in reference to the state park at Yosemite):

"To conserve the scenery and the natural and historic objects and the wildlife and to provide for the enjoyment of the same in such a manner and by such means as will leave them unimpaired for the enjoyment of future generations."

Congress passed the act creating the National Park Service in 1916. Mather became its director, and Horace Albright (his eventual successor) was named his assistant.

Only an overriding national emergency now could endanger the national parks, and Mather found himself confronted by one almost immediately. Early in 1917 the United States entered the war against Germany. Harry Slattery was to summarize the danger many years later in his memoirs: "As Franklin D. Roosevelt later did, Wilson apparently felt obliged to turn right with war coming on, in order to win the cooperation of industrial and financial interests for preparation of the country for the war."

It was a gloomy omen for the national parks when Wilson turned sheep out to graze on the White House lawn. Uncertain of the future, many government officials were susceptible to the exploiters, who now rushed to Washington with predictions about the approaching famine, and imminent shortages of wood and fiber. Faced by rascals wrapped prominently in the flag, Mather had few defenses. Lane bowed to the sheepherders and ordered that their flocks be admitted to graze in Yosemite National Park; the Sierra Club successfully fought the order and limited the livestock invasion to 5000 head of cattle.

There were attempts, some of them successful, to slaughter deer and elk in the parks, in part for the meat they would provide, and in part to wipe out grazing competition for sheep and cattle. Immense areas of grassland in the West, unsuitable for the purpose, were plowed up and planted to wheat. With Lane about to crumble completely before the demands of the cattlemen and timbermen, the national parks held off the profiteers when Herbert Hoover, the head of the Food Administration, issued a statement denying the emergency required the spoliation of the parks. One of the chief invasions, however, occurred at Yellowstone, where mining interests got permission to take coal from a mine there that had been closed for many years. Incensed because he knew the coal was of very poor quality anyway, Mather stepped in immediately after the armistice and ordered the mine's tunnels to be dynamited.

With the war ended and the parks intact, Mather set out to accomplish three things:

(a) to make more Americans aware of their scenic treasures;

(b) to eliminate private holdings within the parks; and

(c) to coax more money from Congress.

The first step was the easiest. Mather's promotional genius, supported by the propaganda turned out by the National Parks Association, flooded the country with information about the parks. The parks, formerly accessible chiefly by rail, now were opened to the growing numbers of people who owned automobiles. To make the parks more attractive to them Mather lowered the high entrance fee charged to cars. (Where it had once cost $10 to bring a car into Yellowstone, Mather brought the fee down to $3.) Tenderfeet flocked to the parks. National Park rangers still like to talk of the fellow who drove into one of the most majestic of the parks, poked his head out the car window, and inquired of the ranger, "Say, where's the scenery around here?"

The elimination of private holdings within the parks was a different matter. Timbermen, for instance, clung tenaciously to their holdings (accumulated mostly by claims under the Swamplands Act*) in Sequoia National Park. Some of the last great stands of Big Trees were threatened by these holdings. When Congress refused to appropriate the money to buy the stands, Mather raised over $100,000 from people sympathetic to the parks and bought the land for the government. Money, however, could not help him at Grand Canyon, where William Randolph Hearst, the immensely wealthy publisher, owned considerable land within the park's boundaries. In order to prevent their seizure by the government, Hearst ordered a cabin built on his holdings and installed one of his employees in it to cement his claim.

"My holdings at Grand Canyon," Hearst said, "are as safe with me as they would be with the government."

Mather's skills were put to their ultimate test by Congress, which was always reluctant to spend money on scenery. Many congressmen knew little about the country's national parks, and cared less. Mather did his best to remedy this deficiency, making frequent forceful appearances before congressional committees to spread his own special gospel, while encouraging people outside the govern-

*See page 91.

ment to make their wishes known to their own congressmen. On one occasion he arranged a tour of the Western national parks for the members of the House Committee on Appropriations; the tour was financed by a number of Western cities. Mather also made large financial contributions to the campaigns of influential congressmen.

Mather believed that one of the difficulties in coaxing appropriations from Congress was the sectional nature of the program. Almost from the first he began to campaign for national parks in the East. The problem seemed insurmountable. The great Western parks had been created from the public domain, but all of the land in the East had long since fallen into private hands. Mather might have left it at that had he not needed a broader base for the support of the National Park system. Again he turned to private enterprise. Perhaps the most spectacular scenery found on the East Coast is that at Mount Desert Island in Maine, which had long been a resort for wealthy Easterners. Each summer hundreds of these families packed up their bags, gathered their children and servants, and set out on steamboats from various ports for the run to Bar Harbor. Samuel Eliot Morison, in *The Story of Mount Desert Island,* has recalled those trips on boats that were not covered by insurance and that therefore scurried into the nearest haven in bad weather. After a long wait in such a haven one day, an impatient passenger approached the skipper.

"Aren't you going on?" he asked.

"Nope," the skipper replied.

"Why not? It's all clear overhead."

"We're not bound that way."

At Mount Desert Island, just as in the Great Smoky Mountains, it was the wealthy landowners who decided to save the land from development. Through gifts of land and money the National Park Service was able to acquire a nucleus of land for the parks, giving it a firm base in the Eastern states.

Mather gave his wealth, his health, and finally his life, in establishing what is certainly one of America's most valuable possessions—its national park system. Dedicated to his vision of parks for the people, he pushed himself beyond the limits of his endurance. He suffered three mental breakdowns while serving as director, and died while still holding that position in 1928. Twelve new parks were created during Mather's regime. He organized the system's dedicated corps of rangers, standardized the concessions operations, and built up a priceless store of good will among both congressmen and the public. Eulogies are often meaningless, but visitors to a number of national parks today may come across memorial plaques dedicated to Stephen Mather. In the light of his achievements the quotation on those plaques, taken from a eulogy to Mather by Representative Louis C. Cramton, does not seem to be flagrant hyperbole:

"There will never come an end to the good he has done."

Part Four

The Fight for Wildlife

17

Hornaday

"Fully ten per cent of the human race consists of people who will lie, steal, throw rubbish in parks, and destroy wildlife whenever and wherever they can do so without being stopped by a policeman and a club."

This was William Temple Hornaday, writing in a spirit of comparative good will, before long familiarity with sportsmen and fellow conservationists dampened his cautious optimism about the human animal. The words appear in his book, *Our Vanishing Wild Life,* which he wrote in 1913. Hornaday's concern for the preservation of endangered wild creatures, and his notable lack of concern for the feelings of those who did not agree with him, brought him fame (and a measure of success) far beyond that of most of the other conservationists of his time. But militants seldom attract eulogists. The directness with which he attacked every problem accounts for the planned obscurity into which other conservationists let his name drop immediately after his death.

Hornaday's passion for wild animals was lifelong, and began as it did for most young men of his time as a passion for the hunt. Born in 1854 on an Indiana farm, and carried by wagon train to Iowa as a child, he spent his days in the out-of-doors. The habits of wild animals and the handling of an old gun absorbed his attention. Yet there was always something wasteful about the hunt, he thought, something senseless about killing an animal and then throwing most of it away.

Later, as a freshman at Iowa State College, he took an interest in its new museum. Hours in the zoology class, where he had watched the instructor mount a crow, convinced him that taxidermy might be a justification of the hunt. After some sloppy and uninspired work on a dead squirrel he had found, one of his teachers turned over to him a white pelican that some marksman had brought down near the campus. With the pelican, the teacher handed young Hornaday a copy of Audubon's portrait of the bird. Hornaday, inspired now by both the drawing and its subject, turned out a finished specimen that earned him regular work in the museum.

"I shaped his future," Hornaday said of the pelican, "and he shaped mine."

From Iowa State he went on to Ward's Natural Science Establishment in Rochester, New York, where he began to master his trade, and from there to the wild places of the world: the Everglades, the South American jungles, the Nile, India, the East Indies, and the plains of the American West. He shot alligators and crocodiles along muddy streams, elephants in bamboo thickets, tigers at jungle watering holes, and buffaloes on the Great Plains. In Borneo he visited headhunting Dyaks to observe the trophies hung about their houses and noted, with a young scientist's objective wit, that "none of the skulls is labeled with locality, date, sex, and species, as crania always should be, to be valuable." He skinned and preserved somewhat more legitimate specimens of his own. And in the evenings, sitting about a campfire with his native help, he could think, with some justification, "This is the jolliest life that was ever led."

Yet Hornaday's emotional horizons were far broader than those of the usual killer of game. He took time out to write a little book based on one aspect of his African experience, *Free Rum on the Congo*, which was published in 1887 by the Woman's Temperance Publication Association. Like Gifford Pinchot, he was a prohibitionist, and his book was a fire-and-brimstone account of the black man's corruption by the white man's hard liquor. In tone and approach, *Free Rum* resembles Hornaday's later conservation publications

("Let cowards shirk the encounter and sophists befog it, after the manner of the cuttlefish, with an impregnable cloud of theories, if they must; but the dragon that threatens to devour the people of Africa shall be unmasked and revealed in all his hideousness.").

Hornaday also worked with a dramatic, if defter, hand as a taxidermist, pioneering in the creation of lifelike animal groups for leading museums. He conceived, and became the first super-intendent of, the National Zoological Park in Washington. This project was characteristic of his vision and energy: at the time, he happened to be working on a paper for the Smithsonian Institution dealing with the extermination of the bison, and wondered why the nation's capital should not have a zoo of its own in which to preserve a handful of the last specimens. It was also characteristic that, with his project's completion in sight, he resigned after a dispute about the zoo's physical layout. He retreated in a huff to Buffalo, New York, where he entered the real estate business and wrote articles, a novel, and a manual of taxidermy. But the passion for wildlife, preferably alive, still gripped him and he heeded the call to come to New York City as the first director of the Bronx Zoo. It was from this position that Hornaday, by dealing alternately in persuasion and anathema, would rally the wildlife preservation enthusiasts during the next third of a century.

The destruction of the great buffalo herds had sobered him. So had the dwindling flocks of birds of all kinds, now approaching their all-time low around 1910. He could detect no concerted effort within the federal government, except perhaps at Yellowstone Park, to protect America's wildlife. Turning to the scientific organizations he saw even less interest.

"Seeking a hookup with some organization of bird men," he wrote in his autobiography, "I went exploring backward through the annual reports of the American Ornithologists' Union. I came upon a funny record made in 1894 stating that the Bird Protection Committee of the Union 'asked to be discharged, the need for such a committee being no longer urgent of late, its function having been merely advisory and its services not often required.' That report led me to abandon my intention of trying to connect with that organization for anything like real work."

Perhaps in later years, with their peace of mind in view, the AOU's members considered themselves fortunate that Hornaday decided to connect with other organizations. He was fast becoming that kind of preservationist, berated for "sentimentality" in our own time as well, who passionately and loudly contends that halfway measures will not do. His sense of urgency was justified. To the profligacy with which Americans had always approached their wildlife resources was now added a whole new set of circumstances that helped them on with the work of destruction. The increasing use of trains and automobiles to bring hunters to formerly remote areas put added pressure on the game; and the increasing use of bird dogs helped these hunters to locate the game once they had arrived on the scene. As fishing and hunting clubs proliferated around the country, the exchange of information became easier, and modern methods of communication lifted the exchange to a new level of efficiency. E. H. Forbush, the Massachusetts naturalist, described this process:

"A flight of birds is seen some day on the shores of Cape Cod. This news is immediately telephoned to Boston. The favored ones get it, and that night trains and automobiles take them to the ground. The next morning they join with the local gunners in what is virtually an attempt to kill every bird. If the daily papers publish the news, every gunner who reads it can take advantage of the opportunity and be on the ground within twenty-four hours."

One area in which the Establishment (conservationist and game-hog alike) united was in opposition to the "alien" hunter. Forbush, again, describes the situation as it existed in the early years of this century:

"A comparatively new element of danger to the song birds, and, for that matter, to all birds, is the fast-increasing horde of foreigners, mainly Italians, who come here from their native lands to engage in contract labor. Most of these men seem to be sportsmen, hunters or trappers in their way, but they regard everything that wears fur or feathers as game. These people go out in small parties, most of them armed with guns, and, in some cases at least, shoot at nearly every living thing within range. I have been told that if so much as a song sparrow gets up, the whole party shoots at it. Some of these gentry came into my yard in Medford in 1895, and shot a pair of bluebirds that were nesting there. The birds are not shot for profit, for their little bodies will not pay for half the ammunition fired at them. They are shot for sport, and afterwards eaten."

The reports were accurate, as any tourist who has survived a hunting season in modern Italy can testify; the toll of song birds was heavy enough to alarm the Audubon Societies, which urged their members to "do all they can to suppress the alien gunner and bring him to justice." In 1905 New York State passed the Armstrong Fire-Arms Law, prohibiting aliens from carrying fire-arms in "public places." Hornaday had the satisfaction of seeing one of his guards at the Bronx Zoo apprehend a couple of aliens in the act of killing song birds. The culprits were hauled before the bar of justice and (in lieu of $450 in fines) sentenced to serve ten weeks in jail. Meanwhile the slaughter of robins and other song birds went on unpunished in the South for a number of years, remaining legal in most states until the passage of the Federal Migratory Bird Act in 1913.

But the introduction of modern transportation and communications, skilled hunting dogs or an alien hunting ethic (not alien at all to anyone who had observed the attitude to game shown for so long by Americans of more ancient lineage) were overshadowed by still another innovation. This was the increasing manufacture and use of automatic weapons. No longer did the hunter have to take the gun from his shoulder and reload it after each shot. With the new automatic rapid-fire guns he could sweep his field of vision of every living thing. Hornaday was the leader of the crusade to harness the nearly unlimited potential of the new weapons.

"For fifty years the makers of shotguns and rifles have taxed their ingenuity and resources to make killing easier, especially for 'amateur' sportsmen, *and take still greater advantage of the game,*" Hornaday thundered in 1913. "The sole and dominant thought of many gunmakers is to make the very deadliest guns that human skill can invent, sell them as fast as possible, and declare dividends on their stock. The Remington, Winchester, Marlin, Stevens, and Union Companies are engaged in a mad race to see who can turn out the deadliest guns, and the most of them. On the market today there are five pump-guns that fire six shots each, in about six seconds, without removal from the shoulder, and two automatics that fire five shots each in five seconds or less, by five pulls on the trigger! The autoloading gun is reloaded and cocked again wholly by its own recoil."

The arms manufacturers were not obtuse. They recognized that by their own technology they might eventually wipe out the wildlife on which their livelihood depended. Increasingly their representatives could be heard among those who called for shorter gunning seasons and lower bag limits; but in no case would they assent to restrictions on "inventive genius."

Still, the post-Roosevelt era saw a gathering momentum toward effective legislation to save the nation's wildlife. Roosevelt's initiative in establishing wildlife refuges did not yet give widespread protection to endangered species; the programs of individual conservation organizations continued to lead the way. To counter the destruction caused by organized local "shoots," in which gunners earned points for every bird or mammal they collected, the National Association of Audubon Societies organized the annual Christmas Bird Census; in 1900 hardy and devoted birdwatchers (twenty-seven men and women in twenty-five localities) set out at Frank M. Chapman's urging to spend "a portion of Christmas Day with the birds," and send to the Audubon Societies a report of all the species and individuals they saw. (The census continues on a much greater scale all over the United States today.) Meanwhile, the American Ornithologists' Union took a belated interest in the passenger pigeon. In 1909 it organized a search for pigeons in the wild, offering $1220 to anyone who discovered either a nest or a colony of that bird; an offer of $100 for a dead pigeon was quickly reconsidered and abandoned. But it was too late for either project. The last of her species was even then living out her days in the Cincinnati Zoo.

A more rewarding private program was carried out by Hornaday. In 1905 Hornaday and several members of the Boone and Crockett Club in New York organized the American Bison Society. At their urging, the New York Zoological Society gave fifteen buffaloes to the federal government, which installed them as the nucleus of a new herd on the Wichita Mountains Wildlife Refuge in Oklahoma. The animals were protected by the "Page Wildlife Fence," a woven wire fence patented by J. Wallace Page and later adapted and publicized by Hornaday for the protection of large animals both in zoos and on the Western range. The buffaloes, flourishing on the Wichita Refuge, proved that they could build back up from the edge of extinction into imposing numbers, and similar refuges completed what once had been considered only a remote possibility.

If the buffalo program moved smoothly forward, another drama was to be played out in the violent manner that suited Hornaday's temperament. This was the struggle to save the northern fur seal, an attractive mammal whose rich, impermeable coat attracted the relentless hunters who nearly drove it into oblivion. The Russians had taken a heavy toll of the seals before the United States completed the purchase of Alaska in 1868, hunting the great herds in the Pribilof Islands, a remote volcanic group in the Bering Sea. The United States government leased killing privileges on the islands to private companies, which slaughtered two million seals during the next forty years.

This slaughter in itself was not sufficient to destroy the teeming herds that came to the cobbled beaches of the Pribilofs to breed. Like the Russians, the United States prohibited the hunters from killing females, and thus the heavy losses were in some measure recouped. But pelagic hunters upset the balance. These international harvesters (Americans, Canadians, Russians, and Japanese) worked from boats outside the three-mile limit, shooting seals without respect to age or sex. The hunters collected only a small portion of their indiscriminate kill, many of the dead seals sinking almost immediately and the wounded swimming off to die unnoticed somewhere in the fog and rain that shrouded the islands. An enormous toll was taken among the pups, which starved on land after their mothers had disappeared.

For some time there had been calls in the United States for action to stop the pelagic sealing. Since the calls often were based on economic rather than humane grounds (the fur trade itself was beginning to suffer), the government made several attempts to intervene. American citizens were forbidden to take part in pelagic sealing. Washington made some overtures to Great Britain (most of the pelagic sealers were Canadians) to put a stop to the practice by treaty; and when Great Britain ignored the overtures the United States seized some Canadian boats, thus setting off a controversy that was settled only when Washington paid damages to the owners of the offending vessels. By 1909 the uncounted millions of fur seals had dropped in number to an estimated 150,000. They seemed to be headed the way of the buffalo.

Though the Bering Sea was one of the few areas of the world in which Hornaday had not observed wildlife, he turned his attention to the plight of the fur seals at about this time. His interest was aroused by Henry Wood Elliott, who had studied the seals in the Pribilofs and later campaigned for their preservation. Constant rebuffs, however, caused Elliott to grow bitter. "At last he became so wild with anxiety to save his beloved seals from extinction,"

Hornaday wrote, "that his insistence turned savage, and his relations with certain scientists and bureau officers of Washington became a complete wreck."

Elliott spoke to Hornaday at the Bronx Zoo, and Hornaday agreed to try to do something for the seals through the Campfire Club, an organization of outdoorsmen he had founded several years earlier. The time was right. In 1909 the "killing lease" which the government had granted to the North American Commercial Company was to expire. The lease had declined considerably in value. Only a few years earlier the company had butchered over 100,000 seals annually, while now it could not quite reach the new government quota that had been set at 15,000 seals. Hornaday took the matter to Congress, first arming himself with maps, facts, and figures supplied by the distraught Elliott, whom he had warned to keep in the background for fear of antagonizing any further a number of important personages in Washington.

"And then—ye gods and little fishes!" Hornaday exclaimed in retrospect. "There started, and continued right down to the end, the bitterest and most brutal fight ever waged around the fur seal."

He was the only witness to appear at a hearing called by the Senate Committee on the Conservation of Natural Resources to discuss a bill to protect "the fur seal fisheries of Alaska." Delivering Elliott's facts and figures in his own forceful voice, Hornaday swayed the assembled senators. By a unanimous motion the committee instructed its chairman to "communicate to the Secretary of Commerce and Labor the views of the Committee that a new lease for the killing of fur seals should not be made, and that steps should be taken to secure treaties with foreign governments for the prevention of pelagic sealing."

A bill was drawn up in the office of Charles Nagel, Secretary of Commerce and Labor, apparently carrying out the wishes of the Senate Committee. One variation, however, was that in place of Hornaday's suggestion that the killing of all seals for commercial purposes be halted for a few years, Nagel included a phrase that gave him discretionary powers in the matter. Then, when he applied to Congress for $100,000 to buy the private holdings of the old lessees in the Pribilofs, he also asked for $50,000 to compensate the natives for the earnings they would lose after the killings were halted. Hornaday, and apparently Congress, believed the matter had been settled to their satisfaction.

But trouble broke out early in 1910 when the Bureau of Fisheries, in whose hands the management of the seals had been placed, announced that the killing would be carried on again that summer. Bad blood already existed between Hornaday and Secretary Nagel, who had objected to his interference through Congress with the department's seal-killing programs; representatives of the department had called on high officials of the New York Zoological Society suggesting, in Hornaday's words, "that Hornaday should be supressed." Now Hornaday dispatched a bristling letter to Nagel, protesting the proposed killing and suggesting that at least one of the men advising the department on the management of the seals be replaced. Nagel, equally indignant, replied:

"Now, Mr. Hornaday, you have considerable responsibilities in your official employment, and I shall endeavor not to molest you. I hope that you will accord me the same privileges in my capacity. I always welcome advice; I do not fear criticism; but I do discourage unnecessary comment upon other men engaged in my bureau who are charged with responsible duties, who are expected to be loyal, and who are not in a position to defend themselves."

The killing took place as scheduled. More than 12,000 seals were slaughtered by the Bureau of Fisheries and shipped to auctions in London markets, a procedure duly noted by Hornaday in New York; further, he noted that the official records in London revealed that 8000 of the seals were pups. Hornaday immediately put together a pamphlet entitled *A Square Deal for the Fur Seal*, containing copies of his correspondence with Nagel, the attempts to "suppress" his campaign among congressmen for fur seal protection, and records of the London auctions. Though he published the pamphlet as an "open letter" to the American people, it was read with considerable interest in Congress. The Senate opened a hearing into the matter of Nagel's interference with legislation affecting his department.

As in the congressional investigation of the Ballinger-Pinchot controversy, the committee report split along party lines, the Democratic members this time supporting the administration's handling of the matter. But the revelations that the Department of Commerce and Labor had tried to suppress Hornaday's testimony before the Senate committee irritated many congressmen; that the government was killing and selling seals of an illegal size shocked them. The affair ended as a clear-cut triumph for

Hornaday. Congress rapped a variety of administrative knuckles and passed a law forbidding the killing of seals for five years. (Under careful management the herds have been rebuilt to over a million and a half animals, a percentage of which are killed each year by the Bureau of Commercial Fisheries in the Department of the Interior, and sold at auction.) Prodded by Hornaday's revelations, the government concluded a treaty with Great Britain, Russia, and Japan in 1911 that put a stop to pelagic sealing.

The treaty produced a significant dividend: almost as an afterthought it prohibited the killing of sea otters. At that time they were considered extinct, or nearly so, on our shores. Under protection, that delightful little animal has reappeared, to the nation's esthetic profit, in some numbers off the coast of California.

18

Milestones

Hornaday had mounted what was to become his permanent frontal attack on bureaucratic inertia. Meanwhile, more conventional conservation leaders were uniting to lift wildlife protection out of its dark ages. There were signs already of the split that would send the uncompromising, often distressing, sometimes immensely appealing Hornaday on his lonely way through the last two decades of his life, but for the time being he fought shoulder to shoulder with the other great names of the conservation movement through the bitter struggles that took place in the New York State Legislature and in Congress during the years 1910–13. Winning, the conservationists established wildlife protection for the first time on a sound gridwork of law.

There were four major legislative battles, and each deserves to be considered in some detail.

I.   The Audubon Plumage Bill

The sordid nature of the plume hunting business, as revealed by Guy Bradley's murder, had to some extent aroused public sentiment against the use of wild birds' plumage in fashion. Unfortunately, the milliners' flourishing trade in plumes survived through their political influence and the public's confusion. Subterfuge and specious arguments prevailed. The milliners, for instance, contended that they used the plumes of only non-native birds. Since the plumage of native white herons is almost indistinguishable from that of their African and Asian relatives, no one was likely to prove them wrong. Therefore, birds killed illegally in one state and shipped to another (a violation of the Lacey Act of 1900) were palmed off as "foreign" birds. Nor did the Lacey Act apply to plume birds killed in the Southern states that did not protect them.

The leaders of the National Association of Audubon Societies realized that only a bill that struck at the milliners concentrated in New York State could put an end to the subterfuge. T. Gilbert Pearson, the Association's secretary (and later its president), was dispatched to Albany to prepare the ground for an effective "feather law" in the state.

A Southerner by birth and an experienced lobbyist in that part of the country, Pearson looked forward to his assignment in Albany with some anxiety. He knew no one in the state capital, he tells us, and was not sure how to conduct himself with Northern legislators. He was a good mixer, however, and made a point of striking up conversations with the legislators in the Kenmore and Ten Eyck hotels. Apparently they found his anecdotes of life in the South, told in Negro dialect, excrutiatingly funny. Thus, though Pearson never quite overcame his distaste for beer, he managed to become one of the boys and soon was a familiar and well-liked figure in Albany's legislative circles.

Pearson arranged for a bill to be introduced in the legislature, outlawing the sale in New York State of the plumes of all native American birds. The milliners responded with a great show of force in Albany, where they were represented in the legislature by Assemblyman Alfred E. Smith. The future governor of the state accepted the milliners' contention that thousands of New Yorkers would be thrown out of work by the passage of the bill, and the industry itself destroyed. Another of the milliners' strong points seemed to be their claim that not a single species of New York's song birds was used in the millinery trade. Pearson was equal to the occasion. Before attending a legislative hearing he scoured the shops and came up with a number of "Chanticleer Bows" which were then on sale in Albany's department stores. This item was made of a pretty ribbon, onto which had been sewn the head of a skylark, a European bird enjoying a short-lived existence around New York City after its artificial introduction by local admirers of birds and English poetry.

An even greater blow to the milliners was Pearson's destruction of their story that herons and egrets need not be killed to collect their plumes. According to the milliners, they bought their plumes from Venezuelans, who gathered them under the trees in which herons and egrets gathered to molt. "Everywhere on the ground," wrote the milliners' authority, "as well as on the tree branches and on the bushes and thickets, they leave their feathers which at that moment must form the happiness of the natives and of the workmen busy with the harvest thereof."

Pearson in turn produced an American who had worked as a plume hunter in Venezuela for ten years. He proved to be an arresting and effective witness, pointing out that the few plumes, called "dead feathers," that were picked up from the ground were damaged and far less valuable than those torn from the bodies of birds that had been shot.

"The natives of the country, who do virtually all of the hunting, are not provident in their nature and their practices are of a most cruel and brutal nature," he testified. "I have seen them frequently pull the plumes from wounded birds, leaving the crippled birds to die of starvation, unable to respond to the hungry cries of their young in the nests above. I have known these people to tie and prop up wounded egrets on the marsh where they would attract the attention of other birds flying by. These decoys they leave in this position until they die of their wounds or from the attacks of insects. I have seen the terrible red ants of that country actually eating out the eyes of these wounded, helpless birds."

The Audubon Plumage Bill became law in 1911. The millinery industry, shorn of a particularly bloody aspect, managed to survive.

II. The Bayne Bill

George Bird Grinnell, in 1894, had been the first prominent American to call for the abolition of the sale of game. By 1911 nineteen states had passed laws restricting to one degree or another the sale of game within their boundaries. But there was a fatal weakness in all the laws of this kind. New York, for instance, prohibited the sale of grouse, quail, and woodcock *killed within the state*. The loophole enabled the city to be the center of the game market in this country; gunners shipped game to New York dealers from states that had no such law, and within New York itself birds and animals were killed and sold with impunity because the authorities could not prove their point of origin. One New York City dealer, August Silz, claimed to have sold one million game birds each year.

The situation seemed to be accepted until the market hunters unwittingly antagonized William Hornaday. In the fall of 1910 Hornaday received a visit from a "good sportsman" in his office at the Bronx Zoo.

"The market gunners of Long Island and the game dealers of New York have formed three strong organizations," the sportsman said, "and they say that next winter they are going to wipe off our statute books all the laws for the protection of feathered game. They are going to send a man to the legislature expressly to do whatever they tell him about game. And they intend to make a clean sweep of all the wildlife protection laws that they don't like."

This was the challenge that Hornaday, in love with the dramatic confrontation, always relished. "Well then, damn their souls," he claims to have replied (and probably did), "we will give them the fight of their lives. We will introduce a bill to stop the sale of game, and carry the war right into the enemy's camp."

Hornaday ordered circulars printed and raised funds for the fight ahead. He also collected facts on the quantity and the kinds of wild birds sold in the New York markets. He pointed out that, only a few years before, thousands of grouse, quail, and ducks had been found in one cold storage house there, in addition to 8058 snow buntings, 7607 sandpipers, 5218 plovers, and 788 yellowlegs (a species then approaching the vanishing point). The bill, which Hornaday ordered drawn up by a lawyer, was named for Howard R. Bayne of Staten Island, chairman of the Senate Judiciary Committee, who lent his prestige to the campaign in Albany.

At first Hornaday ran into heavy opposition from organized groups of market hunters and the Hotel Men's Association of New York. After they took the measure of the support Hornaday had gathered in the legislature, however, the bill's opponents offered several amendments, which Hornaday accepted: the new law would permit the sale of certain European deer and game birds in the state, as well as pheasants, mallards, and black ducks raised on American game farms. With the last obstacle cleared, the bill sailed easily through both houses of the legislature and became law in 1911. Similar laws passed in Massachusetts and California the following year virtually ended the large-scale traffic in native wild game in the United States.

"And what did I get out of it?" Hornaday wrote many years later. "Nothing but a few brief mentions of my name by my jealous rivals far down in the list of those who 'assisted in passing the Bayne law.' Not one publication (so far as I am aware) ever gave me one-half the credit for initiative and leadership to which my efforts were entitled; and the same spirit has continued right down to this day—save in the inner circle of my most devoted and generous allies."

This was something more than an old man's petulance. It reflected the ripples of bitterness that increasingly agitated the unity of wildlife conservationists and sportsmen during the first third of the twentieth century.

III. The Federal Tariff Act

The states had taken the initiative. Now conservationists hoped to prod the federal government into legislation that would close the loopholes through which the shadier milliners and game dealers still carried on their trade. Hornaday joined forces with the National Association of Audubon Societies to halt the importation of all wild birds' plumage into the United States. A relatively simple path suggested itself to the conservationists in 1913 just before Congress was to debate the Tariff Bill sponsored by President Woodrow Wilson's new administration. Hornaday and Gilbert Pearson, who was representing the Audubon Societies, went to Washington to try to have a clause banning wild birds' plumage inserted in the bill.

Hornaday, predictably, went for broke. He submitted to the House Ways and Means Committee a clause reading: "The importation of birds-of-paradise, aigrettes, egret plumes or so-called osprey plumes, and the feathers, quills, heads, wings, tails, skins or parts of wild birds, either raw or manufactured, and not for scientific or educational purposes, is hereby prohibited."

Pearson, meanwhile, submitted a clause banning the plumage only of American species that migrate to foreign countries or of birds that are indistinguishable from American species. In the face of Hornaday's criticism, Pearson maintained that an alternative should be offered to congressmen who could not swallow the stiffer clause. ("If we could not have the whole loaf we wanted a half loaf.") The dispute was rendered academic when the committee accepted Hornaday's clause and the full House approved it with hardly a dissenting vote.

The milliners finally awakened to the danger. Their lobbyists appeared in force in the hearing room of the Senate Finance Committee, which was then considering the Tariff Bill for that body. Working around the clock, they persuaded the committee to amend Hornaday's clause so that the plumage of any bird commonly recognized as "edible or pestiferous" could be imported. As Pearson pointed out, such a measure would "nullify the effect of the anti-importation proviso." It would be difficult to find a bird that is not considered "edible" somewhere in the world; and even herons and egrets are considered "pestiferous" by the operators of fish hatcheries.

To the milliners' arguments was added the menace of viewpoints like that of Senator James A. Reed of Missouri. His attack on the plumage clause resembled in tone, if not in detail, the speeches of legislators in every era who cannot comprehend a view of life that is not based solely on economics.

"I really honestly want to know," Reed asked his colleagues, "why there should be any sympathy or sentiment about a long-legged, long-necked bird that lives in swamps, and eats tadpoles and fish and crawfish and things of that kind; why we should worry ourselves into a frenzy because some lady adorns her hat with one of its feathers, which appears to be the only use it has? . . . If the young are then left to starve, it would seem to me the proper idea would be to establish a foundling asylum for the young, but still let humanity utilize this bird for the only purpose that evidently the Lord made it for, namely so that we could get aigrettes for bonnets of our beautiful ladies."

In the end the milliners could not find enough men of Reed's sensibilities in the Senate, and the plumage clause remained intact. On October 3, 1913, President Wilson signed the bill into law.

Within a few days fashionable ladies, just stepping off ocean liners on their return from buying sprees in Paris and London, were met by customs inspectors who relieved them of their millinery adornments. Eight years after Guy Bradley's murder, the traffic in wild bird's plumage went wholly underground.

IV.   The Federal Migratory Bird Act

The heretical notion that migratory birds could be protected only by the federal government, and not by the states to which the game "belonged," was first promoted in legislative halls by George Shiras III, perhaps the outstanding wildlife photographer of his time. Born near Pittsburgh, Shiras came from a family of distinguished public servants, and early in this century he was prevailed upon to run for Congress. During his brief service in Washington, Shiras concentrated on conservation legislation. It occurred to him, while working on a public health measure designed to protect the public against polluted water served on railroad trains, that if the government was able to eradicate germs in interstate traffic, it ought to be able to protect game birds that moved from state to state.

Accordingly, in 1906 Shiras introduced a bill in the House of Representatives providing "that all wild geese, wild swans, brant, wild ducks, snipe, plover, woodcock, rail, wild pigeons and all other migratory game birds which do not remain permanently within the borders of any State or Territory shall hereafter be deemed to be within the custody and protection of the Government of the United States."

The chief idea behind the bill was that the Biological Survey would take over the regulation of the hunting of these birds and set a closed season on them. Sportsmen were beginning to realize that spring shooting had decimated the flocks of wildfowl which once had seemed inexhaustible. Wild ducks, for instance, pair in the South before starting on their long northward flight in the spring. If one or both of the pair are killed in migration, the young birds which they could be expected to raise during the summer naturally will never be produced. In drawing up his bill, Shiras was reflecting the sentiment of sportsmen who called for hunting seasons restricted to the fall and winter, when the young of the year had swelled the total numbers of wildfowl.

But Shiras' bill came a cropper. The states were not yet ready to surrender jurisdiction over migratory wildfowl. Even congressmen friendly to the bill doubted its constitutionality: migratory game birds, they reasoned, could not by any stretch of the imagination be covered by the Constitution's interstate commerce clause.

It was not until 1912, as the great flocks continued to dwindle, that life was breathed back into Shiras' proposal. Shiras himself had left Congress. His bill reappeared in much the same form, but now was named after its new sponsors, Representative John W. Weeks of Massachusetts and Senator George P. McLean of Connecticut. The old bugaboo of unconstitutionality still clung to it, however, and there did not seem to be enough enthusiasm in Congress to challenge the notion. Though they supported the principle, many conservationists were not working assiduously in behalf of a bill whose chief purpose seemed to be to improve the duck hunter's sport.

The Weeks-McLean Bill was salvaged by the "dicky-bird amendment." Gilbert Pearson, speaking for the Audubon interests, naturally had been hopeful that *all* migratory birds might be covered by the legislation. He felt that the inclusion of song birds, insectivorous species among them, would attract support from farmers, foresters, and homeowners who could be convinced of these birds' beneficial feeding habits. But many sportsmen continued to be contemptuous of "dicky-birds." It was only when all prospects for the bill's passage seemed lost at the end of 1912 that Hornaday, George Bird Grinnell, and other prominent conservationists came around to the Audubon point of view.

Hornaday plunged into the struggle with his usual abandon. He sent out telegrams to influential people, story ideas for newspapers, and a copy of his book, *Our Vanishing Wild Life*, to each member of Congress. He also prepared and distributed a circular entitled *Slaughter of Useful Birds: A Grave Emergency*.

"The sockdolager at the end," he wrote afterward, "was a picture of two glass jars containing the dead bodies of forty-three valuable insectivorous birds that were taken from two Italians in October 1905, in the suburbs of New York City, by field agents of the New York Zoological Society. As pertinent bird pictures we threw in a snipe, killdeer, plover, robin, martin, nighthawk, shrike, and golden-winged woodpecker; and believe me, the text was good reading for the farm block."

The bill still faced formidable opposition in Congress. Senator Elihu Root, who had been Theodore Roosevelt's Secretary of State, opposed the bill on constitutional grounds. However, when conservationists brought their case to him, he agreed not to take an active part in the debate, but rather would seek to provide constitutional support for it by other means; toward that end, he later introduced a resolution in the Senate calling for negotiations with Canada that would sanctify the bill's major points in a treaty.

Other congressmen were more difficult to win over to the bill. Its most outspoken foe was Representative Franklin W. Mondell of Wyoming, who presented the case for states rights:

"This is, in my opinion, the most revolutionary, the most far-reaching legislation, in its possible and probable effect on our system of Government, that has been presented to Congress in the sixteen years during which I have been a member of this body. If this bill should become a law no man who voted for it would ever be justified in raising his voice against any extension, no matter how extreme, of the police authority and control of the Federal Government. It takes from the States control over everything that flies, save some birds of the grouse family, bats, and butterflies, and it authorizes a clerk in a bureau of the Agriculture Department to designate as crimes, punishable in Federal penitentiaries, the slightest infraction of the prohibitions contained in the bill against the capturing, the killing, or taking of any bird that flies anywhere in the Union save those few which never migrate."

These remarks were delivered, says Gilbert Pearson, who heard them, with "great vehemence."

Just at this point an unlikely birdwatcher entered the campaign for the Weeks-McLean Bill. Birds had become a chief source of diversion for Henry Ford, as they were for Theodore Roosevelt. He enjoyed watching them on his estate and, when he wasn't reading about machinery, he could usually be found absorbed in a good book about natural history. Ford admired the writings of John Burroughs so ardently that in 1912 he sent the seventy-five-year-old naturalist a new automobile and a man to teach him how to drive it. Burroughs failed to master "the blind, desperate thing," which carried him into and through the side of his barn one afternoon, but this did not diminish his respect for Ford, of whom he wrote: "His interest in birds is keen and his knowledge considerable."

When Ford learned of the nature of the Weeks-McLean Bill he

called in Glenn Buck, one of his advertising men, and ordered him to drop whatever he was working on and proceed at once to Washington.

"And don't come back until that bird bill has been passed," Ford told him.

Prospects for the bill brightened considerably once Ford threw his influence behind it. "For the first time, big business has been called upon for help, by a voice strong enough to compel attention," Hornaday exulted. Congressmen began to hear from powerful constituents. The volume of publicity increased. The bill, now known as the Migratory Bird Act, passed Congress as a rider on the Agriculture Appropriations bill in the waning days of the departing Taft administration, and was sent to the President for his signature on March 4, 1913.

And then the conservationists profited from one of those happy turns of fortune that sometimes alter the course of history. Taft said later he would have vetoed the bill if he had known what it contained because he believed its contents to be unconstitutional. But the bill arrived for his signature on his last day in office along with dozens of other documents and he signed it without reading it.

Later the bill was challenged in the courts. Conservationists held their breath while negotiations, complicated by the outbreak of World War I, were carried on between the United States and Canada toward a Migratory Bird Treaty. The treaty finally was signed in 1916, and ratified by Congress in 1918 (the legislation from then on being called the Migratory Bird Treaty Act). At that moment the Supreme Court dismissed all challenges to the federal government's jurisdiction over migratory birds: the provisions of a treaty, signed with another nation, take precedence over the rights of individual states.

The Biological Survey was free to set regulations for the management of migratory birds. It reiterated the ban on spring hunting (first imposed when the original act had been passed in 1913) and market hunting. It limited the open season on waterfowl to three and a half months, and set daily bag limits of twenty-five ducks and ten geese. Finally that bureau took a drastic and courageous step toward preserving the sandpipers, plovers, and other shorebirds. These vulnerable birds, as we have seen, could be slaughtered by the dozen with one blast of a shotgun as they gathered in dense masses on rocks and beaches. No extensive move had been made to protect them before; as someone has said, the season on shore-birds was always "open" during the height of their migrations, and "closed" when they were out of state. Now the Biological Survey prohibited the shooting of most members of the family (except for woodcock and snipe), a moratorium that is still in effect.

Conservationists celebrated the most important legislative mile-stone in the history of wildlife protection. They had won every point they had set out to achieve. Ironically, in the Biological Survey's administration of the Migratory Bird Treaty Act lay the seed of another violent upheaval within the conservation movement.

19

War

World War I stimulated an excess of patriotism in the breasts of a great many market hunters who had been forcibly retired, as well as in that of William T. Hornaday. This sentiment manifested itself among the market hunters in their enthusiastic offers to provide fresh game at a reasonable price to lighten the burden of America's war effort. Hornaday, who did his best to fend off the market hunters, channeled his patriotism into various lusty battles against Army brass, "socialistic" schoolteachers, and his fellow conservationists. As in most outbursts of patriotism, an ugly strain could be detected running through the high-minded exuberance.

The exploiters made their move immediately upon America's entry into the war in 1917. As we have seen, they demanded grazing, cutting, and mining privileges in the national parks and forests. State legislatures were asked to waive all restrictions on hunting for the duration of the war. Western cattlemen wanted to kill elk and other dwindling big game on the public domain in order to wipe out the grazing competition for their own livestock.

Conservationists in and out of government banded together to resist this sudden assault on wildlife. They laid their case before Herbert Hoover, chief of the United States Food Administration, and drew from him an acknowledgment that "no emergency has as yet arisen sufficiently acute to warrant the Food Administration advocating the destruction of game, which forms a valuable national asset." Theodore Roosevelt, from his sickbed, ridiculed the notion that America's food resources had dipped so low as to open the doors to the exploiters: "To the profiteering proposal of the Pseudo-patriots, the Patriots for revenue only, that protection of wildlife in wartime be relaxed, the united hosts of conservation reply: 'You shall not pass'."

If there was any need to justify their stand with hard facts, the conservationists were ready to provide them. Among the most strident calls for a war on wildlife was that made by Jeremiah Hezikiah Williams, the State Game Commissioner of Florida. Williams asserted that a million brown pelicans lurked off Florida's shores, devouring $950,000 worth of fish *every day*. A similar report came from Texas. Williams and his supporters wanted the Food Administration to strike a blow for liberty by killing all the pelicans.

Gilbert Pearson of the Audubon Societies led an expedition to the Gulf Coast to investigate the pelicans' depredations. Close counts of the various areas frequented by pelicans indicated there were no more than 65,000 of these birds all along the coast. Some pelicans were collected at random to analyze the contents of their stomachs, while thousands of nests were examined to determine the types of fish they fed to their young. The results of this study proved what biologists have since learned time and again when investigating the reports of some wild animals' toll of man's resources: the reports were exaggerated, and the bulk of their diet consisted of species seldom used as food by man. The pelican scare quickly subsided.

Vigilant men marshaling sound facts were able to keep the damage to a minimum in the forty-eight states. At the Bronx Zoo Hornaday even found time to fulminate at length in various tracts and pamphlets against targets outside the sphere of conservation. Even before the United States entered the war he had thrown himself vigorously into Belgian relief work, alternately raising funds for victims in that unhappy country and agitating for America's entry into the war in support of the Allies. When war came he increased the intensity of his anti-German pamphleteering, demanding severe postwar punishment for the "German den of mixed wolves and mad dogs." Hornaday reserved some of his most virulent prose, however, for his campaign to ferret out "cowards, traitors, socialists, pacifists," and all the other demons who peopled his nightmares in those days. Anti-Semitism was part of his bag; in pamphlets he applauded the dismissal of "alien socialists of the most dangerous type, many of them Russian Jews," from the New York City school system when they refused on constitutional grounds to sign a loyalty pledge.

But early in 1918 Hornaday returned to the conservation wars. The telephone rang one morning in the offices of a number of distinguished conservationists, including that of George Bird Grinnell.

"Are you aware of the fact that mountain sheep, moose, and caribou are now being killed in Alaska, in large numbers, to sell to contractors to feed laborers?" an excited voice demanded to know.

The inquirer was Hornaday, who had just read the transcript of a bill then before Congress to change Alaskan game laws. Hornaday later recounted the exchange: "Each inquiry elicited a surprised and horrified, 'No! I have heard nothing about such doings.' And my reply was 'I thought not!'"

Alaska always has been a sticky conservation problem. It is America's "last frontier," and sportsmen and conservationists in the forty-eight contiguous states have hoped that it would escape the wildlife and environmental destruction which has blighted much that was good in their own regions. Alaskans, perhaps naturally, have not always felt as apprehensive. Like any frontiersman, they have wanted to get what they could from their own natural resources, meanwhile displaying an appropriate resentment to what they believed to be outside interference.

World War I intensified this problem. If food scarcity was a myth in the United States, the case was somewhat different in the Territory of Alaska, from which ships usually available to transport foodstuffs had been diverted to war service. Alaskans complained of scarcities and high prices. Perhaps most of all they complained of the profiteers who took advantage of the territory's isolation. Alaska's congressional delegate, Charles A. Sulzer, drafted a bill with the help of the Biological Survey that would permit the sale of game killed legally north of the 62nd parallel.

At first most conservationists (including Theodore Roosevelt) opposed the Sulzer Bill on the grounds that it would turn back

the legislative clock. They had worked hard to win state laws that prevented exactly what the Alaskans were then demanding. But soon some of these conservationists, led by Charles Sheldon of the Boone and Crockett Club (who had had much experience hunting big game in Alaska), began to feel that the Sulzer Bill might not be wholly obnoxious. They reasoned that, in the absence of any semblance of enforcement procedures throughout the vast interior of the territory, gunners were already engaged in the sale of game. The opinion of Alaskans, Sheldon said, "was so absolutely unanimous that the people were entitled to this relief from the beef monopoly, that the officers of the law could not convict anybody for breaking the game laws, and they stopped trying to convict anybody." And further, by adapting themselves to Alaska's wartime problem, conservationists might soften up its residents for needed reforms in game protection later on. Some sort of an accommodation seemed to be possible until Hornaday read the transcript of the hearings held on the Sulzer Bill.

Hornaday's attention had been caught by the testimony of Thomas W. Riggs, a commissioner of the Alaskan Railway. In his appearance before the House Committee on Territories, Riggs revealed that the railway had fed its workers on 6000 pounds of the meat of big game animals, purchased at between fifteen and twenty-five cents a pound from Alaskan market hunters. When this figure is applied to moose and caribou, it is clear that probably no more than fifty of these animals were needed to meet the demand. But Hornaday now had a figure of 6000 pounds and he made the most of it.

The inevitable pamphlets rolled off the presses. Stories were distributed to newspapers, and editorial comment invited. Hornaday, mustering all the support (lukewarm and otherwise) that he commanded among conservation organizations, rushed to Washington to testify against the bill at the next hearing held by the Committee on Territories. Whatever the merits of Alaska's case, it was overwhelmed by Hornaday's impassioned rhetoric.

"In one hour after the hearing opened," Hornaday said afterward, "that bill was as dead as Julius Caesar."

There was some hand-wringing among other conservationists that Hornaday's outspoken attack on the motives and competence of Alaskans might set off a chain of reactions far more damaging than the intentions of the Sulzer Bill. And indeed, there was for a time a violent reaction in Alaska, not only against Hornaday, but against Roosevelt and other conservationists as well. (Sheldon claimed that Hornaday had been less than honest about the extent to which many of these men and organizations opposed the bill.) At any rate, with childish petulance the Alaskan newspapers began a crusade against the Alaskan brown bear, a species which Hornaday had mentioned kindly in his attack on the bill. Editorial writers magnified the danger presented by these bears to both livestock and human beings. There were calls for their "extermination." When Dan A. Sutherland, a friend of Hornaday's, ran for Territorial Delegate to Congress, the Juneau *Empire* coined a campaign slogan: "A vote for Sutherland is a vote for Hornaday and the Alaskan brown bears."

Both Sutherland's campaign and the brown bears survived the slogan. After a time passions cooled and a sounder game code was written for Alaska in 1925, a code on which Hornaday and other conservationists could agree. Meanwhile, Hornaday had gone on to other, more wide-ranging, wars.

20

Dead Ducks and Brickbats

I. *The Slaughter*

During the Taft and Wilson administrations, the bird protection movement in this country had made startling gains. The song birds, the plume birds, and the shore birds for the most part found shelter under the terms of the Migratory Bird Treaty Act. The upland game birds, propagated and given respites by closed seasons, found shelter of a sort under various state game laws. Only the waterfowl (except for the wood duck, shot so close to extinction that it was accorded complete federal protection from 1916 to 1941) remained a festering subject of dispute.

Americans never followed the "sustained yield" approach to waterfowl that has characterized many of the peoples of northern Europe. There the populations not only of ducks, but of puffins and other sea birds as well, remained constant for centuries; the people restricted their kill to the annual surplus produced by the mating birds. The relentless slaughter of eider ducks along the Atlantic Coast (early in this century there were less than a dozen pairs breeding in Maine) brought this comment from the ornithologist C. W. Townsend:

"There is no reason why the eider, which furnishes the valuable eiderdown of commerce, should not be made a source of considerable income without any reduction of its natural abundance. The principles of conservation can be as well applied to the eider as to a forest. The conservation of the common eider of Europe, a species that differs but very slightly from the American bird, has been practiced for many years in Iceland and Norway. The birds are rigidly protected during the nesting season and offered every encouragement. They are not allowed to be shot, and even the discharge of a gun in their vicinity is forbidden by law . . . The people are allowed to take the eggs and down during the first of the season, but the birds are permitted to hatch out and rear a few young in order to keep up the stock. The last down is taken after the birds have left."

American fowlers never had any qualms about killing the geese that laid golden eggs until it was almost too late to salvage the survivors. Whatever restrictive steps they took of their own accord generally were prompted by the desire of individuals to keep others from bagging the greater part of the game. Wildfowlers in North Carolina's Currituck County traditionally observed "lay days," three days each week when no one was permitted to kill ducks. Lay days were not designed as a humanitarian gesture toward the groggy ducks; rather, since an occasional respite kept the ducks from abandoning the area altogether, they served in the end to increase the local kill.

As early as 1848 Frank Forester, a noted sportsman, mentioned another instance in which local people united in the face of a threat to their own sport. The locale was the Bush River near Chesapeake Bay:

"For the last three years a man has been occupied on this stream with a gun of great size, fixed on a swivel in a boat, and the destruction of game on their feeding flats has been immense; but so unpopular is the plan, that many schemes have been privately proposed of destroying his boat and gun, and he has been fired at with balls so often, that his expeditions are at present confined to the night."

But even such large-scale assaults on waterfowl as these became commonplace as the century proceeded. Ducks and geese were the principal targets of market gunners during most of that era (replaced only very briefly by the buffalo), and every conceivable destructive device was brought to bear on them. Swivel guns, charged with a quarter-pound of black powder and a can of shot, massacred whole rafts of ducks. Gill nets, set just underwater, entangled ducks as they dove for their food, holding them under until they drowned. Surface boats, or batteries, were towed into favorable locations, amidst hundreds of wooden decoys, and left with a man heavily armed hidden in the bottom, well out of sight of the approaching ducks. (These boats, which resembled wooden coffins, were surrounded by a platform attached to its upper edge so that the boat and the man in it actually floated beneath the surface of the water.) Other waterfowl were lured to concealed gunners by the use of live decoys, or corn and other bait spread on the ground in front of a blind.

One of the most curious methods of luring waterfowl was "tolling," described by the ornithologist A. C. Bent. The hunters tolled with "a small dog, especially trained for the purpose,"Bent wrote. "Some quiet place was selected where a large flock of canvasbacks was bedded a short distance offshore and where the hunters could conceal themselves in some suitable ambush near the water. A small dog was kept running up and down the beach after sticks or stones, with a white or red handkerchief fluttering from some part of his body, which would so arouse the curiosity of the ducks that they would raise their heads and swim in toward shore to study the cause of such peculiar actions. Often the discovery of their hidden danger came too late, for as they turned to swim away they would receive a broadside from a battery of guns and large numbers would be killed."

In many places the carving of wooden decoys was raised to an art form by the need to beguile waterfowl made wary by many narrow escapes. Some masters of the art shaped marvelous images of various ducks, using their dextrous hands and precision tools to convert solid wood into the sheen of feathers, laid one upon another and grading into the graceful outline of a bird that almost breathed.

As market hunting increased late in the century, factories opened to provide the gunners with mass-produced decoys that, in the water, assumed a perpetual position of "tipping up," as in the act of feeding; the decoy was simply a block of wood, rounded off in the image of a duck's rump, and equipped with a small anchor to hold it in position. Wooden geese, fitted to a bellows that worked by wave action, ceaselessly honked to their flesh-and-blood lookalikes in rough weather. For the gunner bent on violating local laws against Sunday hunting the factories provided decoys representing the smaller shorebirds, so that decoys and dead birds could be thrust into the pocket upon the approach of anyone likely to disapprove. When game protection laws finally drove the market hunters out of business, the decoy factories closed down.

Meanwhile, the gunners took a mounting toll of ducks and geese. At Big Lake, Arkansas, in the winter of 1893–94 market gunners sent 120,000 mallards to market; one man killed 8000. At Malheur Lake, Oregon, in 1908, gunners would fill a wagon with mallards, stop at a street corner in town, and allow the passersby to help themselves as long as the supply lasted. On the East Coast, though prices varied around the turn of the century, a gunner received about $1.60 for a pair of redheads, and $2.75 for a pair of the tastier canvasbacks. In November 1905 four men on Currituck Sound sold 2300 ruddy ducks for $1700.

Market hunters were by no means alone to blame for the increasing decimation of waterfowl. Sportsmen belonging to private hunting clubs took so many ducks each year that they grew reluctant to divulge the totals. Like the market hunters, sportsmen used live decoys and baited the ground in front of their blinds. The slaughter was performed very efficiently; at a Florida club men were hired to go out in boats and drive the ducks from secluded areas toward the blinds, where a hunter lay concealed with two pump guns (each able to fire six shots in six seconds), while another hired man kept the guns constantly loaded. In Massachusetts sportsmen utilized duck stands, warm buildings where they could drink, eat, and play cards, while live decoys tethered on the beach called in wave after wave of ducks. As each wave approached, a sentinel would sound the alarm. The sportsmen would lay aside their cards and refreshments and rush outside to take their positions behind a screened fence erected for the purpose. As the ducks came within range, tolled ever closer by the live decoys, the men fired at them with heavy guns through portholes in the fence. Then the sportsmen retired inside to their less exhausting diversions while men hired for the purpose set out in boats to pick up the dead birds and chase down and shoot the cripples.

The following account of a day's pleasure in California was written for a Western magazine by a sportsman in 1913. It reveals to the modern reader what waterfowl hunting was like in the days before bag limits and restrictions on automatic shotguns were established:

"February 5th, I and a friend were at one of the Glenn County Club's camps. Neither of us having ever had the pleasure of shooting over live decoys, we were anxious and could hardly wait for the sport to commence. On arriving at the scene we noticed holes had been dug in the ground, just large enough for a man to crawl into. These holes were used for hiding places and were deep enough so the sportsmen would be entirely out of sight of the game.

"The decoys are wild geese which had been crippled and tamed for the purpose. They are placed inside of silk net fences which are located on each side of the holes dug for hiding places. These nets are the color of the ground. After we had investigated everything the expert caller and owner of the outfit exclaimed: 'Into your holes.'

"We noticed in the distance a flock of geese coming. Our caller in a few seconds had their attention and they headed toward our decoys. Soon they were directly over us but out of easy range of our guns. We were anxious to shoot but in obedience to our boss had to keep still, and soon noticed that the birds were soaring around and in a short time were within fifteen or twenty feet of us. At that moment we heard the command, 'Punch 'em,' and the bombardment that followed was beyond imagining. We had fired five shots apiece and found we had bagged ten geese from this one flock.

"At the end of one hour's shooting we had 218 birds to our credit and were out of ammunition. On finding that no more shells were in our pits we took our dead geese to the camp and returned with a new supply of ammunition. We remained in the pits during the entire day. When the sun had gone down behind the mountains we summed up our kill and it amounted to 450 geese! . . . Supper was then eaten, after which we were driven back to Willows; both agreeing that it was one of the greatest days of sport we ever had and wishing that we might through the courtesy of the Glenn County Club, have another such day."

A phenomenon that worked against hunters having many more such days was a by-product of the intensive shooting described in this case. A number-six shotgun shell carries 280 pellets; when fired, the pellets flare, some of them perhaps hitting their target but a great many more falling harmlessly into the water or marshland beyond. It is estimated that 1400 pellets may be spent for every bird killed. In densely hunted marshes tons of these lost pellets build up on hard, shallow bottoms, lying among pondweeds and the seeds of other plants, from which they are indistinguishable to the duck's eye. A duck swallows and digests the seeds; but its gizzard's grinding action and digestive juices go to work on the pellets, eroding their surfaces until soluble lead salts make their way into the digestive tract. Some ducks, having eaten heavily of the pellets, die swiftly of lead poisoning, others lose their appetites and die slowly of starvation.

The incidence of lead poisoning among ducks and geese in hunting marshes was known to many naturalists in the nineteenth century. George Bird Grinnell, writing in *Forest and Stream* in 1894, predicted that the condition "is likely to grow worse instead of better." And indeed, right down to our own day, more than a million ducks a year apparently fall victim to a virulent "lead pollution" for which the sportsmen and ammunition makers are wholly responsible.

Waterfowl, which played so great a part in the sport and recreation of people all over the country, thus were hunted to increasing scarcity. One might have expected to hear of vigorous measures to protect such a resource. Instead, one finds on investigation that sportsmen resorted to some pretty queer diversions in order to avoid confrontation with the real issues. One of these diversions came to be called "The Great Duck Egg Fake." It received influential sponsorship early in 1895 when John H. Mitchell (who later was imprisoned for his part in the great Oregon land fraud) arose in the United States Senate and made a detailed and impassioned speech. The story he told about certain nefarious deeds on the vast waterfowl breeding grounds in Alaska and northern Canada agitated most of the sportsmen in this country.

"It is a fact not generally known that for the purpose of obtaining ova or egg albumen, which is largely used in commerce," Mitchell said, "certain corporations have been formed and large amounts of capital have been invested for the purpose of gathering in these breeding grounds and shipping annually vast millions of the eggs of these ducks and geese. The shipments annually over the Canadian Pacific Railroad of these eggs are said to be enormous. Not infrequently as many as 1000, 1200, or 1800 barrels of these eggs are taken."

The senator's story was not quite a revelation. Rumors of this reputed practice had circulated among sportsmen for several years. Occasionally they had broken into print. Most of the stories seemed to have as their source an organization known as the National Game, Fish and Bird Protective Association. But now the whole sordid story had been set forth on the floor of the Senate, and that body was about to consider Mitchell's demand for an appropriation of $5000 to finance an investigation by Treasury Department agents of the traffic in waterfowl eggs. Calls for restrictive legislation were heard from around the country.

The story certainly had its hair-raising aspects. It was said that Indians, in the employ of unidentified interests, ceaselessly prowled the tundra during the nesting season of ducks and geese. The Indians gathered up all of the eggs they could find, packed them into barrels, and shipped them to confectioners in New York. There the eggs, the potential source of fodder for the sportsmen's guns, were turned instead into egg-albumen cakes, which sold in the shops for twenty-five cents a pound.

Mitchell, though admittedly not an enthusiastic hunter, expressed the fears of every sportsman. "There is little doubt," he said, "but this destruction of the eggs of the canvas and teal duck of the Pacific Coast, which by many are thought to be superior in flavor and other respects to those of the Potomac, has done more in the last few years to diminish their number on the Pacific Coast, in the states of Oregon, Washington, Idaho, Montana, and California, than all the guns and dogs of the sportsmen in that vast region."

Was it a coincidence that the story had appeared just at that time when sportsmen everywhere were beginning to lament the diminishing numbers of ducks and geese? Consider this letter from a duck hunter in Louisiana, written to George Bird Grinnell at *Forest and Stream:*

"Can't your influence with sportsmen help this cause a little? It is a cause that ought to be dear to the hearts of all sportsmen, and not to a sportsman alone, for all the people of this great country are interested in this subject. I know very little how this gathering of the eggs of waterfowls has affected the North and West, but in this country ten or twelve years back it was very little trouble for any darky or poor white man with his old muzzleloader and a few charges of powder and shot to secure in a few hours ducks enough to last his family for a week. Now it is a good hunter who can get half a dozen ducks in a day except under very favorable circumstances."

Grinnell had received other letters on the subject, but increasingly he suspected what he called a "mare's nest"—a grand illusion. His knowledge of hunting practices led him to believe that spring hunting and "game-hogs" were the chief reasons for the decline in waterfowl. As the editor of *Forest and Stream* he assumed the responsibility for learning the extent to which Alaskan Indians were undermining the American sportsman.

He felt that his first clue to the answer might be found in the source of the egg-albumen horror stories. Senator Mitchell's speech, as well as many of the press reports, had been based on figures (1800 barrels of eggs, etc.) supplied by the National Game, Fish and Bird Protective Association. "A careful investigation shows that millions of eggs are gathered and shipped from these grounds annually," an official of that association had told reporters. "Unless they are protected from such wanton destruction I fear we will, in a short time, be forced to enjoy our duck hunting in memories of the past." First, Grinnell delegated one of *Forest and Stream's* staff to bring back some of the results of the Association's "careful investigation." The Association's president, a Mr. M. R. Bortree, replied that he had no facts to give at that time, but promised to try to find some.

Grinnell suspected he would hear no more from Mr. Bortree. Many of the National Fish, Game and Bird Protection Association's members had only recently become rabid protectionists. The growth of their concern had coincided with the disappearance of things to shoot, a phenomenon they were unable to associate with their insistence on spring shooting. The egg-gathering redskins, though only vaguely perceived, offered a more appealing target for reform than the inadequate laws which regulated waterfowl shooting. Grinnell turned his attention to more rewarding sources of information.

"If anything approaching the quantity of eggs mentioned were shipped each season from railroad points on the northern Pacific Coast," he reasoned, "some one would know about it; there would be great coastwise traffic in these eggs. Trains of merchandise are

not loaded up at night and shipped off secretly to unknown consignees, nor are shiploads of eggs received from foreign countries
without entry at the Custom House; a man does not start with an
egg in his pocket from the shores of the Far North, come down
to the border line and smuggle it across and then go back for
another."

Grinnell wrote to the general traffic managers of the Canadian
Pacific and Northern Pacific railroads. After a thorough search
of their books, each replied that not a single barrel of wildfowl eggs
had ever been shipped over their lines. One railroad official suggested that Senator Mitchell had been made the victim of a mon-
strous practical joke. Another was more specific:

"I wonder if Senator Mitchell considered how many wild birds'
eggs it would take to fill 1800 barrels, and how many years it would
take to gather them; for with the exception of gulls' eggs, which
are gathered in larger quantities than those of any other wild
birds, it would simply be an impossibility to gather the large
quantity mentioned in a hundred years if any one did feel disposed
to do so."

Turning from the railroads, Grinnell then questioned officials of
all the custom houses at ports and border towns through which
wild birds' eggs might enter the United States. None reported any
record of either eggs or albumen. "My opinion," volunteered a
customs official, "is that more eggs are destroyed in the Mississippi
Valley by the spring shooters, a thousand, or even ten thousand,
to one than it would be possible to destroy in any collecting that
would be carried out, even if eggs were worth one dollar a dozen
at the breeding grounds."

Finally, Grinnell consulted the albumen dealers in New York.
From them he learned that almost the whole of the American
albumen supply was imported from Russia, Germany, and France,
where hens' eggs cost less than four cents a dozen. "The cheapness
of the foreign article, which is imported free of duty, prohibits
American competition," a leading dealer told Grinnell. "Eggs
imported from Alaska would be likely to spoil or lose their freshness
before arriving here, and would then be unfit for the manufacture
of albumen."

Grinnell published the results of his investigation in *Forest and
Stream* under the title "The Great Duck Egg Fake." His article was
preceded by a mini-fable:

"A Wild Goose (the old original 'wild goose chase' bird) sat on a Mare's Nest and hatched out a Beautiful Fake. And when the National Game Protector (who had stopped shooting when there was nothing more in sight) saw it, he said: 'It is a Good Thing; push it along.' But—you cannot protect Game by pushing a Fake."

By such searching journalism Grinnell helped to draw closer the day when sound hunting laws—including the abolition of spring shooting—became something more than idle chatter.

II. The Combatants

Awareness came early to men like Grinnell. It came much later to many of the sportsmen and legislators whom self-interest should have awakened to the worsening waterfowl situation in this country, but here and there a light was beginning to shine through. In the early years of the new century California reduced the daily bag limit on ducks from fifty to thirty-five. The Migratory Bird Treaty Act of 1918 firmly established the principles of bag limits and the prohibition of spring shooting on a national scale.

Sportsmen and conservationists were joined in the struggle to preserve the beleaguered waterfowl flocks by an entity that hitherto had been solely destructive. With much at stake, the arms industry decided to tag along with the conservation movement. The industry took the first step in 1911, when two representatives of the Winchester Repeating Arms Company called on T. Gilbert Pearson at the New York office of the National Association of Audubon Societies. Their intention, they told Pearson, was to check the relentless slaughter of game birds and mammals; for, as they said, "as game decreases, our business grows less." Their plan was this: they would raise, by subscription among the various arms manufacturers, a sum of $25,000 a year for five years, which would be administered by the Audubon Societies. This sum would have doubled the Audubon Societies' annual income, as well as raised Pearson's annual salary from $3000 to $6000.

Pearson laid the plan before the board of directors. After some bickering among themselves, the board voted to accept the money and devote it to wildlife protection.

"Instantly there was a cry that the Audubon Association had sold out to the gun people who wanted to kill all the birds of the country," Pearson wrote years later. "This came chiefly from men who had no connection with our organization. Some of it was from a man who, we had reason to believe, was chagrined because the money had not been given to him to spend."

Though Pearson did not identify that man, it may be noted that the most piercing outcry against this accommodation came from the Bronx Zoo. In any event, the board of directors hastily reconsidered their action and came to the conclusion that it would leave them vulnerable to charges from their "enemies." The arms companies proceeded to form their own organization. They called it the American Game Protective Association and, on Grinnell's recommendation, appointed as its president John B. Burnham, who had once worked for him at *Forest and Stream.*

Burnham and the new association played an aggressive role in all the propaganda and legislative battles that culminated in the Migratory Bird Treaty Act. Hornaday, however, detested the thought of working hand in glove with the gunmakers. In 1912, when Burnham's name was proposed for membership in the prestigious Boone and Crockett Club, Hornaday worked assiduously behind the scenes and blocked his acceptance for nearly four years. Grinnell expressed his annoyance to another club member:

"I am not crying down or disposed to quarrel with Hornaday, whom I like. He is a good fellow, and a useful man so long as he works in his own job. It is when he goes outside of his own job that he . . . stirs up trouble—not for himself, for he delights in a row, but for others including his employers, who may not like a row so much."

This estimate of Hornaday was certainly true, as far as it went. But many conservationists, noting only Hornaday's twin tendencies toward inflexibility and self-glorification, often underestimated his exceptional talents in salvaging lost causes. In fact, those two not wholly desirable tendencies contributed to his immense success as a propagandist. He believed with religious intensity in the righteousness of his cause, and in his own methods of furthering that cause.

One reason he resented the arms manufacturers' organization was that he happened to be building up a fund of his own to carry on the wildlife struggles of the day. In this, as in so much else, he was spectacularly successful. Beginning with a contribution of $25,000 from Mrs. Russell Sage, the widow of the financier, he established an endowment fund which he called the Permanent

Wild Life Protection Fund. Its purpose was to circumvent the usual frustration of being faced with a fund-raising campaign as each new wildlife crisis presented itself, and instead have at his disposal a "permanent" reservoir of cash. Contributions from Henry Ford, George Eastman, and Andrew Carnegie helped to swell the fund to over $100,000. "Societies may come and societies may go," Hornaday wrote, "but this Fund will go on forever."

His concern for America's waterfowl brought Hornaday into conflict with almost every leading conservation organization and government agency in the country. He never overcame his initial prejudice against the American Game Protective Association. Most of the other organizations incurred his considerable wrath after the administration of the Migratory Bird Treaty Act inevitably took a course in conflict with his own inflexible views.

The Biological Survey, located in the Department of Agriculture and headed by E. W. Nelson, assumed the administration of the act. As we have seen, that bureau set daily bag limits of twenty-five ducks and eight geese for each hunter, and enforced the bans on spring shooting and market hunting. The guiding spirit was to be flexibility: the freedom to alter bag limits and shooting seasons in response to fluctuating waterfowl populations and prospects. A federal advisory board was set up to work with Nelson, "as a liaison group between the government and the public." Burnham was appointed its chairman, and its other members included Hornaday, Pearson, and Charles Sheldon of the Boone and Crockett Club.

None of this mollified Hornaday very much. He believed that the waterfowl could build back to acceptable numbers only under rigid protection. He called for a long-term moratorium on water-fowl hunting in certain areas, and the cutting in half of bag limits and open seasons elsewhere. Indeed, in the face of waterfowl scarcity, eleven states already had set bag limits well below those established by the Biological Survey, a move pointed to by Hornaday as a repudiation of the federal government's "criminal bag limits and outrageous open seasons."

But Nelson, the Chief of the Biological Survey, held the reins and he saw no need to antagonize any further the nation's sports-men, who already had been asked to accept what they considered to be drastic restrictions on their traditional hunting privileges. Added restrictions, he said, might set off a rebellion in Congress that would undo all of the gains achieved by recent legislation.

Most of the members of the advisory board agreed with Nelson, justifying their stand by the fact that ducks and geese seemed to be enjoying a resurgence of numbers under the new regulations. Hornaday, they believed, had exaggerated the crisis.

Hornaday was beside himself with frustration. He worked for the most part outside the advisory board, gathering support for his contention that little had been done to fend off an eventual waterfowl disaster. One of his supporters, Jack Miner, argued that there was really a six-month open season on ducks and geese, rather than three months as set by the Biological Survey: the birds ran a gauntlet of hunters beginning on September 1 near their breeding grounds in Canada and continuing until the southern states closed their hunting seasons at the end of February. Miner also discussed the implications of the daily bag limits set for each hunter by the Biological Survey and supported by the major conservation organizations:

"Some time ago I received through the mail a booklet entitled *Federal Power and Duck Bag Limit Facts,* a study bulletin issued by the National Association of Audubon Societies. Now I am proud to say that I am a member of this society, yet I am disgustingly surprised to think that such a highly respected association would issue a bulletin that has a tone upholding state laws privileging any individual to shoot over 2000 ducks and 800 wild geese in one year . . . Yes, we all know that no sportsman will kill that amount of game in one year. Then why in the name of common sense do we leave that privilege open to those who will?"

Hornaday's fears were justified when the brief waterfowl resurgence ended abruptly in the early 1920s. The catastrophe, however, was related less to bag limits and open seasons than to the far more devastating process of wiping out the ducks' breeding places. All through the northern tier of states and on into Canada great drainage projects were set in motion to reclaim the land for wheat and other crops. The vast swamps, sloughs, and potholes, once the haunts of breeding ducks, disappeared. Increasingly, when the waterfowl flew north in the spring, they no longer could find the wet habitat and its rich food resources they needed to raise their young.

Hornaday lifted the level of his clamor many decibels, but still Nelson refused to lower daily bag limits for waterfowl. He argued, on not very certain grounds, that drainage had reduced the food supply of breeding ducks to such an extent that many would starve if their ranks were not thinned by the hunters. While some states lowered the bag limits on their own initiative to twenty, fifteen, twelve, or even ten ducks a day, those with great concentrations of ducks held firm to the Biological Survey's standards: New York, Massachusetts, Connecticut, Rhode Island, New Jersey, Ohio, and all of the southern states except Tennessee. Hornaday raged on; but Nelson had an even more disagreeable message in store for him.

Like John Burnham of the American Game Protective Association, Nelson believed the administration of any waterfowl program should concern itself with the hunters as well as with the ducks and geese. Wetlands were shrinking; private hunting clubs had bought up many of the prime marshes and other areas where the waterfowl presented themselves in the greatest numbers to the gun. Burnham, Nelson, and the Survey's chief game warden, George A. Lawyer, gathered support for what many conservationists believed to be a capital idea, the intent of which was expressed in the unwieldy title of the bill that was its result: The Public Shooting Grounds-Game Refuge Bill.

Briefly, the idea was to purchase suitable wetlands for use as waterfowl refuges and public shooting grounds. A Migratory Bird Refuge Commission was to be established, whose duty it would be to décide on the areas of land and water to be bought by the government, and the prices to be paid. The purchase of land and the enforcement of hunting regulations were to be financed by a federal hunting license which hunters could buy at any post office. The bill was introduced in Congress in the spring of 1921.

"Public shooting grounds must be established for the rank and file of the gunners who cannot afford to belong to an exclusive club," the *Bulletin* of the American Game Protective Association had said. "This is the duty of the state, but the sportsman must take the initiative . . . With the public shooting ground must come more preserves where the birds must have absolute protection, for as the country becomes settled, shooting would be impossible without them."

Secretary of Agriculture Henry C. Wallace,* in lending his support to the bill, said that it "would maintain for the residents in both country and town large opportunities for continued wild-fowl shooting that will be impossible in any other way. It might,

*The father of the future Vice-President of the United States, Henry Agard Wallace.

in fact, be stated that it would provide Federal shooting clubs for the benefit of the general public at the nominal cost of a federal hunting license of $1 a year."

The notion that the federal government should make it easier for increasing numbers of hunters to kill ducks horrified Hornaday. "This odious measure was not by any means the product of 'the sportsmen of the United States,' nor of any persons chosen by them," he wrote. "But it was doped out by three professional regulators of game-killing, one of them in the Association created and maintained by the manufacturers of guns, gunpowder, and loaded cartridges. The other two were ensconced in the Bureau of the Department of Agriculture that creates the annual game-killing Regulations, *and that would handle all of the millions of dollars that would accrue from the operation of the act! Do you get that?*"

Hornaday gathered his own support, particularly in the West, where the sentiment against interference by "big government" had been sharpened by the increasingly complex bureaucracy spawned during World War I. Hornaday also won over to his side Will H. Dilg, a flamboyant Midwestern advertising man who was one of the founders, and the first president of, the Izaak Walton League. Dilg, however, was a more abrasive personality even than Hornaday. Eventually he was ousted as president and the Izaak Walton League fell into line with the other conservation organizations behind the Biological Survey.

To Hornaday's disgust, the National Association of Audubon Societies was as firmly committed to the Shooting Grounds Bill as any of the others. For a time the Western sentiment against the bill was sufficient to block its passage. By 1926, however, its supporters believed they had mustered the strength to push the bill through Congress. Confidently, they introduced it. Confidently, they watched it approach a discussion in committee. And then, to their consternation, a young representative from New York City named Fiorello H. La Guardia, whom Hornaday had been lecturing at great length, spoke passionately and articulately against the bill. He swayed enough of his colleagues to the opposition side to bottle up the bill permanently in committee.

"If that old bill had been enacted into law," Hornaday said with considerable satisfaction and probably some exaggeration, "I am sure that it very soon would have finished the remnants of the migratory game of North America."

The long squabble over public shooting grounds unfortunately had delayed the acquisition of wetlands to be used as waterfowl refuges. The problem grew increasingly urgent as the drought of the late 1920s took a firm grip on the land. What man had spared, nature dried up with a relentless succession of sunny, cloudless days. Disease appeared among the weakened waterfowl and millions died of botulism.

Man, of course, was still prominently in the picture, creating as much mischief as possible: magnificent waterfowl marshes in both Lower Klamath Lake on the California-Oregon border and Malheur Lake in Oregon were drained to create additional farmland and ranches. Gilbert Pearson, on a visit in 1927 to the site of what had been Lower Klamath Lake, described the desolation: "I did not see a ranch, although I was told that there were a few somewhere. I saw only weeds—miles and miles of thickly growing weeds—and the only living creature we found was a scrawny, venomous snake that crossed the road and paused by the wheel track to shake his rattles at the two perspiring men in the car. Farther on we came to open flats over which whirlwinds chased each other like ghosts of the wildlife that had departed. In despair, almost in bitterness, I fled."

By this time Nelson, Burnham, Pearson, and the others had come around to the belief that lower bag limits must be set. In 1927 Nelson testified before the Senate Committee on Agriculture and Forestry, presided over by Senator Charles S. McNary of Oregon, and revealed an unexpected complication to an already serious problem. Nelson was describing the efforts of the Biological Survey "to safeguard the breeding stock of wildfowl in order to maintain the supply and to permit the utilization of the surplus by sportsmen from year to year."

McNARY: Do you permit any of these wild birds to be sold on the open market?

NELSON: No. They are "bootlegged" however. Since the Volstead Act went into force the bootlegging in wild game has increased tremendously. The same men who are bootlegging liquor bootleg ducks.

McNARY: That is interesting. What is the connection between the liquor and the wild game?

NELSON: The same methods are used. They take orders for ducks, and put them in a gripsack and drive up with an automobile and go into a house with their gripsack and deliver them. Delivering them in that way, undercover, it is exceedingly difficult to get evidence.

McNary: And that unlawful practice has grown up since the adoption of the Eighteenth Amendment?

Nelson: It has tremendously increased. You know how the law was pretty well respected, in that there was comparatively little bootlegging when the Migratory Bird Law went into effect. But the example of the bootlegging of whiskey has had a tremendous influence. It has built up a regular industry, you might call it, of bootlegging wild game.

McNary: That is interesting from the standpoint of criminology. I wonder if it applies generally to other infractions of the law?

Nelson: I do not know, but we know as to this because we are suffering from the consequences. It is really outrageous in many places.

McNary: All right. Then if there is bootlegging in the wild game had we not better cut down the limit a little bit and conserve at that end?

Nelson: I think we will show that we are handling it along that line.

McNary: All right. Go ahead with your bootlegging proposition.

Nelson: The department made it known from the beginning of this work that whenever conditions developed that required restrictions in killing migratory game birds they would be applied. At the time Dr. Hornaday made his original suggestion of a drastic cut in bag limits our information was so positive as to the abundance of wild fowl throughout the country that we were convinced that the birds were in no need of such additional protection. Through the increase in the number of hunters and the tremendous losses of birds through alkaline poisoning in the Rocky Mountain and Pacific Coast states we are convinced that the time has now arrived for a proper reduction in the killing of birds that the supply be maintained.

But the promised reforms did not materialize at once. Three weeks after announcing that the daily bag limit on ducks would be reduced from twenty-five to fifteen (the figure long recommended by Hornaday), the Biological Survey changed its plans without explanation and reverted to the higher limits. The year of decision was delayed until 1929, when two events of considerable interest occurred. New legislation, called the Norbeck-Andresen Bill after its sponsors, Senator Peter Norbeck of South Dakota, and Representative August H. Andresen of Minnesota, appeared in Congress. The bill provided for the purchase of wetlands by the federal government for use as waterfowl refuges; the controversial "public shooting grounds" plan had been dropped. Conservationists at once united to support the bill and it quickly became law. At the end of the year Paul G. Redington, who had succeeded Nelson as Chief of the Biological Survey, announced that daily bag limits had been reduced to fifteen ducks and four geese.

The year's events had not been totally gratifying to Hornaday. There were insufficient funds to buy the needed wetlands, and he had not managed to extract a promise from the Biological Survey that its ruling on bag limits might not be reversed in another year or two. (In 1930 a bill originated by Hornaday to make the lower bag limits permanent failed to survive a hostile Congress. The future would demand more vigorous legislation still.)

Nonetheless, he had earned the perverse satisfaction of listening to claims by other leading conservationists and their organizations that measures they had long fought for finally had been attained. Hornaday could not resist delivering a spirited response: "For too long have American bird conservationists been humbly meandering along behind the firing lines, picking up the cripples. To be sure, they are trying to 'save' them. They gather up the fragments of wildlife, 'band' it for reference purposes or pen it up and try to induce it to lay eggs and breed more gunfodder birds, for more shooting by more sportsmen and more crops of cripples."

In one case his attack on fellow conservationists went too far. John Burnham, who recently had retired as president of the American Game Protective Association, sued him for libel. Hornaday settled out of court, and returned to the firing line.

Part Five

God's Plenty, and
What Became of It

21

A Little Black Bag

Alice Roosevelt Longworth, the eldest daughter of Theodore Roosevelt, once described Warren G. Harding as "not a bad man, only a slob." One of Harding's more obvious lapses in discrimination occurred in 1920 when he became President of the United States and began to choose the circle of men who would occupy the highest places in his administration. Among these men was Albert Bacon Fall, an old crony in the Senate whom he appointed Secretary of the Interior. Fall moved into the luxuriously appointed office of his predecessor, Franklin K. Lane, who graciously left behind him the personal gifts he had received from friends all over the world. Fall appraised the rich Chinese rug, the Philippine mahogany table, the handsome ebony screen from India, and all the other treasures about him, then transferred them to the Treasury Department where he claimed them for the sum of $231.25; whereupon he shipped his new-found collection without delay to his ranch at Three Rivers, New Mexico.

The transaction was crudely symbolic of a great deal of what was to follow.

To Fall's colleagues in Washington there seemed to cling about him the quality of a character, either hero or brigand, it did not

227

matter, who had swaggered rather recently from the pages of a
Western pulp magazine. He had grown up in Kentucky and drifted
to the Southwest, where he prospected for gold. Money, like atmosphere, adhered to his lean frame, and he became a successful
rancher and miner with a rapidity possible only within the vast
and vulnerable landscape and the supple moral code of the frontier.
He knew how to ride and shoot and cut a corner. In 1910 Forest
Service rangers detected Fall in the act of grazing 6000 sheep, rather
than the 2000 he was restricted to by law, within a nearby national
forest. Upon investigation, the rangers learned further that he was
grazing the excess sheep under falsified permits and ordered him
to desist. Fall dashed off a letter to the regional forester, bristling
with indignation and threats; the Forest Service, he swore, would
'rue the day' it had decided to pick on Albert B. Fall.

Fall entered politics in the Territory of New Mexico as a Democrat. Disenchantment with William Jennings Bryan led him to
leave the party and join the Republicans, under whose banner he
was elected to the United States Senate when New Mexico became
a state in 1912. His drawl (friendly or not, it was invariably loud)
and wide-brimmed hat became familiar fixtures in the homes and
clubs of a certain type of hero-worshiper in Washington. A reporter
for the New York *World,* perhaps a bit carried away, has described
him for us as "a fighting man whose career to some extent is
reminiscent of Buffalo Bill, though in appearance he is the last man
in the world one would pick for a border hero. He is slight and
spare in physique, with a long, narrow, almost aesthetic face distinguished by blue penetrating eyes—the sort of eyes that one
learned to beware of in early frontier days as indicating a man who
could take care of himself in almost any sort of company."

Fall became a member of the Senate Foreign Relations Committee, where he focused his interest most often on Mexico. He had
explored extensively in that country across the border from New
Mexico, and he held firmly to the view that the only solution to
the "Mexican problem" was its annexation, forcibly or otherwise,
by the United States. In fact, he was in favor of direct action at
all times. No wonder, then, that stories about him that were not
altogether accurate circulated in Washington. It was said that, on
the occasion of Woodrow Wilson's illness in 1919, Fall was dispatched by the Foreign Relations Committee to the President's
bedside in order to gather his views on certain pressing matters

of policy. Fall, it was said, satisfied his suspicions about the serious-
ness of the President's illness by going over to his bed and pulling
back the covers for a long hard look. That the story, though untrue,
gained such wide belief suggests the nature of Fall's reputation.

Certainly Fall had not earned a reputation as a conservationist
in Washington. He was hostile to all progressive conservation legislation. For some reason, however, Gifford Pinchot thought he
detected certain qualities in Fall's colleague in the Senate, Warren
Harding, that would make him favorable to conservation measures
as a President and thus supported him in the campaign of 1920.
To this appallingly inaccurate guess Pinchot added another one
by supposing that Harding might appoint him to his cabinet. The
National Conservation Association had fallen on lean days. Pinchot
was casting about for an appropriately broad avenue back into
public life, while his assistant, Harry Slattery (who was to play an
important role in the sensational events ahead), went into private
law practice in Washington. Curiously, Pinchot's ambition was to
become secretary of that branch of the executive at which he spent
much of his life shaking his fist—the Department of the Interior.

To Pinchot's chagrin, Harding appointed Fall to that position,
then compounded the injury by appointing as his Secretary of the
Navy a former Michigan congressman named Edwin Denby who
had staunchly supported Richard Ballinger during the celebrated
dispute. One observer, noting the men with whom the new President associated, suggested that Harding apparently felt himself in
need of "complete mental relaxation." Pinchot expressed his concern about Fall in a telegram to a friend: HE HAS BEEN WITH EX-
PLOITATION GANG, BUT NOT A LEADER. HAS LARGE PERSONAL HOLDINGS
IN MINING AND OTHER RESOURCES IN THIS COUNTRY AND MEXICO.
TROUBLE AHEAD.

Senator Robert M. LaFollette later was to speak of Interior
as "the sluiceway for a large part of the corruption to which this
government of ours is subjected." Apparently Fall did not find,
aside from Franklin K. Lane's exotic furniture, that Interior was
sufficiently well stocked with treasures to interest a man with large
ideas. Accordingly he reached without ceremony for whatever he
coveted.

Alaska, of course, appealed to Fall's exploitive nature as it had
to Ballinger's. He became interested in the oil seepages near the
Brooks Range, as well as in "the wonderful forests of Alaska, with,

we hope, a future that is bright for the wood pulp and paper industries." Between him and control of the forests' disposal stood, just as it had for Ballinger, the Forest Service. Chief Forester William B. Greeley learned of the impending attempt to spirit the Forest Service out of the Department of Agriculture from Agriculture Secretary Henry C. Wallace.

"The main line of attack would be that 'conservation' as then applied meant only locking up from use," Greeley wrote. "The economic development of the West, her timber and power and livestock industries, were blocked by the theorists in the Forest Service. The prize exhibit of a shackled empire was Alaska. And the scheming centered in the Secretary of the Interior."

The grazing and power interests, the latter rabidly opposed to Pinchot's old principle of government ownership and control of the sources of hydroelectric power, supported Fall's scheme. Fall went so far as to identify Greeley as the "theorist" who stood in the way of the woodlands' full development and whom he would dispose of once the Forest Service had been transferred to Interior. Sensing another Ballinger-Pinchot controversy, Greeley went to Secretary Wallace and offered to resign so that he would be able to reply to Fall without embarrassing the department and the Forest Service. Wallace listened to his story, then refused to accept Greeley's resignation.

"My boy," Wallace said, "don't ever get yourself in a pissin' contest with a skunk."

In November 1921 a bill was introduced in Congress to transfer the national forests to Interior's jurisdiction. By this time, of course, Pinchot had been apprised of the rumors and had rallied his forces. Frederick Olmsted wrote to Pinchot that he looked for a bitter struggle, "for I doubt if anything else will knock sense into their big business heads. I haven't the slightest doubt . . . that the lumber interests are behind Fall and coaxing him along." Pinchot, working closely with the Society of American Foresters, found all his old public relations channels still open. Dozens of newspapers condemned the scheme in their editorial columns. The big farm organizations threw their support behind the Department of Agriculture. Harry Slattery, after conferring with Pinchot, delivered a detailed attack on Fall's conservation policies at a public meeting in Washington.

"I won't answer Pinchot's and Wallace's stooge," Fall told the press.

President Harding had sided until then with his Secretary of the Interior. When the subject arose at a cabinet meeting Wallace protested bitterly, promising that if the national forests were removed from his department he would resign and carry his case against Fall to the people. Harding wavered. Finally he withdrew his support from Fall in his campaign to snatch the forests from Agriculture. He sought to appease him, however, by letting him have his way in another conservation dispute that had been brought to public notice by Harry Slattery. This affair concerned the naval oil reserves that Fall had arranged to lease to private interests.

After a slow start during which the young American petroleum industry used the product of its wells mostly for kerosene during the latter half of the nineteenth century, it had suddenly emerged as a major and immensely profitable business. John D. Rockefeller, the world's most successful oilman, was already a byword for wealth. The development of the gasoline engine was the most important impetus to the industry's growth, but World War I, highly mechanized, had proved oil to be a vital element in the nation's defense. As a result, two areas in California and one in Wyoming had been set aside by the United States government as naval oil reserves against a national emergency. The policy was spelled out during Woodrow Wilson's administration by Franklin Delano Roosevelt, then Assistant Secretary of the Navy: "The government has the right to and must set aside reserve oil lands and prevent absolutely the taking of oil from these lands for private purposes."

Leading conservationists, including Theodore Roosevelt,* had supported this move in a period when the oil industry's extraction procedures were characterized by enormous waste. The naval reserves, however, were eyed as hungrily by private interests as any other part of the public domain. While he was Secretary of the Interior, Franklin K. Lane proposed to grant leases to drill on the reserves, but the outcry from the Navy Department and conservationists forced him to abandon the plan. In 1920 Congress placed the reserves under the jurisdiction of the Secretary of the Navy. The arrangement was short-lived. In 1921 rumors persisted that President Harding would sign an executive order transferring the reserves from the Navy Department to Interior. Pinchot was outraged by this further evidence of Fall's long grasp, which Harry Slattery's investigations had confirmed. He sent Slattery with a note

*Roosevelt died in 1919.

to see Theodore Roosevelt, Jr., the new Assistant Secretary of the Navy.

"I went to the Navy Department with the letter," Slattery later wrote, "and, observing an outer office filled with pictures of TR in every type of action, felt sure when I was ushered in that I would be received on friendly grounds. When I told the Assistant Secretary of the naval oil fight and of my knowledge of it, and the vital necessity of oil for the Navy, I could see he was irritated. When I referred to the well-known anti-conservation record of Secretary Fall, he hit the ceiling. He said that Fall was in his father's Rough Riders and that he would not permit me to say anything derogatory of this great good friend. We sparred back and forth, and he finally admitted he himself carried the executive order, written by Fall and with [Navy Secretary] Denby's approval, to President Harding, transferring the reserves from the Navy to Interior, and that Harding had signed it. I was shocked, but that information was worth the visit. When I told him I was ready to predict Fall would turn over the naval reserves to private interests in the oil industry he showed me the door in anger."

The drama had been set in motion. Early in 1922 Pinchot turned his attention to his successful campaign for the governorship of Pennsylvania, leaving Slattery in Washington to keep an eye on Fall. In April *The Wall Street Journal* confirmed Slattery's worst suspicions in an article which revealed that the Interior Department had leased the 9000-acre naval oil reserve in Wyoming to the Mammoth Oil Company. The site, located fifty miles north of Casper, possessed a remarkable sandstone formation which thrust itself above the surrounding sagebrush like "a disfigured human hand," and which came to be called Teapot Dome.

Secretary Fall, off on an inspection tour somewhere in the West, was unavailable for comment, but his subordinates glowed with enthusiasm. A department spokesman called the lease "one of the greatest petroleum undertakings of the age and symbolizes a notable departure on the part of the government in seeking partnership with private capital for the working of government-owned natural resources." The Mammoth Oil Company had agreed to pay royalties to the government in oil certificates, which the government then could exchange for the company's various petroleum products, or demand cash for the certificates instead.

Slattery, who had dogged Fall's footsteps since the early rumors about his grab for the national forests, felt that the Secretary had overreached himself. In addition to Teapot Dome, Interior had leased the naval reserves at Elk Hills, California, to the Pan-American Petroleum and Transport Company. When at last he made himself available for public comment, Fall justified the California lease on the grounds that the oil there was draining off underground where it could be tapped by private interests (without royalties) outside the naval reserve. He offered no valid explanation for the lease he had approved at Teapot Dome.

Slattery, having poked about behind the scenes, took his suspicions and the facts to Senator LaFollette. He asked LaFollette if he would conduct an investigation in the Senate to determine whether the events leading up to the leases, and the leases themselves, were in order. LaFollette, a progressive Republican and, through his friendship with Pinchot, an interested conservationist, promised to do what he could. Several days later he introduced a resolution that called on Fall to submit to the Senate all the necessary orders and correspondence dealing with the oil leases. The Senate passed the resolution unanimously.

"The times were tense," Slattery recalled years afterward. "When we conservationists started to question his activities Mr. Fall decided he would use some tough tactics. He had a two-gun man named Basocca, who had passed several men over the Great Divide. Mr. Fall sent him around to see me, with a threat. I kicked that gentleman out of my office."

In the face of LaFollette's resolution Fall grew acquiescent. He shipped the pertinent files to the Senate, including a letter in which President Harding affirmed that "the policy decided upon and the subsequent acts have at all times had my entire approval." La Follette, in turn, arose on the Senate floor to ask for a further investigation of the leases. "Who were the real organizers of the Mammoth Oil Company who were to be favored by the government with a special privilege in value beyond the dreams of Croesus?"

At this point it might be worth our while to answer this question by describing the oilmen associated with Fall. Behind the Mammoth Oil Company stood a brash pirate named Harry Ford Sinclair. Sinclair had grown up in Independence, Kansas, where he worked as a pharmacist in his father's drugstore. When oil was discovered nearby, he abandoned his pills and prescriptions to join the

hit-or-miss rush for instant riches. One success led invariably to another, a circumstance that certainly came about in great part
because of young Sinclair's boundless confidence in himself. At a
critical point in his fortunes he challenged the vast Standard Oil
empire and survived.

"Rockefeller hasn't got anything I don't have," Sinclair is reported to have said at the time. "He hasn't got any more brains
than I have. But I've got something he doesn't have—youth and
time."

Nothing daunted Sinclair. He challenged another powerful
American institution, major league baseball, by buying a franchise
in the "outlaw" Federal League. The franchise went down with
the league two years later. Sinclair broke into big-time thor-
oughbred racing with considerably more success, and had the
satisfaction of watching his Zev win the Kentucky Derby in 1923.
By that time (concurrent with the uproar over Teapot Dome) he
was one of the richest and one of the most famous oilmen in the
world.

Edward E. Doheny was the power behind the Pan-American
Petroleum and Transport Company to which Fall had leased the
Elk Hills reserve in California. Doheny came to wealth along a
more circuitous route than Sinclair had followed, and to general
fame only with the revelations about his curious ties with Albert
B. Fall. For years Doheny had drifted through the West like thousands of other seekers after gold and adventure. He worked as a
schoolteacher and a surveyor, traded horses, and, while leading a
band of vigilantes, disarmed and arrested the desperadoes who tried
to ambush him. He prospected for gold and silver, the latter somewhat successfully. But it was in California that he made his fortune,
converting with a pick and shovel his hunch about the Brea tarpits
into a rich oil strike. Greater riches followed. In the course of his
travels Doheny had met Fall. His outstanding contribution to the
election of President Warren G. Harding (whom he rightly guessed
to be a friend to oil) was money for a project to publish the photographs of Harding's parents in newspapers throughout the country,
thus demolishing the canard that Negro blood flowed in the candidate's veins.

The investigation requested by LaFollette and approved by the
Senate was slow to materialize. Few senators were enthusiastic
about an investigation, some for the reason that no substantial or

headline-grabbing charges against Fall could as yet be made, others for the reason that they were unwilling to embarrass the Harding administration. While the investigation hung fire, several notable events took place. Fall was already discredited and under fire because of the manner in which he had turned over the naval oil reserves to private drilling. Conservationists, naval officers, and a number of congressmen were outraged, and there were rumors of his impending resignation. Fall still had a scheme up his sleeve, however. He attempted to push through Congress legislation to create what he called "the All-Year National Park." Upon studying the proposal, one found that it consisted of setting aside a large area in New Mexico, with Fall's own ranch sitting at its heart. It was Fall's kind of national park, as well: it would be open to grazing, logging, mining, and hunting. Congress was not interested.

In January 1923, Fall resigned as Secretary of the Interior. The White House explained his resignation by saying he had joined the administration only at great personal sacrifice and now he was returning to his neglected business affairs. Herbert Hoover, Secretary of Commerce, wrote to Fall that "the vast majority of our people feel a regret at your leaving the Department of the Interior. In my recollection, that department has never had so constructive and legal a headship as you gave it." Hoover's attitude toward conservation during his own administration proved to be consistent with these sentiments.

That summer Warren Harding suddenly died. He was succeeded by his Vice-President, Calvin Coolidge, whose innocence was best expressed when he said on taking office that he did not intend to make any changes in his cabinet. Herbert Hoover observed later in his *Memoirs:* "Had he known what bugs crawled about under the paving stones of the Harding regime, he would not have been so inclusive."

The bugs began to be uncovered when the Senate investigation of Teapot Dome got under way at the end of that year. Senator Thomas J. Walsh of Montana, a Democrat and the chairman of the investigating committee, seemed at first to be no more aware than Coolidge did of the extent to which corruption had proceeded under Harding; but once he began to look into the many rumors that Fall had accepted certain gifts in return for the leases he was very quickly relieved of his illusions. Walsh discovered that Fall, despite many financial difficulties, had made costly improvements on his ranch immediately after he had approved the oil leases to Sinclair and Doheny. Sinclair, in fact, had visited Fall's ranch at the time.

Sinclair denied any impropriety when questioned by Walsh, but Fall claimed he was too ill to testify. In reply to the committee's request for information about his financial condition at the time of the Teapot Dome lease, Fall replied by mail that he had borrowed $100,000 from Edward B. McLean, the publisher of the Washington *Post*. Yes, McLean told Walsh, he had sent checks totaling $100,000 to Fall, but Fall had returned them uncashed several days later. Until then the press and the public had not been terribly excited about the affair. Then Walsh put Edward Doheny on the stand and asked him if he knew anything about a $100,000 loan. Doheny replied that his son, Edward, Jr., had carried $100,000 to Fall in a "little black bag."

Headlines spread the news across the country. Fall, it seemed, was a liar at best, and perhaps much more. A terrific fuss was made over the "little black bag." The only other piece of news that rivaled it in public interest was the conjecture about what might be found in the near future when King Tutankhamen's tomb was opened in Egypt; a cartoonist depicted an archaeologist climbing out of the tomb carrying Doheny's "little black bag."

Even the jaded Senate was shaken by the revelation. Charges and countercharges flew across the aisle. Senator Thaddeus H. Caraway of Alabama thundered his disapproval not only of Doheny but of other cabinet members who seemed to be implicated at least by acts of omission. The rhetoric flowed like boiling lava. At one point Senator J. Thomas Heflin, Caraway's colleague from Alabama, was moved to record the incident in something more permanent than legislative prose:

Abou Dough Heenie (may his tribe increase!)
Awoke one night from a deep dream of peace
And saw within the moonlight in his room
Making it rich and like a lily in bloom
A Senator writing in a book of gold.
Enormous wealth had made Dough Heenie bold;
And to the Senator in his room he said:
"What writest thou?" The statesman raised his head,
And with a look which made Abou boil
Answered, "The names of those who seek for oil!"

"And is mine one?" said Abou. "We will see!"
Replied the Senator, but Abou Dough cheerily
Responded in a still and softer tone,
"Write me as one who loves to make a loan."
The Senator wrote and vanished. The next day
He came again—it looked like CARAWAY—
And showed the names of those whom Fall liked best
And lo! Dough Heenie's name led all the rest.

There were more revelations to come. Archie Roosevelt, one of
Theodore Roosevelt's sons, brought fresh grist for Walsh's mill.
Until recently young Roosevelt had worked for the Consolidated
Oil Company, another part of Harry Sinclair's empire. Quite by
accident he had learned that Sinclair's private secretary had sent
$68,000 to Fall at his ranch. Upon being questioned by Walsh, the
private secretary contended it was all a misunderstanding, that he
had said *"six or eight cows"* had been sent to Fall and that Roosevelt
had mistakenly thought he had said "sixty-eight thousand."

All of this was immensely embarrassing to President Coolidge.
His Secretary of the Navy, Edwin Denby, was under fire for having
collaborated with Fall in persuading Harding to transfer the naval
oil reserves from the Navy to Interior. (When several senators
proposed to impeach Denby, Senator Walsh observed that stupidity
was not grounds for impeachment.) Attorney General Harry M.
Daugherty, already closely linked to unrelated scandals, was under
fire for not having investigated the charges against Fall at an earlier
date. Standing bewildered at the head of an administration fast
being exposed as rotten to its core, Coolidge's prospects for a term
in his own right as President seemed to be dim. They dimmed still
further with the rise of William Gibbs McAdoo, Woodrow Wilson's
son-in-law as well as his Secretary of the Treasury, as a leading
candidate for the Democratic nomination.

But in February 1924 the committee summoned Doheny again
at the request of Senator James A. Reed of Missouri, another
prominent contender for the Democratic nomination. Reed saw
that the proper questions were put to Doheny, a procedure leading
inexorably to the disclosure that McAdoo had received $250,000
for representing Doheny after resigning as Secretary of the Treasury, but while his father-in-law was still in the White House.
McAdoo was now "splashed with oil." A Republican newspaper

succinctly dismissed him as a threat to Coolidge in the coming election: "McAdieu!"

Coolidge was helped further by subsequent events. Fall finally appeared before the Senate committee and, invoking the Fifth Amendment, made no further damaging admissions. Denby resigned as Secretary of the Navy to spare Coolidge "embarrassments." Attorney General Daugherty clung to office with a loosening grip. Skeletons tumbled one upon another out of his closet, among them a young lady named Roxy Stinson, a divorcée whose former husband had been a close friend of Daugherty before meeting his death under mysterious circumstances. Her testimony to the committee seemed to implicate Daugherty in a web of shadiness. Daugherty's grip loosened still further, Coolidge pushed, and another Harding appointee was gone. (Not so quietly as Denby, however: "To my dying day I shall expect Mr. Coolidge to make an explanation of his action," Daugherty complained. Later he was brought to trial for defrauding the government in another matter, but a jury acquitted him for lack of evidence.) "Keep cool with Coolidge," chanted the electorate in 1924, and that rather frigid gentleman was returned to the White House in the fall.

"Most people conserve when there is too little, the oil industry conserves when there is too much," Harvey O'Connor wrote in *The Empire of Oil*. "In fact, the very word 'conservation' when applied to oil must be understood in its Pickwickian sense."

Throughout the administrations of Harding, Coolidge, and Hoover conservation generally was approached from this point of view. "The business of the United States is business," Coolidge had said, and conservation measures that did not fit into this concept tended to be dismissed and starved as "sentimentalism." The spirit, of course, was not wholly *laissez-faire*. No segment of American society sings more ecstatically of free enterprise than the oil industry, while at the same time it works behind the scenes for government subsidies of every conceivable sort. On the whole, then, the industry applauded the conservation measures taken belatedly by Coolidge when he filed suit to restrain private interests from further drilling in the disputed naval oil reserves. Because the market already suffered from a surfeit of oil, thus causing prices to drop, Coolidge simply was making government policy of sharp business practices, conserving a natural resource when there was "too much."

The stain of Teapot Dome was purged from the national conscience by a long series of court actions. The courts eventually canceled both oil leases on the grounds that they had been fraudulently negotiated. The government pressed a series of criminal charges against Denby, Sinclair, and Fall. Denby was acquitted of conspiring to defraud the government. Sinclair, too, was acquitted of these charges, but not before he came a cropper during his first trial when the court learned he had hired detectives to keep jurors under "surveillance;" Sinclair served six months for that infraction and another three months for failing to answer questions put to him by Walsh's investigating committee.

Retribution fell heaviest on the disintegrating figure of Albert B. Fall. The various court cases finally turned up the fact that Sinclair and Doheny had paid Fall a total of $400,000. Convicted of conspiracy to defraud the government, he was sentenced to serve one year in prison and fined $100,000, which he was not able to pay. Fall lived on in poverty and ill-health in a furnished room until World War II, when he died in a Texas hospital.

22

TVA

The Tennessee River emerges from a junction of the Holston and French Broad Rivers near Knoxville and sets off on a circuitous 650-mile journey that carries it into Alabama, northwest into Tennessee again, and finally into Kentucky where it empties into the Ohio at Paducah. During the Civil War the Union Army exploited the Tennessee as one of its avenues to victory; Fort Henry, Shiloh, and Chattanooga lie along its banks. A little farther to the south in Alabama the river once descended for thirty-five miles in a series of rapids that served as a battleground of a different sort during World War I and for some years afterward. The early settlers called this non-navigable stretch Muscle Shoals.

The origin of the name is obscure. Did it refer to the "muscle" needed to pole a boat through the rapids, or was it a valiant but ineffectual stab at the proper spelling of the name by which we know the small shellfish found in the area? History is silent on that score. In any case, local business interests very early proposed a canal to circumvent the rapids. The state of Alabama built the canal, which quickly silted up and became useless. The U.S. Army Corps of Engineers put its mind to the problem and built what it hoped to be a more permanent canal in 1890. But as the century ended other dreams took hold of local businessmen, dreams in which the rapids appeared as a promising source of hydroelectric power.

Alabama congressmen introduced bills to write off the Tennessee as navigable at that point and throw a dam across the shoals. In 1903 a bill to this effect, giving away to private interests the right to build a dam on the Tennessee, passed Congress with little opposition. When it reached the White House, however, the bill encountered a presidential veto. Theodore Roosevelt noted that the "recent development of the application of water power to the production of electricity available for use at considerable distances has revealed an element of substantial value in streams." The river was free to run its turbulent course over Muscle Shoals until it caught the fancy of men with a different vision.

It was during those years that water, for many Americans, was becoming almost the only "conservation" subject that mattered. W. J. McGee, as we have seen, was preaching his gospel of the multipurpose use of our waterways, though many powerful groups could think of only one major use for the precious stuff. The hardy men who had pushed westward to find their fortunes on farms and ranches had put their faith in the increasingly hollow declaration that "rain follows the plow." Once that illusion had been shattered they learned that if the vast reaches of the West were to be worth more than a wooden nickel to them they must divert the little water to places where it would do the most good. The Reclamation Act of 1903 had been an attempt to solve these people's problems by making inexpensive irrigation projects available throughout the West.

But the act became a source of endless squabbles. Speculators bought up large tracts of land that had been proposed for inclusion in irrigation projects, pushing its price from $1.25 an acre to as high as $1000 an acre. Even where farmers held title to good land bought at inexpensive prices they complained that the schedule of repayments to the Reclamation Fund was too arduous. Often they withheld those payments, counting on the government eventually to wipe them altogether off the books. In 1914 the original purpose of the Reclamation Act was considerably weakened when Congress lengthened the schedule of payments from ten to twenty years and withdrew the authority to allocate projects from the Bureau of

Reclamation, reserving that right to its own logrolling mercies.

The Army Corps of Engineers was another group that held very decided views on the use to which America's inland waterways should be put. Because West Point once was the country's only source of engineers, the Corps established an early monopoly in that field. Specifically, the Corps had been instructed by Congress to concentrate its efforts during peacetime on the task of keeping the waterways open to navigation. It made few studies on stream flow and other vital matters which came to claim the attention of the Geological Survey, and indeed saw that bureau as a competitor. Again, as we have seen, the Corps worked strenuously to defeat Senator Newlands' hopes in 1907 to establish an Inland Waterways Commission and devise a multipurpose plan for waterways. Every attempt to revive Newlands' plan during the administrations of Taft and Wilson was defeated, generally with the Corps tipping the balance in favor of Newlands' opponents.

The Corps maintained this stance even though it had assumed vital responsibilities for flood control on our major rivers. Its officers placed no faith in dams, reservoirs, and forest cover to mitigate the great floods that swept down river valleys every few years. Its work on the Mississippi was typical of its approach. During the nineteenth century Congress was hostile to the idea that the federal government should support flood control; it was seen as a local burden, especially by representatives of regions that were not plagued by floods.

But the Corps managed to extend its responsibilities into the area of flood control by masking its work as "improvements to navigation." Along the Mississippi this consisted of building and maintaining levees to stabilize the river banks and wall out the recurring flood waters. Through the years there was increasing criticism of the Corps' position that levees were the Mississippi's sole solution to extensive flooding. Time and again the floods washed out the levees and took appalling tolls of life and property. Yet the Corps continued to dismiss supplementary aids such as dams behind which to store the excess water, or cutoffs by which to divert it quickly into the Gulf of Mexico. Furthermore, despite its considerable influence in matters pertaining to waterways, the Corps did nothing to discourage the settlement of vulnerable portions of the flood plain by homeowners or industries. Gifford Pinchot, after an especially disastrous flood in the 1920s, referred to the Corps' exclusive dependence on levees as "the most colossal blunder in engineering history." Only toward the end of that decade did the Corps' monolithic approach begin to give way to the assortment of remedies that have somewhat mitigated the Mississippi's periodic rampages.

But it was over water power that the great political battles were fought during the years that separated the administrations of the two Roosevelts. Theodore Roosevelt was quick to grasp the enormous tactical value of streams to those who, reaching for great wealth, exploited natural resources that did not belong to them. As Roosevelt remarked shortly before leaving office, at the time he vetoed a bill to build a dam on the James River in Missouri, "The bill gives to the grantee a valuable privilege which is monopolistic and does not contain conditions essential to protect the public." Yet large utilities kept up their assault on the federal government, trying time and again to secure the rights to favorable power sites in perpetuity, without charge or government supervision. The classic battle raged over Muscle Shoals.

After Theodore Roosevelt vetoed the bill to turn Muscle Shoals over to private interests in 1903 there were further sporadic attempts on the site until World War I. Each of these met firm opposition raised in the Roosevelt manner by Gifford Pinchot. Through the National Conservation Association, Pinchot lobbied incessantly for the requirement that private interests pay for such rights through a system of annual fees, which came to be called (in reference to Pinchot's known predilictions) "conservation charges." A further compliment to Pinchot's influence was paid in Congress by Senator Charles S. Thomas of Colorado.

"The average conservationist—I will not say it applies to all of them," Thomas told his colleagues, "is very much concerned about conserving other people, but when it comes to a personal application of the doctrine he is not so enthusiastic. I believe the gentleman who claims to be the progenitor, the father of conservation, is the Hon. Gifford Pinchot, at one time the chief adviser to President Roosevelt, Forester of the United States, and one of the founders and leaders of the late lamented Progressive Party. He it was who discovered that the way to conserve was to reserve, and that the way to develop was to keep everything petrified and stagnant."

When World War I jarred the plug from many of the reserves

stopped up by Pinchot's policies, natural resources began to flow as freely as ever into the hands of persistent exploiters. Muscle Shoals presented them with a unique opportunity. The submarine scare had shaken the country's faith in the dependability of nitrate imports from Chile. If the supply line was cut, so many congressmen reasoned, the Germans would have struck a crippling blow at our munitions industry. Congress passed a bill to construct nitrate plants near Muscle Shoals and a dam to supply them with power. Surplus nitrates, not needed in the manufacture of munitions, would be used to provide cheap fertilizer for American farmers.

But the war ended before either the nitrate plants began production or the dam (named the Wilson Dam in honor of the President) was completed. There was considerable criticism of the whole project. The *laissez-faire* crowd expressed a horror of government participation in any such business, looking on it as another step down the road to socialism. Others believed the entire project was a great waste of the taxpayers' money (though Bernard Baruch, the financier, claimed that the announcement of the plan enabled the United States to save many millions of dollars by extracting a better bargain from Chilean nitrogen interests). But, with the accession of Harding to the presidency, one thing was certain. The administration would try to divest itself of these socialistic trappings as soon as it could find a buyer.

The interested buyer who presented himself to the government in 1921 was no less a personage than Henry Ford. It is difficult for us today to understand the extent to which Americans of the period revered this autocratic industrialist. In the public mind he was the creator of cheap transportation and the "five-dollar day." Edgar A. Guest reflected the emotions of the common man in verses he wrote about humanity's debt to Ford.

'Tis a happier world for his living here, there is
   joy where but grief was known,
Contentment reigns where misery once builded his
   hateful throne.
The children laugh where they used to wail, and the
   eyes of parents glow
With the happiness they used to think only the rich
   could know.
And this is the work of Henry Ford—all this shall
   the future scan,

And find in him a friend who lived and thought of
  his fellow man.

Ford was a maker and shaker of things, an inventor and an
industrialist of genius ("Henry can make 'em faster than you can
wreck 'em," contemporary wags said of his Model T), and a miracle
worker whom many expected would solve the world's largest problems if only given half a chance. The belief was not universal, of
course. A farmer, being selected for jury service in a lawsuit in
which Ford became involved, was asked by a lawyer whether he
owned a Ford car. "Yes," he replied. "But that would not prejudice
me against him."

Ford, as we have seen, was an enthusiastic admirer of nature,
and particularly of birds. On his estate outside Detroit he kept five
hundred bird houses (a martin house there contained seventy-six
apartments) as well as feeders and a large bird bath heated by
electricity. He was also an indefatigable hiker and camper. His long
camping expeditions with his close friends, Thomas A. Edison,
Harvey Firestone, and the bearded dean of birdwatchers, John
Burroughs, were followed so persistently by the press and public
that eventually they had to be abandoned.

An engaging little story, which might even have been true, was
told about one of their earliest trips. When the car in which they
were touring the countryside developed an alarming noise of undetermined origin, they pulled into a gas station. The attendant
looked under the hood and ventured that it might be piston trouble.

"No," one of the party said. "I'm Henry Ford, and it's not motor
trouble."

The attendant poked around a bit more and suggested that the
tires might have been squeaking.

"No," another passenger said. "I'm Harvey Firestone, and I know
it isn't the tires."

The attendant shrugged. "Well, maybe it's faulty wiring."

"No," said a third passenger. "I'm Thomas Edison, and I know
the electric system is all right."

The attendant glared at them, then pointed at Burroughs. "Okay,
okay," he said. "And now I suppose you're going to tell me that
guy is Santa Claus!"

Burroughs himself once described Ford's fascination for running
water and his regret at what he considered the great waste of

potential power at various unharnessed waterfalls. ("His interest in the stream is in its potential water power. He races up and down its banks to see its fall, and where power could be developed.") To his interest in water power Ford added a vision of a decentralized industrial system that might be fitted into the pattern of rural life. No wonder, then, that he seized on Muscle Shoals as the site for a great experiment. He offered to lease the idle nitrate plants and Wilson Dam from the government for one hundred years at an annual rental of $1,700,000. He planned to put the plants to work turning out the cheap fertilizer for farmers that some congressmen had already seen as the chief justification for the government's substantial investment in Muscle Shoals. Ford's offer, however, depended on certain concessions he hoped to extract from the government, including the completion of Wilson Dam.

At first Ford's offer created immense excitement. Not the least of the alluring ideas was the creation along the Tennessee River of a vast city that would rival New York in the size of its population. The difference would be in the dimensions of Ford's dream city: it would blossom as a megalopolis, seventy-five miles in length, but fragmented by islands of green so that in effect it would be composed of dozens of "small country towns." Farm organizations rushed to Ford's support in Congress. Land speculators invested heavily (and ultimately disastrously) in the region to be covered by the sprawling enterprise. Simultaneously a nationwide drive began to put Ford forward as a presidential candidate in the next election.

But, once more, the sentiment in favor of Ford was not unanimous. The giant utilities did not relish Ford as a competitor. Some taxpayers rebelled at the revelation that it would cost $132,000,000 to construct the dam and nitrate plants to Ford's specifications. There were rumors that Ford's plans to operate an aluminum factory at Muscle Shoals aroused the opposition of Andrew Mellon of the Aluminum Company of America, who was serving as Harding's Secretary of the Treasury. Most importantly, as it turned out, Ford's plan met with the dispassionate hostility of Senator George W. Norris.

The issue of Muscle Shoals had been deposited in the Senate Committee on Agriculture, of which Norris was chairman. A chunky man who habitually wore dark suits and "shoestring neckties," Norris may have presented to the public at a distance the image of the old-fashioned senator of cartoons and vaudeville routines. But in action Norris was unique. A newspaperman once said that "George W. Norris is the only honest man in political life in America," and in doing so expressed an opinion that was astonishingly widespread. As a young Republican congressman from Nebraska, Norris had led the successful revolt against the old-line Republican machine and its resident tyrant in the House, "Uncle Joe" Cannon. As a progressive and an independent in the Senate, Norris had fought many brave and lonely battles for what he believed to be right. He never expressed an opinion on a subject with which he was not well acquainted. On looking over the facts concerning Henry Ford's offer to the United States for Muscle Shoals, Norris concluded that it was "the most wonderful real estate speculation since Adam and Eve lost title to the Garden of Eden."

Norris shared Ford's enthusiasm for the potential of water power in creating a better, more efficient, world. However, he held certain strict notions about the way in which it could best be developed in the public interest. "All that is needed to give humanity the full enjoyment of this modern giant is to cheapen its production," Norris said. "If stock manipulation can be eliminated and if financial legerdemain and unconscionable profits can be removed, it is the cheapest source of power and light known to man." And again: "We ought to guard with jealous care against the concentration of water power of the country in the hands of any combination of men." Norris feared that Ford, once he had gained possession of the power rights at Muscle Shoals, might sell them at an enormous profit to the private utilities. Moreover, he harbored well-founded doubts about the feasibility of Ford's plans to produce cheap fertilizer there.

Harding's death removed Ford as a candidate for the Republican nomination in 1924. Coolidge was relatively free of the sinister shadow cast by Teapot Dome, and Ford threw in his lot with the other Republicans who backed the new President for a full term of his own. But Ford's plan for Muscle Shoals remained unchanged. He massed all of his considerable support in Washington for a frontal assault on Congress. That the President of the United States was unaware of Muscle Shoals' value removed the possibility of any passionate opposition from the White House to Ford's plans (or to those of any other private interest); "The problem of Muscle Shoals seems to me to have assumed a place out of all proportion with its real importance," Coolige once said. "It probably does not represent in market value much more than a first-class battleship."

But Norris was the rock on which Ford's ambitious plan foundered. Despite strong support in Congress, especially in the House,
the sponsors of Ford's plan were not able to extract it from the
Senate Agriculture Committee where Norris had entombed it. After
three years of costly effort, Ford abruptly (and without explanation)
withdrew his offer for Muscle Shoals. Apparently being well aware
of Norris's tenacity, he finally despaired of removing that last
formidable obstacle. But the larger issue of Muscle Shoals was still
very much alive. On one side, Ford's grandiose scheme had stimulated new interest among the leaders of Southern Utility companies.
On the other side, Norris himself was moving to the offensive; never
content to be simply "against" an issue or a cause, the senator began
to advance an equally spectacular plan of his own.

Norris had thrown himself into the Muscle Shoals issue with his
customary dedication. In an effort to learn everything there was
to know about hydroelectric power and its potential he traveled
widely throughout the United States and Canada. His most lasting
impression was that of the benefits public power had bestowed on
Ontario. Even his experience with American cities that owned their
own power systems had not prepared him for the advantages reaped
by the people of this province who were supplied by the publicly
owned system. After examining the various charts and statistics
showed him by officials there, he set out on his own tour to talk
to the local people. Typical of those he met was a woman named
Cullen in Toronto, who ran her eight-room home (heating, cooking,
lighting, and hot water) almost entirely by electricity. Her bill for
the month was $3.55. Norris compared the charges on her bill with
what homeowners in various American cities would pay to private
power companies for a comparable amount of electricity: in Washington D.C. they paid $23, in Birmingham $32, in Nashville $40,
and in Florida $60.

Though blind to the beauty of an unharnessed waterfall (he was
furious with the Corps of Engineers for their unfavorable report
that denied a power dam for the historic Great Falls on the Potomac), Norris was touched by the dinginess of many lives and felt
they would blossom under the beneficent ministrations of public
power. As early as 1922 he introduced legislation in Congress to
create a government corporation to complete and operate power
dams and nitrate plants on the Tennessee River. The resultant

power and fertilizer made available cheaply to local people would, he believed, revitalize that chronically depressed region. Furthermore, this basin-wide development would serve as an inspirational model for the people of other river basins throughout the country. In this early bill Norris had set forth the design of the Tennessee Valley Authority.

The times were hardly propitious for such enlightened social legislation. To feed the public's conservative reaction to wartime big government, the great private power companies launched in the 1920s a numbing barrage of propaganda that strengthened their hold on the available power sites. They reasoned that the key to success lay in controlling the nation's press. This they set out to accomplish on a small scale by advancing "favors" and canned editorials to some newspapers, and on a larger scale by purchasing controlling interests in others. International Power and Paper bought stock worth $2.5 million in the Boston *Herald-Traveler;* another company tried to buy the Cleveland *Plain-Dealer.* In Maine, when Dr. Ernest Gruening (later a senator from Alaska) bucked the industrial leaders of that "power-ridden state" as editor of the Portland *News,* large advertisers boycotted the paper.

The industry nominally fell under the regulation of the Federal Power Commission. This cabinet agency had been created by the Federal Water Power Act of 1920, which established federal ownership of all navigable rivers from source to mouth, the new commission being charged with the authority to grant fifty-year leases for power development. The cabinet members who made up the commission in those days generally threw their support to the private power companies. Thus these companies remained free of effective supervision until 1930, when Congress reorganized it and provided for five full-time commissioners in place of the cabinet heads. Meanwhile an investigation by another agency during the 1920s, the Federal Trade Commission, had uncovered one colossal hoax: a report issued by the prestigious Smithsonian Institution, highly critical of the publicly owned Ontario Power Authority, turned out to be based on spurious statistics provided and paid for by private power companies in the United States. A power company consultant with tenuous connections to the Smithsonian had managed to persuade its unsuspecting director to allow the privately printed report to appear under the Institution's imprint.

Twice Norris managed to push his Tennessee Valley Authority

(TVA) bill through Congress, only to have it vetoed by Presidents Coolidge and Hoover. The sole advance made against the industry during those years was the approval of the construction of a great multipurpose dam at Boulder Canyon on the Colorado River; though Hoover did not show great enthusiasm for the dam and made certain the power it generated was sold to private interests for distribution, the project provided water for Los Angeles, flood control for the Imperial Valley, and irrigation for large areas of agricultural land. For a time there was considerable confusion whether the project was to be named Boulder Dam or Hoover Dam, a conundrum that Upton Sinclair waggishly suggested could be solved by declaring it "Hoover Dam, constructed during the administration of President Boulder."

The Tennessee Valley and Norris's hopes for its revival were considerably frayed by the onset of the Depression. Indeed, in 1930 Norris's opponents in Nebraska, including the Nebraska Power Company, concocted an ingenious scheme to bring about his defeat: they prevailed upon a grocery clerk named George W. Norris to run against his namesake in the crowded Republican primary. Norris survived the consequent confusion to win re-election to the Senate. In 1932 Norris threw his support in the presidential campaign to Franklin D. Roosevelt, who had endorsed his Muscle Shoals bill. Roosevelt's election ensured its passage; the message with which he urged Congress to establish TVA eloquently expressed Norris's cherished hopes:

"It is clear that the Muscle Shoals development is but a small part of the potential usefulness of the entire Tennessee River. Such use, if envisioned in its entirety, transcends mere power development: it enters wide fields of flood control, soil erosion, afforestation, elimination from agricultural use of marginal lands, and distribution and diversification of industry. In short, this power development of war days leads logically to national planning for a complete river watershed involving many states and the future lives and welfare of millions. It touches and gives life to all forms of human concerns.

"I, therefore, suggest to the Congress legislation to create a Tennessee Valley Authority—a corporation clothed with the power of government but possessed of the flexibility and initiative of a private enterprise. It should be charged with broadest duty of planning for the proper use, conservation and development of the natural resources of the Tennessee River drainage basin and its adjoining territory for the general social and economic welfare of the nation."

TVA was the crowning achievement of that branch of the conservation movement dealing with resource management. There were vast land problems still confronting the new administration; the nation's soil itself was in jeopardy. But, in the circumscribed area of an historic river, a few "visionaries" had united to turn every facet of the landscape to work for man's material well being. "Three fortunes had been taken off that country—forests, oil and gas," said Arthur E. Morgan, Chairman of the new Tennessee Valley Authority. "The wreckage of the rugged individualism has been handed to us with a request that we try to do something about it."

A series of giant dams, admirable in their architectural purity, arose on the river and its tributaries. The Tennessee Valley stirred in the throes of economic rebirth. Harnessed to one encompassing plan, the river provided its people with the cheapest power in the country, and gave the country itself a yardstick with which to gauge the charges of other producers. The nitrate plants at Muscle Shoals became the center of the world's research on fertilizers. Forest fires and soil erosion on the neighboring slopes were checked, and flood damage mitigated. The production of farms and forests increased. Navigation and recreation flourished on the transformed river.

The wilderness of Muscle Shoals had been enveloped by a technological marvel. As each phase of the grand TVA plan unfolded another stretch of untamed river subsided into a placid lake. "It is emblematic," Norris said of the bill which established TVA, "of the dawning of that day when every rippling stream that flows down a mountainside and winds its way through the meadows to the sea shall be harnessed and made to work for the welfare and comfort of man."

A day dawned when a great many people would not tingle with Norris at the prospect; they would judge the spiritual cost of that physical comfort too high if all rivers were to go the way of the Tennessee. Economically, too, the cost in productive land disappearing under water behind the new dams would be prohibitive if it were repeated endlessly across the continent. But in its time and place Norris's unfailing vision received its fitting monument in TVA. This unique project had provided thousands of Americans with the physical springboard from which to move on toward an even higher concept of conservation.

23

Geological Suicide

In 1909 the Department of Agriculture's Bureau of Soils put its official stamp on this scrap of traditional wisdom: "The soil is the one indestructible, immutable asset that the Nation possesses; it is the one resource that cannot be exhausted, that cannot be used up."

A quarter of a century later Hugh H. Bennett, who became known as "the Father of Soil Conservation," took the measure of such traditional wisdom. "I didn't know so much costly misinformation could be put into a single brief sentence," he said wryly.

In between, he and a few other agricultural dissenters had mournfully traced the nation's rush toward what Bennett liked to call geological suicide. All this was nothing new to be sure. Ever since man relinquished the hunter's life to till the soil and build civilizations he has proceeded sooner or later to undo both of them. Eroded hillsides, gullied fields, deserts whose purity is simply an absence of life, testify to his quaint notion that physical and biological laws are subservient to those of economics.

Before the federal government turned its attention to the soil there were attempts to conserve the minerals beneath it and the forests that rose above it. Unlike forests, wildlife, and fisheries, minerals are non-renewable resources. Yet incredible waste attended their extraction from the ground. Drill-and-run projects squandered much of the oil and left a string of ghost towns across the country. Even where the miners treated the minerals themselves with a certain care they devastated neighboring resources. In California, where they practiced hydraulic mining for gold, prospectors washed untold tons of precious soil into the rivers, and ultimately into the sea. (Down to our own time, "gypsy" strip miners gouge the land for the wealth it contains, then leave behind the gaping holes and heaps of debris that go on oozing sulphuric acid and other pollutants like running sores.) Legislation helped only a little. The Minerals Leasing Act of 1920 further opened, through favorable leases, federal lands to mining interests, but included clauses that encouraged minimal conservation practices.

Forestry, chiefly because of Gifford Pinchot's influence, had moved boldly out ahead of most other areas of resource management. For at least a decade after he left government, Pinchot's National Conservation Association served as an efficient watchdog on government forest policy; and as early as 1911 helped to push through Congress one of the most important resource bills of the time. This was the Weeks Law, sponsored by Representative John Wingate Weeks of Massachusetts, who served later as Secretary of War under Presidents Harding and Coolidge.

Weeks, though his bill aimed at the protection of forests on non-government land, nicely evaded constitutional pitfalls by tying it to the preservation of navigable streams. Although Weeks was not able to justify the purchase of these lands on the basis of public improvements or national defense, he felt that the bill's provisions fulfilled the government's responsibility to protect forests in threatened watersheds. The courts ultimately agreed. Congress, by passing his bill (under pressure from Pinchot and other conservationists), enabled the government to buy lands in the East for inclusion in the national forests and laid the basis for federal-state cooperation in forest fire protection.

Pinchot's lobbying forays were designed to hold earlier gains as well as to fight for new ones. For years he helped the handful of congressmen friendly to the conservation cause to fend off attempts by the power companies to remove the fees charged for permits on water power sites. Another more immediate threat was the movement within Congress to cut the appropriations for the Forest

Service, including those for fire fighting. Pinchot had long before laid the foundation for a successful defense in this area by the enormous favorable publicity he had generated for the service while he was Forester. After he left the government, the Deity seemed to lend a hand; a spate of damaging fires swept the great Western forests. The newspapers recounted the heroic measures taken by rangers ("Pinchot's boys") in fighting the fires. In Idaho a forest ranger named Pulaski was trapped by a raging fire. A former miner, he located an abandoned mine shaft and led his crew into it for protection. As the flames approached, he soaked one blanket after another in water from a pool he found in the mine and held them across the entrance to keep out the flames and smoke.

"The men were about to break out, crazed with the intense heat," Harry Slattery, Pinchot's aide, wrote, "but the Forest ranger with gun in hand kept them back. The fire rushed over the shaft and in its wake the men were all saved. But the intense heat so affected the Forest ranger, who stood like Horatio at the Bridge, that he lost his eyesight."

While the Forest Service maintained the *esprit de corps* that Pinchot had breathed into its acolytes, it did not quite function as the divine instrument of conservation he had hoped for. As it aged, the Service (like other worldly institutions) smelled increasingly of mortality. Its unalloyed purpose as a resource development agency became somewhat diluted following the success of the National Park Service, which forced foresters to put some of their own lands at the disposal of a public hungry for recreation. Pinchot, on the outside looking in, grumbled, but was diverted by more fundamental conflicts over oil and water power.

So the Forest Service sometimes moved in directions he had not foreseen. Younger foresters were making their voices heard within the service, and these voices called on their superiors to preserve wilderness values in the national forests that had nothing to do with economic exploitation. Among these younger men was Aldo Leopold.

In a sense Leopold followed Pinchot's path to professional excellence, yet he brought to his work another dimension of passion. He grew up hunting and fishing and observing wild things along the Mississippi River in Iowa. Although not of the "patrician" class like Pinchot, Leopold's parents were well-to-do, and sent him to the best schools—in this case Lawrenceville School and Yale. His enthusiasm for the outdoors persuaded Leopold to enter the Yale Forest School (endowed by the elder Pinchots) in 1908. From there he proceeded inevitably into the Forest Service.

Here was a forester who could see not only the trees, but the forest and all the land around it as well. A serious illness, which almost cost him his life, heightened Leopold's sense of man's littleness when confronted by the natural world. He saw man's destruction of that world not as a mystic does, but as a scientist and a sociologist.

"If in a city we had six vacant lots available to the youngsters of a certain neighborhood for playing ball," he said, "it might be 'development' to build houses on the first, and the second, and the third, and the fourth, and even on the fifth, but when we build houses on the last one, we forget what houses are for. The sixth house would not be development at all, but rather stupidity."

He carried this analogy over into the Southwestern wilderness where he was stationed. "It was here that I first clearly realized that land is an organism," he said, "that all my life I had seen only sick land, whereas here was a biota* still in perfect aboriginal health."

Leopold was a forester evolving into an ecologist. He detected all the strands in the web of life, their fragility as well as their links to each other, and man's fundamental dependence on the whole. But his concern went beyond man's arrogance and stupidity in his relationship to his environment; he saw the problem ultimately in ethical terms.

"A system of conservation based solely on economic self-interest is hopelessly lopsided," Leopold said. "It tends to ignore, and thus eventually to eliminate, many elements in the land community that lack commercial value, but that are (as far as we know) essential to its healthy functioning. It assumes, falsely, I think, that the economic parts of the biotic clock will function without the uneconomic parts. . . . All ethics so far evolved rest upon a single premise: that the individual is a member of a community of interdependent parts. His instincts prompt him to compete for his place in that community, but his ethics prompt him also to cooperate (perhaps in order that there may be a place to compete for). The land ethic simply enlarges the boundaries of the community to

*The total of all a region's plant and animal life, considered as an ecological entity. See Leopold's description of the prairie biota, page 258.

include soils, waters, plants, and animals, or collectively: the land
. . . A thing is right when it tends to preserve the integrity, stability,
and beauty of the biotic community. It is wrong when it tends
otherwise."

Accordingly Leopold put into practice his belief that wilderness
was of considerable scientific value as well as a potential source
of board feet for the market. In 1924 he and his associates in the
Forest Service designated in New Mexico the first of the "wilderness
type" areas in the national forests. The idea was to preserve forests
of exceptional beauty and interest; these areas were reviewed from
time to time by the service to see if they measured up to "wilderness
quality." If it was determined that they did, they were classified
by such terms as "primitive," "wild," and "wilderness" areas and
preserved for recreation. Otherwise they were opened to the ax.
The New Mexico forest, which later became the Gila Wilderness
Area, was the first of eighty such areas set aside by the Forest
Service during the 1920s and 1930s.

Unfortunately Leopold's spirit did not spread among the mass
of foresters. Selective logging was preached by the service, but its
practice very often fell under the definition given it by conservationist David R. Brower: "First you select a forest, and then
you log it." Brower went on to characterize the man wielding the
ax. "The sawlog forester, you find after painful study," Brower
added, "is the man who somehow thought that the College of
Forestry was a trade school. He majored in Machinery Against
the Land and learned almost nothing about the mechanism of land
. . . There are very many of him and he does not see the forest
for the sawlogs."

Pinchot felt that this sinister figure represented the entire private
timber industry in the United States. He charged that the industry
was bent on destroying the forests through its neglect of sound
forestry, and during the early 1920s he repeatedly called on Congress to regulate timber cutting on private lands; to support such
regulation he suggested that Congress prohibit the interstate shipment of wood and other forest products harvested in violation of
Forest Service directions.

The bitterness with which Pinchot campaigned against industry
practices caused a split between him and William B. Greeley, who
was then the Chief of the Forest Service. Pinchot complained that
Greeley was simply a dupe of the timber interests. Whatever the

extent of Greeley's faith in the industry's ways, however, he shared Pinchot's general concern for the forests, and supported the idea of further federal legislation. To his way of thinking, fire, not foresters, was the problem.

"Stop the forest fires," he told Congress.

Congress responded in 1924 by passing the Clarke-McNary Act, which provided for cooperative plans to enable the Forest Service to work closely with state and private foresters in planting trees and protecting them against fires. Further legislation in 1928 provided for cooperation among those three groups in forest research. This has always been a controversial area. Congress is traditionally reluctant to pay for research that does not show immediate results; and some of the Forest Service's critics have claimed that its leaders often publish low estimates of available timber supplies in order to extract from Congress more generous appropriations for research.

Whatever the truth of these charges, it is certain that the service has directed its research less toward imaginative projects than toward those that would confirm its traditional policies. Ashley L. Schiff* has traced the distortion of its research to the service's early days when Pinchot needed spectacular achievements to persuade Congress of the need for a strong Forest Service. The shrewd publicist and his assistants seized on the ability of forest cover to retard the runoff of surface water, blowing it up out of all proportion to reality. It became their position, staunchly defended, that forests were able to prevent floods. The Forest Service expended a great deal of time and effort in trying to prove this, even in the face of disinterested research that showed otherwise.

"An intensive campaign of public education, designed to arouse an apathetic nation to the dire consequences of profligacy, unknowingly carried these erroneous notions into the hinterlands," Schiff writes. "Evangelism and the appeal to 'mob psychology' won converts to 'the cause.' In so doing, it created a commitment to promulgated doctrine, and this inevitably impaired the ability of the service to retract statements later demonstrated by research to be inaccurate . . . Publicity is more than a mere tool of the administrator. Invariably, publicity becomes an inextricable part of the policy that it is intended to serve."

More disinterested research had shown that a watershed's forests

*See Ashley L. Schiff, *Fire and Water: Scientific Heresy in the Forest Service,* Cambridge, 1962.

retard the flow of surface runoff chiefly over limited areas and during times of limited rainfall. Under heavier rainfall forest soils quickly become saturated, permitting water to run off them almost as freely as it does from a concrete parking lot. A watershed's forests are unable to prevent major floods. The Forest Service came around only very slowly to this truth and the need for additional safeguards such as dams to retard flood waters.

Yet the Forest Service's mistakes were those born of enthusiasm or misinformation, and the forests in general escaped disaster. No one took responsibility for the land itself. The ruined soils of the East had imparted no sense of caution to the settlers as they made their way onto the richer lands of the West, the complexity of which was described by Aldo Leopold:

"The black prairie was built by the prairie plants, a hundred distinctive species of grasses, herbs and shrubs; by the prairie fungi, insects, and bacteria; by the prairie mammals and birds, all inter-locked in one humming community of cooperations and competi-tions, one biota. The biota, through ten thousand years of living and dying, burning and growing, preying and fleeing, freezing and thawing, built that dark and bloody ground we call prairie."

Farmers tore into the rich sod with their plows, pushing westward into ever drier country, depriving the land of the grass cover that held it together. The rains they had counted on seldom came to wet down the displaced earth. Drying, the upturned land became vulnerable to every wind that swept the unobstructed plains. The topsoil that gave the land its life swirled off in dense clouds that blotted out the sun. When the rains came, as they sometimes did in torrents, the uprooted soils lay at the mercy of what once had been a benign, quickening force. The land became scoured by ever-deepening gullies and, in Leopold's words, "rivers washing the future into the sea."

Ranchers, who despised both sheepmen and homesteaders, con-tributed to the destruction of the land. It has been said that grass is a rancher's product, and livestock his manner of marketing it. In that case ranchers failed utterly to manage their primary crop. In their greed they turned out to the range far more cattle than it could carry. The foraging cattle devoured or trampled the food grasses, depriving the land of its natural cover and opening the way for an invasion of mesquite and other pest species which flourish in dessicated soil. The vegetation could not recover in the hot, dry summers of the West.

An ecological disaster was set in motion: rodents, rabbits, and other small mammals, which seldom build up to large numbers in healthy grasslands, invaded the weedy landscape and undermined the soil; the rodents themselves attracted coyotes, which entered the range to feed on their exploding populations, then turned their predatory eyes on the nearby livestock. The ranchers inevitably called on the government for broader rodent and predator control programs, blandly ignoring their own guilt in creating the problem in the first place.

Ignorance lay at the root of the land disasters which overtook the United States in the 1930s. The men who worked the land, whether farmers or ranchers, were largely untutored in the principles of their stewardship, depending for their success on folkways that, more often than not, already had stripped the lands in which these dubious practices had had their origins. "Trial and error" was the settlers' technique. They used up the land, then moved on to more fertile ground until they had used up the frontier itself.

Even the "experts" were paralyzed. Sir Richard Livingstone once defined a technician as "a man who understands everything about his job except its ultimate purpose and its place in the order of the universe." And so, as another observer has said, the experts watched from their ivory towers as gullies ran through ineptly farmed fields, "cutting right up to the rim of college campuses held intact and comely under trees and sod." The value of stable land cover did not occur to them. The stage was set as the old order vanished in the accession to power of Franklin D. Roosevelt.

Few men have brought to the presidency so strong a love for the land as the second Roosevelt. From early manhood he was obsessed by the strength of trees, "the lungs of our land, purifying our air and giving fresh strength to our people." He saw the good life against a natural setting—more particularly against the greenness he had helped to create at his beloved Hyde Park, high above the majestic Hudson. (The geological wonders of the great Western parks did not touch his heart, as they did those of his cousin, Theodore; before the Grand Canyon, Franklin could only stare and turn away: "It looks dead. I like my green trees at Hyde Park better. They are alive and growing.") As governor of New York he actively promoted reforestation throughout the state.

Roosevelt expressed his conservation philosophy during his acceptance speech at the 1932 Democratic Convention. "Let us use common sense and business sense," he told his audience, "and just as one example, we know that a very hopeful and immediate means of relief, both for the unemployed and for agriculture, will come from a wide plan of the converting of many millions of acres of marginal and unused land into timberland through reforestation. There are tens of millions of acres east of the Mississippi River alone in abandoned farms, in cutover lands, now growing up in worthless brush. Why, every European nation has a definite land policy and has had for generations. We have none. Having none, we face a future of soil erosion and timber famine. It is clear that economic foresight and immediate employment march hand in hand in the call for the reforestation of these vast areas."

In his attempt to restore America's economic health Roosevelt used conservation as one of the building blocks of the New Deal. Conservation meant, to Franklin as to Theodore, the wise use of the nation's natural resources. Though Gifford Pinchot was not a member of the New Deal, many other Progressive Republicans supported Roosevelt in his campaign against Hoover (Harry Slattery organized a "League of Progressives for Roosevelt" during the 1932 campaign) and they played an important role in his administration. One of Roosevelt's first acts in the White House was to help George Norris secure the passage of the bill which established the Tennessee Valley Authority. But no Progressive Republican was more visible or more vocal during the Roosevelt years than Harold Le Claire Ickes.

Blunt and outspoken ("on only one other occasion have I tasted worse champagne," he complained once after a White House party), Ickes had been a newspaperman and a lawyer in Chicago. He had also been involved in reform politics, mostly behind the scenes, for a good many years before Roosevelt chose him as his Secretary of the Interior. If he had had no broad experience in natural resource problems (few Interior Secretaries have) Ickes was nonetheless bold, imaginative, and utterly obsessed by his own wisdom and probity. He threw himself into his new job with the euphoria which Roosevelt breathed into so many of the men he had gathered around him at the outset of his Great Experiment.

"It's more than a New Deal," Ickes exclaimed. "It's a new world. People feel free again. They can breathe naturally. It's like quitting a morgue for the open woods."

He assembled in Interior some of the familiar faces of the early conservation movement. He named Slattery his Personal Assistant (Slattery later became Under Secretary of the Interior). He also called back to service Louis R. Glavis who, as a young employee in the General Land Office, had uncovered the irregularities in the Guggenheim Alaskan claims that set off the Ballinger-Pinchot explosion almost twenty-five years before. It was a heartwarming episode except that, like many fairy-tale dénouements, it was all too sugary to last. Ickes found Glavis's enthusiastic investigations too self-righteous even for his own decorous taste, and they soon had a falling out.

But Ickes moved with relentless singlemindedness against many of the evils then current in American natural resource policy. The deteriorating Western range was one object of his concern. He supported legislation to reform the government's policy toward grazing on the public domain. When the wealthy cattlemen fought this legislation, Ickes moved in and threatened to indict them because they had fenced and appropriated vast stretches of public lands for their own use. The cattlemen dropped their opposition and the Taylor Grazing Act of 1934 came into being; the act closed the public domain to homesteading and established a program to regulate grazing in "districts," thus preventing erosion and the other disastrous consequences of overgrazing. The Grazing Service created to administer the act was snatched out of the Department of Agriculture's grasp by Ickes' deft political maneuvering, and the old interagency war began again.

Ickes envisioned Interior as a many-armed Department of Conservation that would gather all of the government's natural resource agencies under its jurisdiction. At one time, several years later, it seemed that with Roosevelt's active assistance the new department would become a reality; but the President had more important fish to fry, and Ickes never realized his dream. Meanwhile he reached for that prize coveted by so many of his predecessors at Interior— the United States Forest Service.

The battle was, as usual, fiercely fought. Ickes wanted the Forest Service not for personal gain but to fulfill his boundless sense of his own unimpeachable public benefaction. Forests, he believed, simply *belonged* in Interior. Henry A. Wallace, Secretary of Agriculture under Roosevelt and son of that Henry C. Wallace who had struggled against a similar onslaught by Albert B. Fall during the Harding administration, gallantly defended his preserve. Inevitably,

Gifford Pinchot rushed into the fray to take issue with Ickes, his old friend and comrade in the Progressive movement. Pinchot revived all those old fears about Interior's motives that had haunted conservationists for decades and which Ickes was trying to bury.

Ickes reacted first with only minor annoyance at Pinchot's defense of his old service, and then with increasing hostility. As he mulled it over, the Interior Secretary became convinced that Pinchot, that "Lot's wife of the conservation movement," had all along been a thorn in the side of progress. Increasingly he began to sympathize with Ballinger and other public servants who had felt the sting of Pinchot's righteous wrath. Finally, unable to contain himself any longer, Ickes wrote an article for *The Saturday Evening Post* called "Not Guilty," in which he revived the Ballinger-Pinchot controversy, reasoned that Pinchot was the unprovoked aggressor, and described Ballinger as the "American Dreyfus." The article made lively reading, but did little for Ickes' cause, which expired like that of his predecessors.

While Ickes hatched plots in the Interior building, Roosevelt was moving ahead with conservation plans of his own. With the banking crisis under control after the early days of his administration, and Prohibition demolished, the new President turned his attention to his cherished ideas about reforestation. He had a dream, and that dream consisted of a million young men, marching shoulder to shoulder into the forests to rejuvenate the despoiled American land; since America's youth was similarly despoiled by the great Depression, Roosevelt's dream reached into many areas of national recovery.

"I think I'll go ahead with this," said Roosevelt, "just the way I did on beer."

The President thereupon sent a message to Congress asking it to create the Civilian Conservation Corps. The legislation proved to be one of the most ambitious conservation projects in history, providing useful work and training for unemployed young men. The opposition, of course, was instant and violent. Even (one might instead say, naturally) organized labor got its back up, one labor leader telling Congress that the scheme "smacks, as I see it, of fascism, of Hitlerism, of a form of sovietism."

Nevertheless Congress quickly authorized the CCC in the spring of 1933, and within thirty days the first camp opened in Virginia. Other camps sprang up in national parks and forests, and on many state lands. Soon two thousand camps, each housing two hundred young men, were in full operation. The young men received $30 a month, most of which they were required to send home to their dependents. During the CCC's existence, two and a half million Americans served in the program, thus providing help for many of the people hardest hit by the Depression—an estimated eight million young men and their dependents.

The CCC workers themselves, mostly city boys, thrived in their unaccustomed environment. As they increased their skills, the land blossomed: they worked on forest planting and protection, soil conservation, recreational development, range rehabilitation, flood control, and other projects vital to conservation. They planted 3,000,000,000 trees, built 1,000,000 miles of roads and trails, 85,000 miles of telephone lines, 4000 fire towers, and 100,000 small bridges and buildings. These city-raised young men quickly became skilled at the dangerous work of fighting forest fires.

"In the early days of the CCC," a regional forester in Montana said, "the general feeling throughout the field units here was that it required three enrollees to equal one hired firefighter. Today the reverse is true. Most supervisors feel that they would sooner have one organized twenty-five-enrollee unit than fifty or seventy-five men recruited on the street. It actually is heartwarming to see how efficiently these units operate from the time they leave their base camp until they return."

It was not to be expected that resourcefulness always would appear in equal measure among the young men confronted by a great new experience. Conrad L. Wirth, who worked with the CCC and later became Director of the National Park Service, has recalled some of the program's early difficulties:

"We had one camp in Yellowstone that came from the Bronx, New York. It was a two hundred-man camp. The camp had been back in the remote section of Yellowstone for barely two weeks, when the superintendent got a call for help from the camp commander, who was a reserve officer in the Army. He had a riot on his hands.

"The superintendent sent some rangers in to help the commanding officer and in short order they had the boys quieted down again. The investigation routed out about nineteen boys and they were shipped back to the Bronx. The only thing they could get out of these boys was that they just could not stand the quiet nights and the coyotes howling . . . It is funny, but it is pathetic. They had to get back to the concrete, the noise, the subways."

There is no doubt, however, that the CCC was one of Roosevelt's most successful projects. "The CCC left no bad taste," Hubert Humphrey has said. "Even the bitterest opponent of the New Deal has to admit that the CCC was a sound investment in both people and the land." Forests, trails, bridges, and other tangible reminders of the CCC's brief existence survived the neglect of World War II and the indifferent years that followed, supplying a base on which a later generation was able to build. "I feel almost as if I owned that land," one city boy said of his experience. "Some day when those trees I planted grow large I want to go back and look at them."

The CCC was a crisis project, doomed once the country seemed to be regaining its economic balance. With the onset of war the CCC lost its glamour, and Congress killed it (against Roosevelt's recommendation) in 1942.

Out of the crisis of the 1930s there appeared a tall, broad-shouldered Southerner with a vision and a fund of knowledge sufficient to create a more enduring formula for the land's rejuvenation. His name was Hugh Hammond Bennett. Like Pinchot and Steve Mather, "Big Hugh" was a superb salesman of his own brand of reform. Unfortunately, he possessed neither the wealth nor the high connections to win a respectful hearing for his views, and they languished in comparative obscurity for many years. It was the nation's loss.

Bennett had grown up on a farm in North Carolina's Pee-Dee Basin. His earliest memories were of men whose lives ebbed away under the burden of cultivating wornout land. After his graduation from the University of North Carolina, where he studied geology, Bennett became a government worker in the Bureau of Soils. In the early years of this century he surveyed soils in the South, looking at them with a fresh eye and describing for the first time the destructive phenomenon of "sheet erosion." He carefully documented this process—the erosive action of water as it removed inch after inch of precious topsoil from the cultivated land. (A later agronomist described it as "stealthily removing topsoil as sheets of paper are taken from a pad.") Bennett noted the soil held intact by forest cover in adjoining plots of land, while that which the farmer counted on for his livelihood disappeared. "The red, yellow, and black colors of floodwater running away to the sea are no reflection from the sky," he said of the Southern countryside. "The color of such floodwater is produced by the color of the soil material in suspension. This material comes from the surface of the ground, the best part of our fields, and thus impoverishes our land."

For years Bennett's was a voice crying in the agricultural waste-land as he poured contempt on the American farmer's unbounded ignorance of the land to which he was tied. He saw America's wealth washed off the land with its organic matter, and the vital plant-growing minerals it contained leached away to the sea. Yet slowly his name became known among people who cared for the land. The Union of South Africa, plagued by erosion, commissioned him to devise a remedial plan; Bennett was able to put into practice many of his theories of sound agricultural practice, including plowing the land along its contours (rather than in undeviating rows through which rainwater eventually rushes unchecked with its pilfered burden of topsoil). In South Africa, too, he put into practice the idea of conducting demonstrations of these conservation techniques for farmers in each district.

He finally became a prophet in his own land. "Erosion probably modifies the character of the earth's surface more than any other natural force," he wrote in 1927. "Volcanoes, earthquakes, tidal waves, and tornadoes modify the earth but little in comparison. Over the United States erosion on one day moves soil material exceeding the weight of all the car loadings and all the freight entering and leaving the ports of North America for a period of twelve months."

Bennett was a master of such comprehensible descriptions of the ills he attacked. His stature slowly increased within the government. After more than a quarter of a century his message made its greatest impact on an administration sorely in need of help as the great drought of 1934 threatened to wipe out the early economic gains of the New Deal. Indeed, there was a link between man's abuse of the natural world and the financial catastrophe that overtook him. "In a sense," Stewart Udall has said, "the great Depression was a bill collector sent by nature, and the dark tidings were borne on every silt-laden stream and every dust cloud that darkened the horizon."

The drought dried the thin soils of the overworked West to a fine powder. When the storms came the very land itself seemed airborne. Great clouds of dust blackened the sky so that in Kansas it was said the visibility was sometimes cut to three hundred yards at midday. "Blown like the driven snow," Franklin Roosevelt said, the earth was transported thousands of miles across the continent, and then sometimes hundreds more out across the ocean; parts of the American Midwest were whirled through salt air to be deposited on the decks of ships at sea. "Okies" fled the Dust Bowl in their battered Fords, joining the fruit tramps and stoop labor in the illusory promised land of California.

Alerted to just such a storm Bennett purposely delayed a hearing before a congressional committee that was to consider an appropriation for soil conservation. Then, while Bennett read his remarks on the destruction of the land, the sky in Washington darkened almost supernaturally, and the congressmen watched in awe as the wind-driven particles of Western America swept across Capitol Hill. They briskly appropriated the needed money.

Harold Ickes, quick to grasp the importance of soil conservation and aware of Bennett's reputation, plucked him out of the Department of Agriculture to direct the new Soil Erosion Service in the Department of the Interior. It was one of the few positive steps, and a short-lived one at that, that Ickes took in his campaign to build a giant Department of Conservation. Bennett had nearly a free hand in applying his ideas about soil and water conservation. He was a superb salesman, writing articles about the need for soil conservation, organizing demonstration districts, and carrying his message to Congress. He used plain language (couched in a drawl varying in intensity with the origin of his audience) at the many committee hearings he dominated, but his presentations were both entertaining and instructive. Among the props Bennett brought to these hearings were jars of fine honey produced from legumes or other effective ground cover he advocated for use on farms, or fence posts that had to be imported to a land denuded of its trees. One of his favorite demonstrations consisted of pouring water on the tabletop in the committee room, and then on an absorbent towel; the difference in "runoff" converted more than a few listeners to Bennett's ideas about the value of planting protective cover on the land.

In 1935 Congress passed the Soil Conservation Act, changing the name of Bennett's agency to the Soil Conservation Service and ordering it to carry out soil and water conservation programs on a national scale. The Act transferred both the service and its director from Interior to the Department of Agriculture. The deed was done while Ickes was away from Washington on vacation. (He charged afterward that Agriculture Secretary Wallace had told him he looked run down and solicitously suggested he take a few days off from the grind; Ickes, not suspecting treachery, had complied.)

But it was "Big Hugh" Bennett, not Harold Ickes, who revolutionized the American farmer's approach to his land. Under Bennett the Soil Conservation Service became a prominent force in the rural landscape, and helped to shape that landscape for the better. The dams it built plugged gullies on the land; the streams it straightened restored the banks they had eroded; and the fences it built allowed farmers to restrict their livestock to more productive pastures.

"Agriculture is an exciting profession," Louis Bromfield, the novelist and gentleman-farmer, once wrote, "one of the most exciting on earth," and he gave Bennett credit for reviving that excitement among farmers. Bennett was one of the few conservationists who was able to tell his fellow Americans how to use *their* land—and make them take notice.

24

Of Muskrats and Birdwatchers

I

One morning in 1932 Mrs. Rosalie Barrow Edge of New York City opened an envelope containing an annual financial statement and various other printed matter sent to her by the National Association of Audubon Societies, of which she was a life member. In her customary fashion she began to study the financial statement with great care, as a stern and suspicious parent might go over the report card brought home by a recalcitrant little student. Under the classification described as "Rentals" she came across an item for more than $100,000 that piqued her curiosity. She made up her mind to find out more about it, and when she did she set off an explosion that shook the Audubon Society to its heels and very nearly destroyed it.

Mrs. Edge, whose husband was a wealthy New York stockbroker, already had earned a formidable reputation among conservationists. She did not fit that common stereotype of a female birdwatcher as "a little old lady in tennis shoes." Indeed, *The New Yorker* once described her as dressing "with conservative elegance for office and for society, wearing black satin dresses, and hats with imposing superstructures compounded of things like bristles, fruit, flowers,

nets and buckles"; of everything, it might be added, but plumes.
For Mrs. Edge had transferred her passionate interest in feminism
to birds one summer during World War I when she began to notice
their lively and colorful forms about her country home in Rye, New
York. She carried this interest back to the city with her in the fall.

From that point she proceeded along a path taken by thousands
of urban birdwatchers. She watched for birds in Central Park,
gossiped with fellow "birders," and eventually became interested
in the problems of survival that confronted birds and other wild
creatures in a generally hostile world. Mrs. Edge differed from most
of her newfound colleagues, however, in that she possessed wealth
as well as an inclination to spend it liberally in support of her
passionately held beliefs.

"I have exhausted a large part of a once considerable fortune
in this work," she told a reporter who had asked about her conservation activities, "and while I do not regret one cent of it, I am
now in comparatively straitened circumstances. For example, I need
a new coat, but I propose to spend that money on a pamphlet about
coyotes."

In pamphleteering Rosalie Edge found an outlet for both her
sympathies and her outrage. She readily agreed when a zoologist,
who felt that his official ties kept him from speaking out on controversial matters, approached her with the proposition that she publish under her own name certain material that he would channel
to her; asked what sort of material she would be willing to sign,
she replied, "In a general way, anything."

Like most zealots, Rosalie Edge shunned permanent collabo-
ration and fought many of her most spirited battles with her former
allies. She had joined the Audubon Society early in her birdwatching days, but became increasingly disenchanted with that organization's efforts on behalf of bird protection. She detected weakness
in each conference with the enemy, treachery in each compromise.
She attended the Audubon Society's annual meeting in the manner
of an angry stockholder, charging mismanagement and dereliction
of duty by the society's leaders. Members crowded to these once
tame affairs, anticipating the spectacle of Mrs. Edge in action. After
one such tumultuous meeting at the American Museum of Natural
History, Audubon President T. Gilbert Pearson complained that
she "had spoiled the meeting and there was no time to show the
moving picture which was to have been the feature of the morning."
Pearson retaliated by refusing to mail her a group photograph taken

of the assembled members. William T. Hornaday, however, sent her a message of encouragement and told her that she had "the courage of a lion."

Mrs. Edge shared Hornaday's distaste for the Bureau of Biological Survey, in part because of its refusal to set lower bag limits for waterfowl hunting. (She liked to refer to that federal agency as "the Bureau of Destruction and Extermination.") By 1932 she was certain she had unearthed proof of the Biological Survey's treacherous collusion with the Audubon Society.

One can only imagine her grim satisfaction as the details slowly unfolded themselves under her relentless questioning. Those innocuous "rentals" she had noticed on the Audubon Society's financial statement proved to be euphemisms masking receipts paid to the society by muskrat trappers; and further, the trappers had plied their trade on the grounds of the society's huge Paul J. Rainey Wildlife Sanctuary in Louisiana. The society's receipts of $100,000 represented its share from the sale of 289,940 pelts of muskrats, mink, racoons, and opossums trapped in the sanctuary during the preceding three years.

The whole affair seemed innocent enough to the society's board of directors, which was operating under the principles of game management prevailing at the time. The Rainey Sanctuary harbored thousands of wintering waterfowl, including the blue goose, a color phase of the lesser snow goose that was considered comparatively rare around 1930. On the other hand, muskrats abounded in the sanctuary's marshes, feeding on plants preferred by the blue goose. Two prominent officials of the Biological Survey happened to be serving on the Audubon Society's board of directors. They recommended that the society reduce the muskrats' numbers by allowing the local "marsh men" to come in and trap them.

The board members accepted the plan because it promised to solve two nagging problems at once; the food supply of the blue goose would be preserved and the society's treasury, depleted during the Depression, would receive a welcome infusion from its share of the proceeds. It was a costly mistake. Rosalie Edge appeared at the next annual meeting, wrapped in a stunning mink coat, and demanded that the board put a stop to the practice at once.

"Mrs. Edge, why are you so concerned about the muskrat?" one of the directors asked. "Look what you're wearing on your back."

She might have answered that, at all events, she was not wearing an animal trapped by a conservation organization on a place called a wildlife sanctuary; but she refused to be diverted to personal issues. She repeated her demand, and also asked that the assistant treasurer stop hiding blood money under the guise of "rentals." The board rejected both of her demands.

She was back again the following year, brandishing a resolution asking the society to stop the practice of trapping muskrats and other animals on the sanctuary for a period of three years in order to observe the effect on the wintering wildfowl. When the resolution was defeated she asked that the society substitute box traps (in which the animals could be caught alive and transported to other areas) for the lethal steel traps then in use. The board members, calling the idea impractical, would have none of it.

Mrs. Edge decided to take her case to the society's rank and file. She prepared pamphlets that told her side of the story: "The deed of gift which created the Rainey Sanctuary defines the word 'sanctuary' as 'a place where the killing, trapping or destroying by any means of wild birds and wild animals shall not be permitted' . . . At the last annual meeting of the National Association of Audubon Societies efforts were made to induce the directors to abandon the use of the inhumane steel-trap on the Sanctuary. No progress was made. The only step forward during the past year is that orders have been given, so we are told on reliable authority, that the mink traps on the sanctuary shall no longer be baited with birds, as in the past."

With a crusader's eye, Mrs. Edge illustrated her pamphlets in a manner that would make them most effective in the hands of people concerned about wild creatures. "It looked awful," says one of the Audubon Society's officials who remembers those days. "She printed pictures of muskrats caught in steel traps, which were not very pleasant." After her pamphlets were printed, she asked the society for a mailing list of its members. The society stubbornly refused. Again, Rosalie Edge was not to be put off. She hired a prominent New York lawyer to bring court action against the Audubon Society and force it to disgorge its mailing list. A rather bitter legal battle ensued, during which the society referred to Mrs. Edge as "a common scold." The court decided in her favor. Armed with the mailing list, she distributed her pamphlets to the society's members, many of whom reacted with indignation and withdrew their financial support.

"She decimated the membership in a short time," an Audubon official recalls. "People dropped off like proverbial flies."

The Audubon Society's board of directors backtracked hastily, and terminated its muskrat program. The blue goose apparently suffered no ill effects from the belated decision, for its numbers increased, just as those of Audubon members declined. Rosalie Edge, triumphant and with her Audubon Life Membership intact, proceeded to other good causes, including the establishment of the Olympic National Park in Washington and the Hawk Mountain Sanctuary in Pennsylvania (to both of which she contributed vital time and money).

She died at the age of eighty-five in 1962. Only a few days before her death she flew to the Audubon Society's annual convention in Corpus Christi, Texas, where the resurgent membership gave her a standing ovation as she was led, smiling graciously, to her place on the dais. Time heals.

II

Rosalie Edge was something more than just a quaint character in an insignificant backwater of the conservation movement. She was an activist in an era of change; a radicalized amateur thrashing about among the autoanaesthetized professionals. Science and personal values were altering men's conception of those other creatures with which they share the planet. For one thing, in the light of harder scrutiny men were beginning to grow suspicious of the "moral" qualities they had tacked onto non-human things. Does the concept of "good animals" and "bad animals" play a valid part in the practices of game management? Zoologist Durward L. Allen recalls his grandmother's reaction when the dog next door killed her favorite cat.

"Oh, Lord," she exclaimed in frustration, "why can't they be *nice?*"

More experienced naturalists than Dr. Allen's grandmother revealed similar confusion. Theodore Roosevelt, describing a cougar hunt on the rim of the Grand Canyon, spoke of his prey as "the big horse killing cat, the destroyer of the deer, the lord of stealthy murder, facing his doom with a heart both craven and cruel." Roosevelt was simply echoing the West's boiling hatred of predatory birds and mammals. J. Frank Dobie wrote of a Texas rancher who would saw off the lower jaw of a coyote caught in his trap, then turn the helpless beast loose so that he might have the pleasure of watching his dogs tear it to pieces.

"Crow shoots" and "jay shoots" were popular pastimes not many years ago. In the 1920s William T. Hornaday reported that a boy named Willie Hall of Watson, Saskatchewan, won a provincial competition by collecting 1445 eggs and 5216 legs of crows and magpies; the totals for all competitors in the contest reached 696,201 eggs and 239,901 legs. Hornaday reported the incident not to condemn the competitors but to comment that "in the face of these figures there can be no doubt about the necessity of eliminating a lot of those superfluous birds." Though he did not urge the destruction of predators with the all-encompassing invective favored by many of his fellow naturalists, Hornaday compiled his own little blacklist that included horned, barred, and screech owls, goshawks, Cooper's and sharp-shinned hawks, and golden eagles. Of the peregrine falcon, "another hated destroyer of game birds and song birds," he wrote: "Each bird of this species deserves treatment with a choke bore gun. First shoot the male and female, then collect the nest, the young or the eggs, whichever may be present. They all look best in collections."

But Rosalie Edge had focused on the real villain. Indiscriminate predator control programs had become national policy. As we have seen, the Biological Survey under Dr. C. Hart Merriam gradually had shifted its emphasis during the closing years of the nineteenth century from economic studies to "biological surveys."* The change in course was short-lived. Congress, believing that the Survey's work had become overly theoretical, summoned Merriam before the Committee on Agriculture in 1907 to discuss his work on the distribution of skunks.

"While we understand the significance that may on general principles be inherent in this odious representative of the animal kingdom," the committee's official report read, "we feel bound to concede that we are still uninformed as to his importance as a potential factor in producing results sought to be accomplished by the application of geographic distribution to and for the country at large."

Merriam left the Survey soon afterward to take up the study of

*See pages 39 and 40.

another maligned creature, the American Indian. His successor, writing in the *National Geographic* in 1908, indicated a return to the Survey's original function as an "economic" agency: "The pursuit of science solely for its own sake, however commendable it may be, is not the spirit that animates our government in its support of scientific research. In its aims and ambitions this is a practical age." Under pressure from agricultural and livestock groups the practical direction the Survey's work took was toward predator control. A great rabies epidemic among coyotes in 1915 prompted Congress to appropriate $125,000 for the Survey to begin "West-wide programs on a large scale. The Survey turned its interest to developing poisons and refining the practice of den-hunting (predators such as wolves and coyotes are most vulnerable in the spring, when control workers attack their dens with poison gases and other weapons and wipe out whole litters). Traps for mountain lions and bobcats were scented with oil of catnip.

Taking a leaf from the book of the Forest Service, its sister agency in the Department of Agriculture, the Biological Survey learned to compose an artful publicity release. Its yearbooks detailed "the many fiction-rivaling episodes having to do with the duels of wits between the Survey hunters and some more than ordinarily wily stock-killing wolves, coyotes, cougars, and bears." Other survey workers kept on good terms with Western stockmen. According to a Survey spokesman, one of its men told a meeting of the American National Livestock Association in Salt Lake City that "the Survey was not interested in a game conservation program that would interfere with grazing interests and the raising of livestock, and deplored the radical utterances of fool conservationists, with which he said the Survey did not agree." The Survey's supporters introduced a bill in the House of Representatives in 1918 to levy a tax of one dollar on every dog in the United States; the funds were to be earmarked for killing predators and "bad dogs." Although the idea tickled their fancy, the members of the Agriculture Committee raised doubts about the bill's constitutionality and killed it.

By convincing the stockmen and the public of their needs, the Biological Survey strengthened and enlarged its predator control programs. (These programs were carried out under the Survey's "Division of Economic Investigations.") In 1929 the Survey's official historian could report that predator control was "far and away the biggest part of the job the Survey does today . . . It has killed, and is killing, as many predatory animals as it could be expected to kill with the men and money at its disposal."

So wrapped up in the technique, if not the logic, of their control programs were the Survey's officials that they extended them to areas remote from any sheep or cow. They killed coyotes and mountain lions in mountains where no herds would ever penetrate, but the body counts of dead "varmints" sounded fine to congressmen back in Washington. The animals were "bad," and so they had to be killed.

Supplementing the Survey's programs were bounties, an age-old panacea for man's losses at the hands of wild animals. Bounties, generally varying with the size and alleged destructiveness of the bird or animal, often were established by the state legislatures. In 1917 the Territory of Alaska's legislature established a two-dollar bounty on the bald eagle, which was felt to be preying excessively on salmon; between that year and 1952, when the bounty was finally lifted, Alaskan bounty hunters collected 128,273 bald eagles. Maryland, in the six years between 1925 and 1930, paid bounties on 89,858 hawks. (The biological illiteracy of bounties and indiscriminate predator control programs continues in most states right down to our own day: for instance, Pheasants Unlimited, an organization of South Dakota sportsmen, presses a massive campaign against the fox, which its members feel threatens the local pheasant population. Through a variety of incentives and "education" programs, the organization has collected 124,344 dead foxes in recent years.)

But "fool conservationists" have not been impressed very often with the wisdom of predator control and bounty programs, whether they are conceived on the federal or state levels. Most of them concede the necessity for some kind of controls over birds and mammals harmful to man's economic interests. The trouble is, such programs generally are planned before any scientific evidence of the "villain's" depredations has been collected. Wherever bounties, for instance, are intensively studied they prove that they are not at all helpful to the game animals they were designed to protect, and even work against them.

Aldo Leopold was among the first to raise his voice against the wrong turn that "game management" had taken. From the chair in game management created for him at the University of Wis-

consin after he had left the Forest Service, Leopold spoke out
against the prevailing view of predators.

"When we attempt to say an animal is 'useful,' 'ugly,' or 'cruel,'"
Leopold reasoned, "we are failing to see it as part of the land. We
do not make the same error of calling a carburetor 'greedy.' We
see it as part of a functioning motor."

Well-intentioned people sought to protect certain species such
as deer and game birds by wiping out their predators. But Leopold
and other naturalists, carefully examining the evidence in the field,
noted that this sort of approach invited disaster. Given strict protection from mountain lions, coyotes, and other predators (including man), the mule deer herd at the game preserve on the Kaibab
Plateau in northern Arizona expanded in only a few years from 3000
animals to around 30,000. By 1924 the herd overbrowsed its range,
and both starvation and disease were beginning to set in.

Wildlife specialists had asked that the herd be substantially
reduced by public hunting, or even by a slaughter carried out by
federal workers. At this point the pendulum shifted to the opposite
extreme. Public opinion challenged the decision to kill these deer
on their preserve. Nature took its ruthless course: the deer grew
emaciated, stripped their range of every available bit of plantlife,
and then began to die by the thousands. Not until the 1930s did
men working in the young science of game management finally
put into effect the regulated hunting that controlled the size of the
herd, thus preventing the deer from destroying their range and
finally themselves.

As Leopold pointed out, the problem often began with the
destruction of the predators. In most cases, the predators do not
take the number of game animals and livestock suggested by local
folklore; wolves, coyotes, and foxes, for instance, subsist mainly on
small rodents. The deer and game birds they take are the "surplus
crop"—chiefly the weaker and the diseased (and therefore the most
unwary) individuals from the prey population; the survivors retain
those qualities of fleetness and wariness that made them excellent
game species in the first place.

But where man interfered unthinkingly, the familiar disasters
unrolled themselves. Leopold described the grim process:

"I have lived to see state after state extirpate its wolves. I have
watched the face of many a newly wolfless mountain, and seen the
south-facing slopes wrinkle with a maze of new deer trails. I have
seen every edible bush and seedling browsed, first to anemic desue-

tude, and then to death. I have seen every edible tree defoliated to the height of a saddlehorn. Such a mountain looks as if someone had given God a new pruning shears, and forbidden Him all other exercise. In the end the starved bones of the hoped-for deer herd, dead of its own too-much, bleach with the bones of the dead sage, or molder under the high-lined junipers.

"I now suspect that just as a deer herd lives in mortal fear of its wolves, so does a mountain live in mortal fear of its deer. And perhaps with better cause, for while a buck pulled down by wolves can be replaced in two or three years, a range pulled down by too many deer may fail of replacement in as many decades. So also with cows. The cowman who cleans his range of wolves does not realize that he is taking over the wolf's job of trimming the herd to fit the range. He has not learned to think like a mountain. Hence we have dust bowls, and rivers washing the future into the sea."

Leopold's vision slowly crystallized as orthodox game management principles. The realization crept up on thinking naturalists that the greatest enemy of both a farmer, stockman, and sportsman was not the carnivore but the herbivore. The deer and the mountain lion, the fox and the rabbit, lived together for countless thousands of years, and the prey flourished as well as the predator. It was only when man bumbled onto the scene and began removing the predators that the prey first expanded to unmanageable proportions (destroying man's crops and its own wild fare) and then succumbed to disease and starvation brought on by overpopulation.

The revolution in the professionals' attitude toward game, then, was ecological. They began to take into consideration not only the *true* relationship of predator and prey, but the relationship of both to the land. Wildlife flourishes only on land that is healthy and diverse. Game management people learned that it is sound economics to improve an animal's habitat rather than to try to exterminate its predators. The idea is not to raise the largest possible deer herd, but to confine the size of the herd to the land's "carrying capacity." No region is able to support deer (or any other species) beyond the capacity of its winter food supply. If predators and regulated hunting do not provide the necessary checks on that species' population, then starvation takes its toll.

Unfortunately game management practices continue to be dictated in many cases not by science but by politics. The federal predator control program survived even a massive administrative shakeup: during 1939–40 the Biological Survey was removed from the Department of Agriculture, and the Bureau of Fisheries from the Department of Commerce, to be unified under the new designation of the U.S. Fish and Wildlife Service in the Department of the Interior. But predator control workers in the West went right on telling stockmen how badly the control services were needed, and the stockmen went right on telling their congressmen how badly funds were needed to continue those services. Only in very recent years have the new agency's officials begun to alleviate the excesses of their predator control and "eradication" programs in the West.

The Biological Survey and its successor wrote a much brighter conservation chapter with their waterfowl programs. "Every head of wildlife still alive in this country is already artificialized, in that its existence is conditioned by economic forces," Aldo Leopold wrote in 1933. Under Jay N. "Ding" Darling, a former cartoonist and newspaperman, and later under Ira N. Gabrielson, the Biological Survey/Fish and Wildlife Service concentrated increasingly on finding a place for waterfowl within America's economic framework. Vast commercial drainage projects in the waterfowl's northern breeding grounds and coastal marshes left no room for ducks. To preserve a measure of suitable waterfowl habitat Darling and Gabrielson lobbied for more refuges; the growing chain of refuges, when added to the effect of lower bag limits, cut into the sharp decline in waterfowl numbers despite the rising numbers of hunters who came into the field every year. (Private refuges, especially those maintained by the Audubon Society, also played an important role in restoring several bird species.)

Congress, under pressure from hunters and conservationists, reluctantly began to include wildlife's welfare in more of its deliberations. It had often been swift to approve drainage projects that ruined prime waterfowl land. Now, in 1937, Congress passed the Pittman-Roberston Act which provided for a ten per cent excise tax on sporting arms and ammunition, the proceeds going to wildlife restoration projects around the country.

Congress was much slower in reacting to the depletion of the country's best fishing waters. The dam-building craze converted such excellent fishing grounds as the swift-running Columbia River into chains of placid lakes. Industrial pollution, domestic wastes, and pesticide runoff began to transform once-pure fishing streams into repulsive sewers. But it was not until 1952 that Congress passed the Dingell-Johnson Act (a counterpart of the Pittman-Robertson Act) which placed an excise tax on fishing tackle to raise funds for fisheries research and restoration.

The emphasis often shifted to the restoration of damaged habitat. Ironically there was a long and bitter internal struggle in Congress over the attempt to preserve that teeming reservoir of life, the Everglades. Man had done his best to "make something of it." The dark, rich soil invited farmers to drain the land and plant their crops; thousands rushed to this promised land.

"I feel that no more complete botch has been made of any project attempted within the lifetime of my readers," wrote Charles T. Simpson in *Florida Wild Life**. "Apparently no one knew whether the soil would produce, how much rain fell annually, and how much within a given time, or whether any system of canals they proposed to dig would carry off the waters in time to save the crops . . . Hundreds of poor, trusting people have gone into this land of promise, only to waste their little all and to find there was nothing more substantial than promises."

That dark, rich soil proved to be deficient in potash and phosphoric acid. The fruits and vegetables grown there consequently lacked sweetness and firmness, and when someone conceived the idea of turning the Everglades into the world's "sugar bowl" the scheme reached an abrupt end when the sugar itself lacked sweetness. Where the Everglades had been drained to start these ill-considered projects, the surrounding mats of vegetation dried out and great fires swept the "river of grass."

Under these circumstances the state of Florida was willing to turn a large stretch of the Everglades over to the federal government so that a national park could be established there. Bills to that effect were introduced in Congress, but many congressmen demurred. The struggle reached a climax early in Franklin D. Roosevelt's first administration, with congressional Republicans branding the land "worthless" and referring to "a snake swamp park." Many of these congressmen, so solicitous to real estate interests in their own states, contended that the whole idea had been conceived by Florida real estate men to increase the value of land in which they held an interest nearby.

With Roosevelt's support a bill to establish a park (consisting

*New York, 1932.

of 2,000,000 acres) was passed by Congress in 1934. No appropriations were included in the bill however, and it was not until after World War II that funding and planning were completed. Everglades National Park was dedicated by President Harry S. Truman in 1947.

III

The urge to give objects in nature a name has had an enormous (but understated) effect on the conservation movement in this country. Men and women who begin by wanting to give names to wildflowers, butterflies, or sea shells usually proceed to a greater awareness of the landscape in which they find these objects of their interest, and finally to a desire to preserve the landscape and its integral life. More often than not conservationists come to the cause through this single initial interest. Their earliest bibles are their field guides. If this is true, and I think it is, few proselytizers have drawn so many people to an active participation in conservation organizations as a writer-painter-photographer-lecturer-ornithologist named Roger Tory Peterson.

As a journalist, and as a conservationist who had approached the fold along the path described above, I sought out Peterson several years ago. I met him for the first time in the living room of his shingled, many-windowed home that stands on a hillside above the Connecticut River estuary. He is a tall, white-haired man with a long face and a diffident manner. He is also something of a paradox. A man who hates to get up early, who suffers from hay fever once he makes his way into the field, and who has no academic background in the sciences (his doctorates are honorary) is an unlikely candidate to be the world's most famous and influential ornithologist. Yet the shoe fits.

Peterson brings to his subject the intense concentration that is the hallmark of so many specialists. Books on birds lined the walls of the room. Cameras and lenses for photographing birds lay on the sofa. A canvas blind had been set up in the center of an adjoining room, where Peterson was able to remain concealed while taking pictures of birds that wandered near the large sliding glass door to the back yard. One end of the living room itself had been converted to glass, giving us an unobstructed view of the birds that flocked to the feeders. And in the basement there was a 600-pound freezer, holding for Peterson's further study the dead birds (ranging in size from chickadees to a swan) picked up by friends and neighbors.

Now, in his living room, Peterson spoke in a soft, husky voice of that fascination with birds that goes back to his early boyhood. He was born in 1908 in Jamestown, a furniture-manufacturing town in western New York where his father designed locks. Shy and moody, he shunned the games that occupied his classmates. Then he began to notice birds. He could only grope at an explanation.

"Birds seemed to me to reflect some kind of life force," he said. "Every outstanding ornithologist I know felt much the same way at a very early age."

Hand in hand with his interest in birds grew his skill in drawing. "Our teacher had us copy some of Louis Agassiz Fuertes' bird portraits and I became very good at it," he said. "After school I was interested in nothing else. I can remember going to the library when I was eleven years old and dragging home E. H. Eaton's *Birds of New York* in a little wagon. When I saw a new bird, it was a special day for me. I still know my grandmother's birthday because I saw my first cardinal on that date.

"Birds are associated with almost every event in my life. I suppose you could say I've even acquired my culture through birds. I went to the Acropolis primarily to see the rock nuthatches there. My memories of Versailles are bound up with a grasshopper warbler I saw near the reflecting pool."

Once, while he spoke, Peterson turned toward the broad window. The grating note that had caught his attention sounded again. "A rusty blackbird," he said. Getting to his feet, he walked to the window. "Yes, it's a rusty all right. See its white eye? It's always best to check the first time you hear a bird in the spring."

He came back to the sofa and sat down. "I can hear birds anywhere—over the conversation at a cocktail party, or in the midst of traffic in a city. Sometimes the birds on a sound track can spoil a movie for me. I remember some years ago sitting through a picture that was supposed to be set in the Vienna Woods. Then all of a sudden I heard a wrentit, which is confined to our West Coast, and the illusion was gone."

Peterson's school days ended when he was sixteen. He left Jamestown to study in New York City at the Art Students League and, later, at the National Academy of Design. To support himself he painted little Chinese figures on furniture in a Bronx factory. He moved ceaselessly from one furnished room to another in those days—in the Bronx, Brooklyn, the Harlem YMCA, and Greenwich Village.

"There were lively parties in the Village every weekend," Peterson recalled, "and a number of our group went on to become famous—people like Van Heflin, James Agee, and Vincente Minelli."

A companion of his during the 1920s, the late ornithologist Robert Porter Allen, once painted a sightly different picture. He recalled Peterson as a morose young man who hung out in a greasy-spoon restaurant near Sheridan Square, joylessly playing a pinball machine until the early hours of the morning. At parties, Peterson rarely spoke unless the conversation came around to birds.

"Roger was being consciously anti-social," Allen wrote to a friend years later, "which meant he was still maturing, still adjusting to a world he felt was all wrong. It was especially difficult for him, because he was farther away from it than most of us are to begin with."

Peterson's move to the city only increased his interest in birds. He was the first "outsider" to be admitted to the Bronx County Bird Club, a group of exceptional young men whose skill and enthusiasm in the field were to set a standard for birders all over the country. Joseph J. Hickey and Allan Cruickshank went on from the club to become outstanding ornithologists; John Kieran was a sometime member. The club's guiding spirit was Ludlow Griscom, an older man whom birders claim was the most remarkable of the field ornithologists. Before Griscom, professional ornithologists did not believe that many of the smaller birds could be distinguished with any certainty in the field. Identification could be clinched only with a shotgun. The bird's presence was established by terminating its existence. Hail and farewell.

Yet, by the 1920s, modern binoculars had enabled experienced field observers like Griscom to sort out even the migrating fall warblers in their drab plumages. Griscom converted his conservative elders by singing out, before the guns went off, the names of the elusive birds wrapped in the treetop foliage. Among such skilled birders, Peterson found the competitive aspect of birding that he has always prized.

"Each one of us tried to outdo the other—in listing the most species, or finding the first spring migrants, or even imitating bird calls," Peterson said. "We bought an old Buick for $50 and drove all over the city and the suburbs to find birds. We combed cemeteries and sewer outlets and dumps for rare species. You know, they've ruined some beautiful dumps around New York by turning them into parks."

It was Griscom's idea that each bird could be distinguished from all other birds in the field by one or more telltale "field marks." Peterson went a step beyond the process of taking notes on Griscom's pointers. He made patternistic sketches of the more difficult birds and took them into the field with him.

One chilly, misty morning in the winter of 1930, the members of the Bronx County Bird Club set out in the communal Buick for Croton Point along the Hudson River to look for eagles and canvasbacks. Among the group was a young man named William Vogt, who later became a prominent conservationist. Peterson showed him his sketches.

"Bill was quite excited about them," Peterson said, "He thought they were very helpful, and he said I should put together a bird guide. I didn't take him seriously at first. But he kept after me. He said he would take the guide around to the publishers himself, because he had been a drama critic and knew a few people in publishing."

The Depression put an end to Peterson's courses in art school. He found a job teaching art and natural history at a boys' school in Brookline, Massachusetts. It was there, in his spare time, that he began to prepare the bird guide that was to make him famous.

"When I finished it I sent it to Bill Vogt," Peterson said. "He took it around to six publishers in New York, and they all turned it down. I got it back from him and brought it to Houghton Mifflin in Boston. A couple of editors there liked the guide well enough, but they didn't have much confidence in it. They didn't give me any advance payment, and they said that the plates would cost money so they couldn't pay me any royalties on the first one thousand copies sold, either. They printed a first edition of two thousand copies."

The first edition of *A Field Guide to the Birds* (it included only those species found in the Eastern United States) appeared in April 1934. It sold out within a week. Five thousand additional copies were printed and sold almost as quickly. Every year the guide continued to sell more copies than it did the previous year, until there were over a million copies in print.

The success of the guide can be traced to the plates, which illustrate what has come to be called "The Peterson System of Identification." Each plate contains a group of related species, two-dimensional birds perched on abbreviated twigs. Slender black "pointers" indicate the features (patch of color, shape of bill, crest, etc.) by which the bird "tells its name." The text includes basic information on each bird's voice, range and habitat.

Going to a bookcase, Peterson pulled down a copy of the first edition. Vladimir Nabokov has spoken of his most celebrated book as a comforting presence in the house, the very thought of which "instantly results in a quiet little explosion of warmth." No such glow suffuses Peterson's breast when he turns to the first guide.

"I shudder every time I look at it," he said. "The drawings are horrible. I revised it completely in 1939, and spent a full year revising it again after the war, but I'm still not satisfied. I plan to do the whole thing over in the next couple of years."

Nevertheless, the first edition altered Peterson's life. The National Association of Audubon Societies offered him a position as its Educational Director. Requests for books and magazine articles flooded in on him. (His *Guide to Western Birds* was published in 1941.) He spent his holidays traveling around the country, not only watching birds but painting and photographing them. He also began to give public lectures. The debut of perhaps the most popular natural history lecturer of our time was hardly auspicious.

"My friend, Allan Cruickshank, arranged for me to give a lecture at the Brooklyn Academy of Music," Peterson said. "The audience had to sit through the lecture before they could see a Douglas Fairbanks movie. I brought glass slides of the birds I was going to talk about, but I had prepared too much material for the first slide—the chestnut-sided warbler. Pretty soon I could hear the kids in the audience giggling. While I was up there talking the slide was melting in the projector.

"The climax of the program was supposed to be bird calls. I would imitate a bird and Cruickshank, whom we'd planted in the balcony, would call back to me. We began with the screech owl, and it was very impressive. But then all the kids began to whistle and yodel too and the lecture broke up in an uproar."

But the sport of birdwatching had become established. "The

Peterson field guides laid the groundwork," Roland C. Clement, a vice-president of the National Audubon Society has said. "They made bird identification easy. Before they were published a birder had to work a lifetime at it." According to a recent report by the U.S. Census Bureau, eight million Americans now identify themselves as birdwatchers and another three million as bird and wildlife photographers (the total is two million short of the number of American hunters).

"The Peterson field guides have had their impact on the professionals, too," John Bull of the American Museum of Natural History has said. "Students must learn identification before they can proceed to behavioral studies, wildlife management, and similar fields. Peterson has handed them a short cut."

Indirectly the guides have affected the birds themselves. Homeowners, their curiosity aroused, try to attract more birds by spreading seed on the lawn or by putting up feeders. There is no doubt that artificial feeding, especially in winter, has helped a few birds like the cardinal to extend its range into northern areas where it has never before been able to survive.

But the artificial feeding of birds is not an unmixed blessing. To increase interest in birds some years ago, the Audubon Society encouraged people to attract them to their backyards.

"People misinterpreted this as meaning that they *had* to feed the birds to sustain them," Clement says. "But unless there's some disastrous change in the weather most birds can take care of themselves. Some of the insectivorous birds, of course, should be encouraged by planting shrubs and trees for cover and nesting sites, or by putting out small feeders or bits of suet. But the commercial interests have twisted our statements to imply that seed should be spread lavishly. This only encourages large flocks of cowbirds, starlings, and other pest species."

Roger Peterson has compiled, or served as the general editor of, a score of field guides (each stoutly bound and waterproofed) to natural history. The sales of his own various books about birds approach four million copies, and his illustrations have been reproduced in hundreds of other books and magazines. Because of his unrelenting concentration his prodigious output remains extraordinarily accurate. He came a cropper seriously only once, when an Arctic three-toed woodpecker he drew for a book on Newfoundland birds slipped into print with four conspicious toes.

"But we were able to use the same plate for a book on the birds of Nova Scotia," Peterson said with satisfaction. "The printer simply buffed one of the toes off the plate."

"Do you regret having no formal training in science?" I asked him.

Peterson considered the question for a moment. "No," he replied at last. "My art studies really made possible my special contribution to ornithology. I made a science of recognition—I gave order to it. If I had been a scientist I probably would have felt that my guides were presumptuous, and abandoned my system.

"Still, I've had a lot of inner conflict about it all. There's a basic contradiction in trying to make plain the patterns of birds. An artist tries to create form. Nature, by camouflaging birds, tries to obliterate it." Here Peterson indicated the walls of the living room, on which hung large reproductions of his own illustrations. "I've seen myself described as a 'modern Audubon.' That's really what I'd like to be, but I've never had the time to show people that I really can *paint*. I'm like a clown who wants to play tragedy. I have an awful feeling sometimes that I've been trapped into doing something I didn't want to do—my work has been mainly schematic."

Ultimately the ornithologist, artist, writer, photographer, moviemaker and lecturer merge in his mind to create a single specimen. "I'm really a teacher," he said, "teaching through a visual medium."

It is impossible to calculate the number of Americans Roger Peterson indirectly stirred to an awareness of the natural environment during the thirty-odd years leading up to the more broadly based awakening of the 1970s. At any rate, it was considerable. Not the least of his accomplishments was pumping into the Audubon movement the new blood needed to replace the faint-of-heart that were scattered by the free-swinging campaigns of Rosalie Edge.

Part Six

The Spirit and the Flesh

25

The Spirit

The collision between Muir and Pinchot in 1897 had sent a fissure through the bedrock of the conservation movement. At times the fissure contracted, only to widen again as outside events (Hetch Hetchy, for instance) tried men's values. Ways of looking at the natural world took hold, and hardened into philosophies. Had modern life forced us to erect figurative fences around portions of the dwindling natural world in order to preserve something vital in the human spirit? Or did modern life require that we use these remnant natural resources to provide ourselves with material comforts and a higher standard of living? In the bitter struggle to pass the Wilderness Bill it seemed that God at last swung over to Muir's side.

"Many times I have thought," J. Frank Dobie, the Western writer, said, "that the greatest happiness to a man—probably not to a woman—is to become civilized, to know the pageant of the past, to love the beautiful, to have just ideas of values and proportions, and then, retaining his animal spirits and appetites, to live in a wilderness."

This sort of feeling was finding a place in many men's hearts just as they were pushing the frontier into extinction. Now that there were few patches of wilderness left to tame they stood back to admire the surviving shreds. "Leave it as it is," Theodore Roosevelt said after gazing into Grand Canyon. "You cannot improve on it. The ages have been at work on it, and man can only mar it." The sight or sound of a wolf had terrorized earlier generations; now men counted themselves fortunate to catch a glimpse of a single wolf making its way across a white northern landscape where its ancestors had once roamed in unchallenged packs. Men approached the wilderness with a new attitude. They were beginning to appraise its value as something more than a nostalgic sounding board for sentimentalists.

"Is it not a bit beside the point for us to be so solicitous about preserving institutions without giving so much as a thought to preserving the environment which produced them and which may now be one of our effective means of keeping them alive?"

This was Aldo Leopold in 1925, picking up Muir's torch and adding to the flame his own notions about wilderness values. He had recently been instrumental in persuading the Forest Service to begin setting aside "wilderness type" areas in the Southwest. Under this plan the Forest Service reviewed wild areas in the national forests to see if their special qualities of grandeur and wildlife habitat merited their exclusion from the ax; such areas were to be periodically inspected and if, for some reason or another, they were found wanting in special interest, their wilderness status could be withdrawn and the logger given the signal to move in.

Other men helped to awaken their countrymen to the splendors of the vanishing wilderness. In 1921 Benton MacKaye, author and planner, envisioned and promoted the idea of an "Appalachian Trail" through the Eastern mountains. MacKaye believed with Thoreau that the best way to get to know the wilderness is to take part in pursuits that harmonize with it. Speaking later of the trail that finally extended as a viable wilderness cord from Maine to Georgia, MacKaye stated a principle that is still foreign to the competitive nature of many Americans: "Of several walkers 'doing' the Trail I'd give the prize to the slowest."

But, after Muir and Leopold, probably no one exerted so sharp an impact on the modern American's approach to a wilderness experience as a wealthy young Easterner named Robert Marshall. His father, Louis, was a famous constitutional lawyer, active in the early labor and civil rights movements and a founder of the Ameri-

can Jewish Committee. (So influential was his word in world Jewry that it was referred to with no little respect as "Marshall Law.") But Bob Marshall's concerns lay elsewhere.

"As a boy I spent many hours in the heart of New York City, dreaming of Lewis and Clark and their glorious exploration into an unbroken wilderness which embraced three-quarters of a continent," Marshall once wrote. "Occasionally my reveries ended in terrible depression and I would imagine that I had been born a century too late for genuine excitement."

Marshall, like that other New Yorker, Theodore Roosevelt, got his first taste of the wilderness in the Adirondacks. There he climbed all forty-six of the peaks that rose to 4000 feet or higher, and developed the great stamina that would allow him to backpack thirty miles through rugged mountainous terrain on an average day, and on some days even more. And yet a certain anxiety gripped him; he imagined the vast Western wilderness "melting away like the last snowbank on some south-facing mountainside during a hot afternoon in June."

Though his family's wealth gave Marshall the opportunity to make extended trips into the remote mountains of the West (including Alaska and Canada) he also was attracted to public service. He received his master's degree in forestry from Harvard and his doctorate in plant pathology from Johns Hopkins before becoming director of the Forestry Division in the Office of Indian Affairs in 1933 (later he was Director of Recreation in the Forest Service). With Leopold in academia, Marshall became the outstanding spokesman for wilderness preservation in the federal government. He supplied the wilderness idea with a foundation in modern philosophy and psychology. Like William James he sought a "moral equivalent of war," and found it in the "harmless excitement of the wilderness," where man's consuming desire for adventure could be appeased. Freudian notions mingled with his love for wild places; civilization has cramped and warped us, Marshall believed, and in frustrating our longing for the freedom of the wilderness we leave ourselves open to such modern ills as tension and anxiety. To plunge into the wilderness and test ourselves against the natural world is to alleviate "the terrific harm caused by suppressed desires."

But what is *wilderness?* Marshall defined it as "a region which contains no permanent inhabitants, possesses no possibility of conveyance by any mechanical means and is sufficiently spacious that a person in crossing it must have the experience of sleeping out. The dominant attributes of such an area are: first, that it requires anyone who exists in it to depend exclusively on his own effort for survival; and second, that it preserves as nearly as possible the primitive environment. This means that all roads, power, transportation and settlements are barred. But trails and temporary shelters, which were common long before the advent of the white race, are entirely permissible."

Marshall called for the country to preserve areas where such an experience would be possible for those people who needed it and could take advantage of it. "There is just one hope of repulsing the tyrannical ambition of civilization to conquer every niche on the whole earth," he wrote. "That hope is the organization of spirited people who will fight for the freedom of the wilderness." Using his own wealth, and with the considerable help of such like-minded men as Leopold and MacKaye, Marshall founded the Wilderness Society in 1935. It was none too soon to provide the means to carry on the struggle for what he passionately believed. Marshall died of a heart attack in 1939 at the age of thirty-eight. Some of his friends believed he brought on death by pushing himself in the mountains beyond the limits of human endurance; if so, he was as much a martyr to his sport as a racing driver, a boxer, or a matador killed in pursuit of his own dreams of conquest. Yet those dreams left an enduring residue in the American conservation movement.

Wildlife and wilderness had suffered little during World War II, but its aftermath posed momentous problems. The explosion of buildings, highways, and babies threatened to leave no room for vestiges of wild America. Even the national parks staggered under the rising number of people who swarmed into them on their summer holidays, overwhelming the very qualities of wilderness and serenity for which they were preserved. Cities grew, and the green spaces around them disappeared under concrete as Pompeii had disappeared under lava. The notion that the land and its resources must be "used" crowded out the hopes nurtured by a small band of conservationists and wildlife enthusiasts that a part of wild America might be preserved for its own sake. Those hopes were nearly extinguished during the Eisenhower administration.

President Eisenhower appointed as his Secretary of the Interior an automobile dealer from Salem, Oregon, named Douglas McKay. Between the Mineral Leasing Act of 1920 and the accession of McKay, the federal government had issued only eleven leases on wildlife refuges for the extraction of oil and minerals; within two years, the Interior Department under McKay granted 60 leases, and an additional 214 leases were granted on other lands administered by the Fish and Wildlife Service.

Public lands again were thrown open indiscriminately to the exploiters. Attempts were made to increase the timber cutting allowances on government lands. McKay's conservation policies drove a number of prominent wildlife specialists, including Clarence M. Cottam, Durward L. Allen, and Alfred M. Day, out of the Fish and Wildlife Service. Another prominent conservationist and author, Bernard De Voto, commented in *Harper's Magazine* in 1954 on the administration's conservation policies:

"In a year and a half the businessmen in office have reversed the conservation policy by which the United States has been working for more than seventy years to substitute wise use of natural resources in place of reckless destruction for the profit of special corporate interests . . . There is a cynicism in the Interior which reminds observers of the aromatic days of the General Land Office. Yet some things that look like cynicism may be mere ineptness. Thus Secretary McKay at a moment when all the conservation organizations in the country—national, nonpartisan, and representing hundreds of thousands of votes—were denouncing his recommendation of Echo Park Dam. Seeking for *le mot juste* to characterize conservationists, he came up with 'punks'."

It was Echo Park Dam that rallied the conservationists. Until then even the prominent conservation organizations were comparatively weak and disorganized, while both business and government grew to unprecedented proportions. For some time the National Audubon Society (the streamlined name assumed by the old National Association after the war) had devoted most of its funds and attention to education programs rather than to reforms through legislative and administrative action. The Sierra Club was still largely confined to a small membership of hiking and canoeing enthusiasts in the Far West. Other organizations pursued their ardent but parochial interests. Sometimes their interests clashed. One conservation leader compared the situation "to one in which the theoretical Society for the Preservation of the Chickadee was constantly warring with the theoretical Society for the Preservation of Sunflower Seeds."

Echo Park changed all that. The federal government had proposed a billion-dollar dam-building program in eleven Western states, to be carried out by the Bureau of Reclamation in the Interior Department, and called the Colorado River Storage Project. A dam 525 feet high was to be built in Echo Park on the Green River in Colorado and Utah. If the dam were completed it would contain six and a half million acre-feet of water,* flooding lovely, unique canyons in Dinosaur National Monument. Conservationists pointed out that this would violate the National Park Act of 1916. David R. Brower of the Sierra Club described what would happen at Echo Park and what Americans would lose:

"There would be construction roads in the canyons and above it, tunnels, the whole power installation and transmission lines, the rapid build-up of silt at the upper end of the reservoir to enable it to fulfill its function—a fluctuation that would play hob with fish and wildlife. The piñon pines, the Douglas firs, the maples and cottonwoods, the grasses and other flora that live on the banks, the green living things that shine in the sun against the rich colors of the cliffs—these would also go. The river, its surge and its sound, the living sculptor of this place, would be silent forever, and all the fascination of its movement and the fun of riding it, quietly gliding through these cathedral corridors of stone—all done in for good."

Brower, Howard C. Zahniser of the Wilderness Society, and representatives of other conservation organizations united in a Council of Conservationists. Old conflicts were forgotten as they mobilized to fight in Congress for the deletion of Echo Dam from the project's enabling legislation. Even Rosalie Edge jumped in. ("The despoilers await like hungry wolves the opportunity to exploit our parks, once a precedent is established," she wrote. "Echo Park is their opportunity. This is a test case.") The specter of Hetch Hetchy reappeared. Pamphlets rolled off the presses; picture books called attention to threatened natural treasures; a motion picture depicted the loveliness of Dinosaur to audiences all over the country. Brower appeared before a congressional committee with precise figures to discredit the Bureau of Reclamation's claim that a

*An acre-foot of water is the amount of water needed to cover an acre of land to the depth of one foot.

reservoir at Echo Park would lose less water by evaporation than reservoirs at any alternate sites on the river.

Western congressmen, supported by "water-users" of all kinds in their constituencies, tried to ram the bill intact through the House and Senate. But the conservationists had planned well. Thousands of letters poured onto Capitol Hill, demanding that the dam at Echo Park be stricken from the legislation. Powerful senators, including Paul H. Douglas, Hubert H. Humphrey, and Richard L. Neuberger, took up the conservationists' cause. At length the Western bloc backed down and Congress agreed to save Dinosaur. The conservationists' victory was written into the bill (at their insistence) that President Eisenhower signed on April 11, 1955: "It is the intention of Congress that no dam or reservoir constructed under the authorization of this Act shall be within any national park or monument."

Encouraged by their successful defense of Echo Park, the conservationists decided to take the offensive. Conservation, of course, is essentially a losing battle: it is the attempt to "conserve" or "preserve" portions of the natural world. A conservationist usually springs to action only when one of these portions is threatened with destruction; he fights his battles, makes his compromises, and usually settles for something less than the whole he originally set out to defend. (During the Colorado River Storage Project struggle, the conservationists retained Echo Park, but lost another natural treasure, Glen Canyon.) But whatever treasures the conservationist saves remain vulnerable; they must be fought for over and over again as each new generation of exploiters casts covetous eyes on them. Whatever the exploiters win, in one great swoop or by persistent chipping away, the conquest is permanent.

The attempt to submerge Dinosaur behind a dam at Echo Park convinced many conservationists that they could no longer afford to wait for the exploiters (under whatever guise) to clean up the last bastions of wilderness in the United States. Commercial interests had mounted their attack from many directions. Late in 1954, for instance, an industrial firm engaged in "cellulose chemistry" paid for two-page, four-color advertisements in both *Time* and *U.S. News and World Report,* attacking the "useless tying-up of park lands" in Olympic National park; scarcely disguising its hankering, the firm lamented the "millions of board feet of prime timber . . .

heedlessly lost each year," and complained that such preservation "does no one any good." Similar despair was expressed by the operators of mechanized ski resorts, who felt that the snow falling on areas set aside as wilderness in California's national forests "should not be wasted."

In most cases all that protected these wilderness areas in national forests, wildlife refuges, and even national parks was an administrator's sense of proportion. As wildlands dwindled, the administrators came under increasingly severe pressure from commercial interests and their spokesmen in Congress. The fears of wilderness enthusiasts seemed to be confirmed by some of the literature issued by the National Park Service during the 1950s. The management of the parks," the service said, "requires that natural forces be regulated to the degree necessary to keep them in scale with the reduced size of the wilderness that remains today." Such comments suggested that the National Park Service thought the wilderness to be of such pitiful proportions that it no longer could take care of itself and must be sprayed and clipped and de-loused like a pet poodle. That the parks' defense hung by a very uncertain thread was admitted in a further statement: "There would be little wilderness and much less of the parks left had the National Park Service been development-minded."

The Forest Service, committed by its very origins to commercial development, was even more vulnerable to excessive pressure. Only public hearings and public pressure kept some tracts from the ax that had earlier been set aside as wilderness areas. But not even the protests of Oregon's Senators, Neuberger and Wayne Morse, could save 53,000 acres in the Three Sisters Wilderness Area from commercial intrusion in the 1950s. Elsewhere the Forest Service opened "wild" areas to roads for public travel, landing strips for planes, mining projects, and grazing lands for sheep and cattle.

"In other cases," Senator Neuberger said, "private interests dictate the terms and conditions under which the general public can go on to federal lands . . . Today the federal government is not the master of all its domain."

Stockmen, for instance, worked to have the public domain turned over to the states so that the rules for using it might be relaxed in their favor. (Many of these ranchers were not enthusiastic about taking over the land in their own name, for then they would be liable for taxes; they wanted to use it, while resenting even the

payment of forage fees to the government.) The Bureau of Land
Management,* dominated by the stockmen and their mouthpieces
in Congress, promoted the interests of these commercial groups over
the broader concerns of the public, who had been lulled into
inattention by the notion of the "multiple-use concept" on federal
lands.

Multiple use is the basis on which the Forest Service manages
its lands. Ideally, it means that the forests are to be open to many
compatible uses, from logging, mining, and grazing to watershed
protection, recreation, and wildlife conservation. But conservationists have often asked how they might interpret multiple
use: Does it refer to the multiple use of every acre in the national
forest, or to the forest as a whole? Apparently only the second
interpretation is valid, for otherwise grazing, mining, logging,
recreation, etc., would take place on every acre of the forest. In
that case, conservationists argued, a system of land classification
should be established so that parts of the forest could be set aside
for commercial use and other parts designated as wilderness.

This ideal has not always been put into practice by the Forest
Service, since the special interests holding the most political power
have tended to exclude other users from the forests they control.
David Brower has called the Forest Service's concept of multiple
use "a political scientist's dream."

"Multiple use was more than what could happen, theoretically,
on land," Brower wrote. "It was also what could be brought to
bear, actually, on people. It could establish a protective cordon of
interest groups that could be played against each other on the
periphery—and at dead center all could be calm. Are the miners
asking too much? Just point this out to the grazers, loggers, water
users, and recreationists. A game of musical chairs out under the
trees."

The "recreationist," low man on the multiple-use chart until
then, began to come into his own in the decade following World
War II. The notion was gaining wider circulation that, in taming
its wilderness, America had become (in William Faulkner's expression) a "gilded pustule." More and more Americans were turning
to the books of writers who celebrated the wilderness ethic and the
natural world: Aldo Leopold (who had died of a heart attack while

*In 1946 the General Land Office and the Grazing Service had merged in the Bureau of
Land Management.

fighting a brush fire in 1948), Sigurd Olson, Bernard De Voto, Hal Borland, and Joseph Wood Krutch.

"There is a penalty for too much comfort and ease, a penalty of lassitude and inertia and the frustrated feeling that goes with reality," Olson wrote. Wilderness was important not only because man needed its experience to refresh his body and spirit, but because it provided man's fellow creatures with a world of their own in which they could live out the timeless drama of their lives without interference from technological man; perhaps it was as a refuge for both man and animals that wilderness found its "highest use." "Great wilderness has two characteristics, remoteness and the presence of wild animals in something like pristine variety and numbers," Lois Crisler wrote in *Arctic Wild*. "Remoteness cannot be imitated in cheap materials; and wilderness without animals is mere scenery."

To preserve what Brower called "the national gallery of primeval art," the conservationists went back to Congress in 1956, this time with a plan of positive action to preserve a few large tracts of wilderness for all time. His colleagues generally give the credit for getting the movement underway to Howard Zahniser, a balding, intense, wilderness lover then in his late forties who had worked as a writer and editor for the Department of Agriculture before finding an outlet for his real interests as Executive Secretary of the Wilderness Society.

"We were deeply concerned at the time with the need for legislative protection for national forest areas which then had no legal standing," Zahniser once said, "and we were concerned with the preservation of the wilderness character of the back country of the National Park System. We were worried then [during the 1950s] about park programs and the apparent move to develop the back country in the parks." And he went on to speak of a need "to secure the preservation of some areas that are so managed as to be left unmanaged—areas that are undeveloped by man's mechanical tools and in every way unmodified by his civilization."

The conservationists presented what was basically a modest proposal. They drew up a bill to create a "wilderness system" that would be composed of areas already set aside as wild in national forests, national parks and wildlife refuges, and administered by the federal agencies in whose care they were already lodged. There was to be no alteration in the purpose (game refuges, national monuments, etc.) each presently served. The bill simply made wilderness preservation a statutory directive from Congress to the administrative agency. The National Park Service, for instance, would then be relieved of excessive political pressure to build roads, reservoirs, or resort hotels in remote areas of its domain. The land involved was only a fraction of the land controlled by the federal government; only eight percent of the 180,000,000 acres in the national forests would be affected by the wilderness bill, and a total of only two percent of the nearly 500,000,000 acres in the entire public domain.

The Sierra Club's David Brower has described the beginnings of the Wilderness Bill: "After seven years study and four wilderness conferences in which hundreds of resource managers and conservationists participated, a bill was drafted to reflect their consensus as nearly as possible. In Washington, D.C. . . . three of us submitted to the Forest and Park Services the first draft of that bill to establish a national wilderness preservation system. We asked for further advice and counsel. Within a few hours—and long before advice or counsel was received—copies of this draft were in the hands of the American Mining Congress, the stockmen and the Chamber of Commerce."

The Wilderness Bill was introduced in Congress on June 7, 1956. Among its sponsors in the Senate were Hubert H. Humphrey, Richard L. Neuberger, Wayne Morse, Herbert H. Lehman, Paul H. Douglas, and Karl E. Mundt; among the House sponsors were John P. Saylor, Lee Metcalf, and Henry R. Reuss. The bill's introduction set up a classic confrontation between those whose appraisal of the natural world arose from entirely different wellsprings. Zahniser expressed one side of the conflict: "Deeper and broader than the recreational value of wilderness, although indeed encompassing it, is the importance that relates to our essential being, indicating that the understanding which comes in its surroundings are those of true reality. Our lives seem so derivitive from wilderness, we ourselves seem so dependent on a renewal of our inspiration from those wild sources that I wonder sometimes if we could long survive a final destruction of all wilderness. Are we not truly and in reality *human*, essentially, as spiritual creatures nurtured and sustained—directly or indirectly—by a wildness that must always be renewed from a living wilderness?"

It is instructive to pick out, from the resultant outcries directed at the Wilderness Bill, the many themes that recur again and again in the opposition to all meaningful environmental legislation in our time. Each opponent raised a dreaded specter:

· *The Red Menace,* as described by A. P. Morris of the Kennecott Copper Corporation: "Certainly the Soviet Union, the enemy of the free world, would be delighted with the passage of such legislation that would limit the development of the natural mineral resources given us by a bountiful providence . . . The enemy of the free world is doing everything possible to explore and exploit the mineral resources of not only its own territory, but that of the countries behind the Iron Curtain."

· *The Predator,* as described by Floyd W. Lee of the New Mexico Wool Growers Association: "For years past the federal Fish and Wildlife Service, our New Mexico Department of Fish and Game, some county governments and the livestock industry have cooperated in a continuing battle against predatory animals. These wilderness areas have been and will continue to be breeding grounds for predators—the enemies of deer, wild turkey and other game birds, as well as sources of losses of the livestock grower's calves and lambs. Why add to the difficulty of predator control by creating more such breeding grounds?"

· *The Waning of the Pioneer Spirit,* as described by G. R. Milburn of the American National Cattlemen's Association: "We do not believe these great resources of the range and timberlands were created for only the enjoyment of the general public. Our Nation was built by the development of our timberlands, our mineral deposits, and our grasslands by those who were rugged enough to do so. Ever-increasing pleasure areas will only lead to the elimination of further development of these resources—the possible destruction of timber and grass by carelessly set fires, the abuse of wildlife, and the destruction of watersheds."

· *The Loss of the Flabby Tourist,* as described by Redford Hall of the American National Cattlemen's Association: "The tourist business is growing in the West because the mountains and plains are being cut up and despoiled by safe, modern, paved highways lined by hotels, motels, and resorts that furnish every modern convenience obtained in the finest eastern hotels."

· And finally, *The Menace of the Common Man,* as described by Milburn: "The cattle producers of the country appreciate the value of a reasonable number of wildlife and wilderness areas in the United States, but we are concerned over the possibility of ever-increasing numbers of such areas in the future. We who live as close to the out-of-doors as anyone, are also concerned over the ever-increasing encroachment by the general public, because of roads and the automobile, and the airplane, on the few un-exploited spaces still remaining in our country."

Clearly the Wilderness Bill faced bitter opposition, not only from Western commercial interests but also from Easterners who had invested heavily in land-use industries. The furniture of these men's minds is frontier modern. All that conflicts with the conquest of the land and the pursuit of a livelihood is chucked out; a viable natural world, in its enchanting variety, is consigned with the other frills to the pragmatic dump.

Even before hearings were held on the bill, some of these men began to spread false rumors. "Word has gotten out in opposition to this bill," Senator Humphrey reported, "that we are contemplating going out here and there and grabbing up lands that belong to somebody else and are really going to upset a whole land-use economy."

This was not true, of course. Only lands already in federal ownership were eligible to be included in the bill's provisions; and within the federal lands only those areas best suited for wilderness preservation and not at present being used for other purposes were to be approved for the system. Yet some of the most effective opposition to the bill came from those agencies whose administrative grip on the lands promised to be strengthened by the bill.

The Department of Agriculture opposed the bill in a statement to Congress in 1957. (In its stand it was supported by the American Forestry Association.) At the heart of the department's opposition was the fear that certain of its prerogatives would be usurped by Congress; but its statement was indirect: "By tending to freeze the status quo of existing wilderness-type areas, the bill would strike at the heart of the multiple use policy of national forest administration. The bill would give a degree of congressional protection to wilderness use of the national forests which is not now enjoyed by any other use."

Though Douglas McKay had departed as Interior Secretary, the department also opposed the bill. Two of its contentions were that the bill would bring Congress into the day-to-day management of the lands and that, while the national parks might fit into the wilderness concept, the national wildlife refuges must be "managed." A third objection was later recognized as valid by the bill's sponsors when they heeded Interior's contention that Indian lands did not properly "belong" to the federal government, and thus removed these lands from inclusion in the proposed wilderness system.

"It's obvious you white people can never agree on this bill," an Apache told a Senate hearing, "so why don't you just give *all* the land back to the Indians?"

The Apache was nearly right when he ventured that the white people would never come to an agreement on the Wilderness Bill. Years of hard work and recrimination lay ahead. Its sponsors were prepared to remove all impractical provisions from the bill, and answer objections to the rest: they showed that they intended to create no "new" wilderness, take no land off the local tax rolls, curtail no current mining, logging, or grazing operations, and abolish no jobs. Each such disclaimer served only to stiffen the will of the anti-wilderness forces.

"We have a fight on our hands," said Ira Gabrielson. "We may as well recognize it. The fight is not against any interests who will be damaged by the proposed bill but rather it is against interests who have hopes of raiding the few remaining areas of wilderness for their own purposes *whenever the future may offer a chance.* The very fact that livestock, lumber and other commercial interests are so ruthlessly fighting this bill is evidence that they are actually opposed to reasonable safeguards for any public areas. Their pious words for wilderness are forgotten when they face a practical program to preserve it."

The opposition to the bill came clothed in many forms. Articles attacking the bill appeared in *American Forests,* the publication of the American Forestry Association, written by men who did not identify themselves as representing certain corporations in the wood-products industry. Men who for years had chafed under the administration of public logging, mining, and grazing lands by federal agencies, suddenly launched a campaign to tell the public how much they admired the Forest Service's wise management of the lands entrusted to its care; stockmen in particular, who had railed against the Forest Service as "despotic," and who had sponsored legislation to take the grazing lands out of its hands, now expressed perfect satisfaction with its policies. Other commercial interests invoked the names of Theodore Roosevelt and Gifford Pinchot in support of their condemnation of the Wilderness Bill. During one of the Senate hearings held on the bill in Oregon, Senator Neuberger pinned down W. D. Hagenstein of the Industrial Forestry Association on this point.

NEUBERGER: When Pinchot himself proposed the forest reserves back in the early days of the twentieth century, what was the position of the Western timber industry on that proposal in general?

HAGENSTEIN: Well, the history is a little bit clouded on that, Senator, but I think that not only the timber industry but I think the people of the West generally at one time were somewhat opposed to the establishment of the national forests, but today you and I, of course, were both born after Gifford Pinchot was no longer spearheading the conservation movement as Chief of the Forest Service, because he was out in 1910. I think that is before your birth date; it is certainly before mine.

NEUBERGER: Correct, but . . . it is a fact, is it not, that most of the Western forest products industry opposed the proposal of Gifford Pinchot and Theodore Roosevelt to set aside the forest reserves as was contained in the bill which TR signed on March 4, 1907? Isn't that a true statement?

HAGENSTEIN: No, it isn't entirely true, Senator. You're trying to put a few words in my mouth, I'm afraid. If you would amend that question to say, "Weren't the people of the West generally opposed?" my answer would be "Yes," but to single out one segment of the West, namely the industry which is the principal industry of this state and the industry by which I have been employed all my life, I don't think is entirely fair.

NEUBERGER: Well, let's even accept your statement. I don't accept it as fact, but let's grant it theoretically. Don't you think those who did oppose Pinchot's proposal in 1907 for the forest reserves were mistaken?"

HAGENSTEIN: Looking back on it, I would agree with you that they were.

And, indeed, strange bedfellows were beginning to speak up from under the blanket of *conservation*. Wrapping themselves firmly in its voluminous folds they were able, by a deft use of semantics, to point an accusing finger at their opponents' philosophical nakedness in much the same fashion that Mao Tse-tung handles a maverick Communist (Mao simply labels him a revisionist and thus, deprived of the magic shield of the party name, the poor fellow is fair game for everybody). In the name of Gifford Pinchot, many exploitive businessmen identified themselves as *conservationists,* while reading their foes out of the movement by branding them *preservationists.*

This position has been neatly stated by one recent historian of the conservation movement* in a discussion of the Sierra Club:

"No one can question the purity of the club's motives; committed to an unwavering position against any infringement on nature, it has never hesitated to do battle with some of the chief vested interests of the economic exploitation of our natural resources. Unfortunately, the preservationists are determinedly uncompromising in their pursuit of absolutes. In their narrow definition of preservation, and their seeming inability to recognize that wilderness pristine is in fact wilderness lost, they have also at times, as in the Hetch Hetchy issue, found themselves on the side of the exploitation interests."

In the fight for the Wilderness Bill the "preservationists" were able to turn this doctrine of guilt-by-association against their foes in the federal agencies and forestry associations, who had aligned themselves with the West's "exploitation interests." All of the stops were pulled out. The Anaconda Company and the Phelps Dodge Corporation urged their stockholders to protest the Wilderness Bill in letters to their congressmen. In an annual dividend notice to its stockholders, Kennecott Copper attacked the bill, contending that it violated the multiple-use principle and discriminated against miners. (One Kennecott stockholder turned over his dividend check of $125 to Howard Zahniser of the Wilderness Society "to counteract the anti-Wilderness Bill propaganda of the Kennecott Copper Company.")

One unfortunate aspect of the struggle was that the battle lines tended to form along sectional boundaries. The anti-wilderness forces, in fact, sometimes did their best to exaggerate the East-West conflict, though the Sierra Club and other ardent sponsors of the bill originated in the Far West. For one thing, all eighteen members of the Senate Committee on Interior Affairs, charged with reporting on the bill, represented states west of the Mississippi River; and all, naturally, came under tremendous pressure from the major contributors to their campaign funds among the mining, lumber, cattle, and petroleum industries.

"Our committee functions very largely on a non-partisan basis," committee chairman James E. Murray of Montana said in 1959. "Whether Democrats or Republicans, we are for Western develop-

---

*Frank E. Smith, *The Politics of Conservation*, New York, 1966.

ment." And Senator Barry Goldwater of Arizona added: "What he says about the Senate Committee on Interior and Insular affairs is true. It is rather exclusive and we frown on Easterners being on that committee."

During a committee hearing in Phoenix, Goldwater, the committee member most outspoken in his opposition to the bill, called it "an unpopular measure which misguided Easterners are trying to cram down the throats of Westerners . . . We don't trust those people back in Washington."

To which Howard Zahniser answered: "Senator Goldwater, you are from Arizona. I am from western Pennsylvania. But aren't we both the people in Washington?"

But as time passed Senator Gordon Allott of Colorado took the lead on the committee by sponsoring amendments that threatened to emasculate the Wilderness Bill. Representative Wayne N. Aspinall of Colorado, who was as well-known as a spokesman for the mining and ranching interests in that state, helped to bottle up the House version of the bill. The 1950s expired along with the Eisenhower administration, to be succeeded by the Kennedy administration, and still the bill languished in the two congressional committees. By now conservationists were beginning to feel a sense of urgency. Succumbing to pressure, the Forest Service opened to the ax certain areas in the North Cascades and elsewhere that until then had presented themselves favorably as permanent wilderness areas. The conservationists sardonically referred to these tactics as "wilderness-preventive logging."

"The concept of this agency," a supporter of the Wilderness Bill said, "still seems to be geared to the concept of 'trees for the loggers, rock and ice for the recreationists'."

At this point another obstacle threatened the bill's progress. The conservationists themselves were beginning to lose heart in the face of repeated frustrations. Charles H. Callison of the National Audubon Society, an experienced and adept lobbyist who was among the leaders of the conservation bloc in Washington, spoke of the sagging morale in 1960.

"The conservation forces were weak and disorganized," Callison said, "because some of the major conservation organizations, formerly effective, were undergoing internal upheaval—perhaps a cyclic development like the periodic decline of a grouse population—and because their leaders seemed less inclined to work together and share the credit for their meager accomplishments."

But the struggle went on, with Zahniser still carrying the load. "What made the difference was one man's conscience, his tireless search for a way to put a national wilderness policy into law," Brower said of his colleague. "The hardest times were those when good friends tired because the battle was so long. Urging these friends back into action was the most anxious part of Howard Zahniser's work."

Writing speeches for friendly congressmen, preparing pamphlets, raising funds, and speaking before both the public and congressional committees, Zahniser kept the bill alive. He had help now from the White House, where President Kennedy urged Congress to establish a national wilderness preservation system. But with their hopes high, the conservationists suffered yet another defeat in 1962.

"More than any other individual in either house, Chairman Aspinall is responsible for the shambles that the 87th Congress made of wilderness legislation," *Field and Stream* told its readers.

The Senate had passed a strong bill by an overwhelming margin; it had appeared that the House would do the same. But Aspinall stalled the bill in his committee, postponing hearings while letting time run out. Public pressure, however, was mounting in favor of the passage of wilderness legislation. Near the end of the session Aspinall trotted out a wilderness bill of his own (called "one massive crippling amendment," by the conservationists) and in submitting it to the full House requested that it be voted on "under suspension of the rules." Such a designation would have brought the bill to a vote without providing House members an opportunity to strengthen its protective provisions by further amendment.

There was a great outcry of protest from Aspinall's colleagues in the House. The bill contained a number of crippling provisions, including one that would have permitted mining to be carried out indefinitely in "wilderness areas," and another that would have submitted each "permanent" wilderness area to review by Congress every twenty-five years. The Speaker of the House, in an unusual move, turned down Chairman Aspinall's request for suspension of the rules. The bill was thrown back in Aspinall's lap. He solved the problem by going home to Colorado, and the Wilderness Bill was dead for another session.

In disgust, President Kennedy ordered the Bureau of the Budget to draw up an administration bill for the next session. The Senate again passed the bill overwhelmingly, but again Aspinall stalled it in his committee. If it was only a matter of time before the bill was passed and put on the President's desk, that time proved to be too long for both Kennedy and Zahniser: Kennedy was assassinated in 1963, and Zahniser, worn out by work, died in 1964.

Concessions were made to the powerful mining and petroleum interests: the Geological Survey and the Bureau of Mines were authorized to make surveys of suggested wilderness areas to see whether they contained valuable minerals (thus providing the industry with surveys made at public expense). Mining, prospecting, and oil and gas development were permitted to go on until 1968, after which no patents within a National Forest Wilderness Area would be issued except for valid claims existing on that date. Grazing would be permitted in areas where it was already established.

With this and a few other amendments, the Wilderness Bill was passed by both houses of Congress and signed by President Lyndon B. Johnson on September 3, 1964. Its passage immediately brought 9,000,000 acres of the national forests into the wilderness preservation system, and provided for the evaluation and inclusion of another 40–50,000,000 acres of other government land in the years ahead.

The nation had a permanent wilderness system at last and (no small accomplishment) a legal definition of wilderness itself. In the beginning of the act one finds the following definition. It was composed by Howard Zahniser, but as one reads, one detects echoes of Aldo Leopold, Bob Marshall—and of John Muir himself: "Wilderness . . . in contrast with those areas where man and his own works dominate the landscape, is hereby recognized as an area where the earth and its community of life are untrammeled by man, where man himself is a visitor who does not remain."

26

The Flesh

In 1948 Dr. Paul H. Müller, a Swiss chemist, was awarded the Nobel Prize for Physiology and Medicine. His was a remarkable achievement—the synthesis of a sophisticated compound that saved countless lives around the world, promised to eradicate the age-old scourge of malaria, and contributed to a rise in the production of food and fiber crops in many countries. But as the years passed Müller's cure-all came to cast a shadow of undetermined substantiality over the future of life on earth; as a byproduct, it altered the nature of the conservation movement in this country.

The substance that Müller developed in the laboratories of the J. R. Geigy Aktien Gesellschaft in Basel is a crystalline, tasteless, and odorless insecticide bearing the technical name dichloro-diphenyl-trichloroethane, and known to friend and foe alike by the initial letters of its trinomial—DDT. Like so many important scientific discoveries, DDT was something of a fluke. Müller was an employee of Geigy, a chemical firm that specialized in making synthetic dyes, and in 1939 he was intent on finding a mothproofing substance that could be added during manufacture to dyed woolens. When he arranged chlorine, carbon, and hydrogen atoms in a certain way, Müller produced a powdery substance that he believed might prove effective as an insecticide. Hopefully, he put some flies into a glass box with his powders and waited for the flies to expire; but nothing happened. Most insecticides worth their salt, he knew, would have killed the flies quickly. It seemed as if Müller would be back at the drawing board the next day.

But when he returned to the lab in the morning he found that all the flies had died overnight. The poison, he decided, worked more slowly than the older insecticides, but with at least equal effect. Without adding more DDT to the box, Müller dropped in more flies, and again found them dead the next day. Other insects suffered the same fate. When this went on for some days (even after he repeatedly scrubbed the box with water and soap) Müller came to the conclusion that he had stumbled upon an insecticide of extraordinary versatility and persistence.

The company applied for a patent on its new chemical compound. To their surprise, Geigy and Müller learned that the formula for making DDT had been in existence since 1874, when a graduate student named Othmar Zeidler had concocted it at the University of Strasbourg while working on a thesis that dealt with certain chemical reactions. Since Zeidler had tossed the stuff away without finding any use for it, thus leaving only a formula for posterity, Geigy was able to obtain a patent to manufacture DDT as an insecticide.

Though DDT was used successfuly against a variety of insects on Swiss farms, the war intervened before it could be put on the international market. The United States government, searching for an insecticide to protect its troops against malaria, yellow fever, and the other insect-borne diseases that have plagued armies for centuries, happened upon DDT in 1943. As a louse powder, DDT worked wonders. It is not nearly so acutely toxic to human beings in small quantities as most other insecticides are; and applied to the bodies and clothing of soldiers and civilians in the Mediterranean theater of war, DDT smothered a potentially disastrous typhoid epidemic. Later DDT proved dramatically effective when it was mixed with kerosene or other solutions and sprayed over the breeding grounds of malarial mosquitoes.

Word of DDT's wartime miracles spread quickly, and a large public was awaiting its production (under licenses granted by Geigy) to non-military markets after the war. It became the chief insecticide used by farmers and public health workers. The world's insect problem seemed to be solved.

Here and there voices were raised against DDT's indiscriminate use. Certain doctors grew uneasy about spreading a long-lasting poison through the environment. The National Audubon Society was among the first to predict that DDT might be disastrous for some forms of wildlife. But the first general reservations about DDT's unmitigated benefits were stirred by the discovery that house flies (and later some species of mosquitoes) had acquired a resistance to it. When DDT lost its effectiveness against these and other insects, scientists were forced to develop even more powerful poisons to supplement it. Insect resistance led to an esclation in both the toxicity and the quantity of the new synthetic insecticides used in pest control.

Neither the federal government, the chemical industry, nor most of the people using pesticides felt any alarm over the fact that man was spreading long-lasting poisons in increasing quantities through the open environment. The magnitude and complexity of the phenomenon escaped them. Therefore, in 1961, when biologists detected significant traces of DDT in the tissue of such marine fish as mackerel and butterfish, the occurrence was dismissed with the explanation that the fish probably had been contaminated by careless spraying within the processing plant.

But the next year Rachel Carson's *Silent Spring* appeared. Rachel Carson's name was better known to the public than the subject of her book. It would be accurate, if somewhat misleading, to describe her simply as a middle-aged woman who had worked for some years as a marine biologist for the U.S. Fish and Wildlife Service. Even her friends found it difficult to catch and hold the many glints of warmth, intelligence and responsibility she reflected— a woman who presented a number of sides to the world but who impressed her friends with the unity of her character. A meticulous scientist; a spinster who spent most of her adult life caring, first for her mother, and later for an orphaned grandnephew; a worker who brightened the routine of Washington's bureaucracy for her col- leagues with high standards in the face of mediocrity and a mis- chievous sense of humor in the face of solemn humbugs; and a rare stylist whose prose brought alive the great blank sweep of the world's oceans for a generation of readers: that was Rachel Carson.

The publication of a best-selling book, *The Sea Around Us,* in 1951, enabled her to leave the Fish and Wildlife Service and devote all of her time to her writing and her domestic duties. She enjoyed a comfortable income, a home in a pleasant Washington suburb, and a summer place on the coast of Maine. Exploring the natural world with a few close friends and translating that experience into a resonant yet precise prose was all the joy and excitement she asked from life. The succession of books she wrote about the sea had assured her of a modest but enduring place in American letters.

That Rachel Carson was a scientist did not necessarily mean she was alert to the degradation of the world's environment (many of her colleagues missed the signals, or chose to ignore them). But her scientific training reinforced her reverence for life, the sort of "ecological conscience" that had driven Aldo Leopold to speak out against mankind's senseless rush to deprive the world of both its loveliness and its diversity.

"It was pleasant to believe," Rachel Carson wrote, "that much of Nature was forever beyond the tampering reach of man: he might level the forests and dam the streams, but the clouds and the rain and the wind were God's. It was comforting to suppose that the stream of life would flow on through time in whatever course that God had appointed for it—without interference by one of the drops in that stream, Man. And to suppose that, however the physical environment might mold Life, that Life could never assume the power to change drastically—or even destroy—the physical world."

But now, in touch with the natural world as well as with the fellowship of science, she was aware of certain disturbing rumblings. The miracles that modern techno-science had produced brought with them a cost that their creators had not counted on. "So it seems time that someone wrote of life in the light of the truth as it now appears to us," Rachel Carson said. "I still feel there is a case to be made for my old belief that as man approaches the 'new heaven and the new earth'—or the space-age universe, if you will, he must do so with humility rather than with arrogance. And along with humility, I think there is still a place for wonder."

Sorting through immense amounts of scientific material and battling the cancer that soon would kill her, Rachel Carson after four years of work finally published her momentous book in 1962. *Silent Spring* broke the information barrier, telling the public just how far man had gone down the dark and dangerous road toward contaminating the world's environment. The book was an attempt to explain what had silenced the voices of spring in town and countryside all over America.

"It is not my contention that chemical insecticides must never be used," Rachel Carson wrote. "I do contend that we have put poisonous and biologically potent chemicals indiscriminately into the hands of persons largely or wholly ignorant of their potentials for harm. We have subjected enormous numbers of people to contact with these poisons, without their consent and often without their knowledge . . . I contend, furthermore, that we have allowed these chemicals to be used with little or no advance investigation of their effect on soil, water, wildlife, and man himself. Future generations are unlikely to condone our lack of prudent concern for the integrity of the natural world that supports all life."

In her book, which became a best-seller immediately, she pointed out that one of the qualities that attracted chemists to DDT and its new sister poisons was their persistence. And yet this persistence—the ability to accumulate and endure in living tissues—was also the quality that made it a threat not only to the target insect but to all living things. Chapter by chapter and case by case she recounted the way in which man (including the "experts") had poured a withering rain of pesticides into the environment, and the paths by which these complex toxins contaminated the earth.

The evidence was clear that DDT had done immense damage to other living things. Its impact on man remained cloudy, but the evidence was disturbing enough to suggest that the DDT residues carried by every human being in his tissues might bring about irreversible physiological changes; the specter of cancer was raised.

Rachel Carson did not call for the abandonment of all chemical pesticides. She asked only that the use of DDT and the other persistent chemicals be waived in favor of alternate pesticides and the biological control methods that were already within man's reach. The chemical and agricultural industries (supported by their spokesmen in government) answered *Silent Spring* not with technological reform but with a public relations barrage. One chemical company official said that Rachel Carson had written not "as a scientist but as a fanatic defender of the cult of the balance of nature." Others called *Silent Spring* a "hoax," and its author a "mystic."

But a great many other people, including President Kennedy, were shocked by the story that she told. Her book survived the industry's attack. Here and there scientists and government workers began to put into action the reforms that eventually vindicated

Silent Spring. In 1963 (the year before Rachel Carson died) the President's Science Advisory Committee recommended that "elimination of the use of persistent toxic pesticides should be the goal."

The goal was still in the distant future. Nevertheless, the message of *Silent Spring* reverberated beyond the pesticide controversy. It was the first "ecological" book to reach a wide audience. In its pages man was shown not only to produce irreversible effects upon his environment, but to be subject to environmental effects as well. For the first time man was coming to see himself in the place of the buffalo, the fur seal, and the plume birds; the passenger pigeon presented itself to gloomier souls.

"There is no question," a government expert on natural resources said, "that *Silent Spring* prompted the federal government to take action against water and air pollution—as well as against persistent pesticides—several years before it otherwise would have moved."

It is curious that so many Americans remained unaware of (or indifferent to) the growing pollution of their environment almost to the threshold of the 1970s. The signs had been there for a long time. Americans had converted their major rivers into sewers, sacrificing all of their other potential uses to that single purpose.

"This area was settled because the river was there," a federal water pollution control official said of the Missouri's banks. "The towns that grew up were *river* towns. Then, when the river became polluted, the people had to look someplace else for their livelihood, their recreation, and their enjoyment of the country's beauty. They had to turn their backs on the river. Their towns became like any other town that doesn't have a river."

Hepatitis, typhoid, and other diseases remained close to the surface, separated from the public only by overburdened water purification plants. But nothing at all protected the urban public from the deadly miasma that steamed up from its own cities. No one wanted to accept the blame for those great "sewers in the sky." It is instructive, for instance, to regard for a moment the studied myopia of the automotive industry.

The automobile became the country's most persistent source of air pollution. Yet the industry did its best to keep this fact a secret, a secret that Kenneth Hahn of the Los Angeles County Board of Supervisors (in one of the most polluted sections of the country) tried to break.

"We feel that the automobile industry has failed its responsibility to the American public and to the health of the community," Hahn told anyone who would listen to him.

He spoke from considerable experience because he began his crusade so long ago that he numbered the Packard Motor Company among his targets. Fortunately this experience is amply documented in a file containing Hahn's correspondence with leaders in the auto industry. Los Angeles, of course, was aware of the source of its smog as early as 1950. The industry paid no attention to the city's complaints. In 1953 Hahn finally wrote to the presidents of the major automakers, expressing the concern of many local citizens. On March 3 he received a reply from a Ford public relations man.

"The Ford engineering staff, although mindful that automobile engines produce exhaust gases, feels these waste vapors are dissipated in the atmosphere quickly and do not present an air pollution problem," the Ford man wrote to Hahn. "Therefore our research department has not conducted any experimental work aimed at totally eliminating these gases. The fine automotive powerplants which modern-day engineers design do not 'smoke.' Only aging engines subjected to improper care and maintenance burn oil. To date, the need for a device which will more effectively reduce exhaust vapors has not been established."

Hahn persisted. At intervals he shot off letters to the industry's Big Three. Invariably the answers were unsatisfactory. A General Motors vice-president (at least Hahn's correspondents were climbing the corporate ladder) assured him that GM was working hard to reduce pollutants in auto emissions.

"I would be less than candid, however," the Detroit executive wrote, "if I failed to point out that we believe that these changes on automotive vehicles alone will have a very limited influence on the total smog problem in Los Angeles."

For the next several years the correspondence lagged. The Ford Company, for instance, seemed to lose interest in Hahn. Intent on developing a brand new car, its executives were wrapped up in a long correspondence with Marianne Moore, during which they hoped the poet would come up with a name for their product. (After Ford pulled the rug out from under Miss Moore by naming its new car the Edsel, the public pulled the rug out from under the car.) In 1958 Hahn was still hammering away. "I have gained the impression," he told the Chrysler people, "that the automobile industry considers that air pollution is not as important to the industry as the new styling, grille design, more horsepower, or any other accessory."

By 1962 Hahn was receiving replies directly from John F. Gordon, then the president of General Motors. Gordon complained that the California Motor Vehicle Pollution Control Board had not seen fit to approve any GM control devices; they had been turned down as ineffectual. A year later Hahn wrote more forcefully to Gordon:

"Your company has done much to improve the performance and appearance of its products with one notable exception. Despite the great advancements in styling and horsepower, the smog-forming capability of the exhaust of your 1963 models is the same or more than the 1953 products."

Later that year a Ford official began his reply to Hahn in a manner that might have been considered a put-on by a man who had had less experience in dealing with the high and the mighty: "Thank you for your letter of July 30, 1963," the Ford man wrote. "We are gratified that you continue to share in our concern with the Los Angeles smog problem."

And so the country's air grew more foul as the people responsible turned their heads. Across the ocean, London had not heeded the warnings presented by centuries of smog. (Indeed, during World War II the British government had *encouraged* the production of smog to conceal the city from Nazi bombers.) But in December 1952 London paid its bill to nature. The prevailing climatic conditions triggered a "killer smog." The acrid smell of sulfur dioxide permeated every street, and every room, in the city. It was the odor of hell, and afterward the city was able to record more than 4000 "excess" deaths during the few days it lay in the smog's grip.

"In the last hundred years only the peak week of the influenza pandemic in November 1918 produced more deaths over the expected normal than did the man-made fog," a British journal reported. "Even the cholera epidemic of 1886 could not equal it."

Yet the most frightening part of the story was that London remained *unaware* of the tragedy it was living through. Radio weather reports gave no indication that conditions were abnormal beyond the inconveniences of the usual "London fog." Newspapers, when they mentioned the dense fog's effects, spoke only of traffic tieups and afflicted livestock. Government health authorities issued no warnings. It was days afterward—when the hospitals ran out of beds and the morticians complained of overwork and the week's vital statistics were recorded—that the smog's full devastation revealed itself to its victims.

This was a grim allegory illustrating the warning that scientists and conservationists had sounded for modern man: long before we discover the extent to which we have contaminated ourselves and our planet we may have determined, irrevocably, our own fate. It was a warning that millions of Americans began to listen to as the 1970s opened.

At this point, in a sense, America itself joined the conservation movement. Most newcomers called the movement by another name—it was "environmental concern," or "ecological action," or whatever, and in most cases their allegiance was prompted not by what was happening to birds or alligators or the wilderness. It was the shouldering to the surface of the seed planted in their minds a decade earlier by Rachel Carson, and nurtured by a thousand conservationists and scientists. Some of the new conservationists took militant action, others gave lip service to the cause.

For the first time the issues of public health mingled with those of the preservation of nature. "Pollution" and "population" became the catchwords. Was all of the sudden fuss simply a reflex action, triggered by the instinct for self-preservation? Was it grounded in a real understanding of man's roots in the natural world? Will it subside as soon as the experts persuasively lay to rest the threats of cancer, hepatitis, and emphysema?

The history of the "new conservation" has yet to be written. It should be a splendid (and hair-raising) adventure story, and the outcome will be in doubt to the very end. In this corner at least the notion persists that unless the new conservationists, a term which by necessity now includes all of us, make the connection between the Everglades and the plume birds on the one hand, and themselves on the other, the story cannot have a happy ending.

Man, our instinct for survival tells us, will undoubtedly persist. He will make an accommodation with the great invisible machinery of nature upon which his existence depends. But he will have blighted for his remaining span of time here those tangible, wondrous, and evanescent blossoms of creation by which he presently measures his humanity.

A Note on the Sources *

As I suggest in my Preface, I approached my subject with a certain bias, a bias that was not seriously shaken by the voluminous reading that led up to and accompanied the writing of this book. From my sources I tended to extract the descriptions of people and events that interested me most, and I plead guilty to slighting certain aspects of conservation history that other writers have thought important. I can only offer what the academicians may consider a lame defense: I am writing chiefly for the reader who shares my own interests and inclinations.

In any case, I hope readers of whatever persuasion will be stimulated to go on to some of the other literature, both old and fairly new, that often made my research a delight. The following books provide a good general background to the subject (they will be referred to, under the discussion of sources for specific chapters, simply by the last names of their authors):

· *A Sand County Almanac* * by Aldo Leopold (Oxford University Press, New York, 1949)

· *Wildlife in America* * by Peter Matthiessen (Viking Press, New York, 1959)

· *Wilderness and the American Mind* * by Roderick Nash (Yale University Press, New Haven, 1967)

· *Adventures in Bird Protection* by T. Gilbert Pearson (Appleton-Century, New York, 1937)

· *The Politics of Conservation* by Frank Smith (Pantheon, New York, 1966)

· *Crusade for Wildlife* by James B. Trefethen (Stackpole, Harrisburg, Pa., 1961)

· *The Quiet Crisis* * by Stewart L. Udall (Holt, Rinehart and Winston, New York, 1963)

PART I: IN SEARCH OF GUY BRADLEY

The literature dealing with the early bird protection movement remains scattered and fragmented, yet might form the basis of an entire book in itself. Matthiessen, Pearson, and Trefethen were all valuable sources, as was *Birds and*

* All of the books marked with an asterisk can also be found in paperback editions.

*Men,** a fascinating book by Robert Henry Welker (Harvard University Press, Cambridge, 1955). I found indispensable the issues for the appropriate years of *Forest and Stream, The Auk* (the publication of the American Ornithologists' Union), and *Bird-Lore* (which became the publication of the National Association of Audubon Societies and finally was transformed into *Audubon*).

CHAPTER 1: Readers interested in the natural history of the Everglades will want to consult *The Everglades* by Marjorie S. Douglas (Rinehart and Company, New York, 1947) and *Everglades—The Park Story* * by William B. Robertson (University of Miami Press, Coral Gables, 1959, 1963).

CHAPTER 2: This chapter was based on "The Cruise of the Bonton," the log of Charles Pierce's journey around southern Florida which was printed in *Tequesta,* the Journal of the Historical Association of Southern Florida (No. XXII, 1962).

CHAPTER 3: Nash provides a thorough and excellent account of the light in which our ancestors viewed wildlife and wilderness. Primary sources for this chapter included Alexander Wilson's *American Ornithology* (the Brewer edition, Boston, 1940); John James Audubon's *Ornithological Biography* (5 vols., Edinburgh, 1831–39); the American Ornithologists' Union's *Destruction of Our Native Birds,* first published as a supplement to *Science,* February 26, 1886; and Frank M. Chapman's *Camps and Cruises of an Ornithologist* (D. Appleton and Company, New York, 1908). The quotation from General Custer's letter appeared in *Remington Arms in American History* by Alden Hatch (Rinehart and Company, 1956). The quotation about the slaughter of shorebirds is taken from Ralph S. Palmer's *Maine Birds* (Museum of Comparative Zoology, Cambridge, 1947). In writing of the passenger pigeon I relied mainly on A. W. Schorger's book, *The Passenger Pigeon: Its Natural History and Extinction* (University of Wisconsin Press, Madison, 1955).

CHAPTER 4: I used early issues of *The Auk* as a source in writing this chapter, as well as various books and articles by William Brewster, including *The Birds of the Cambridge Region of Massachusetts* (Memoirs of the Nuttall Ornithological Club, No. IV, Cambridge, 1906).

CHAPTER 5: Again, I relied on *The Auk,* as well as on *Forest and Stream* and Jenks Cameron's *The Bureau of the Biological Survey: Its History, Activities and Organization* (Johns Hopkins Press, Baltimore, 1929). Other helpful sources included A. Hunter Dupree's *Science in the Federal Government* (Harvard University Press, Cambridge, 1957); E. H. Forbush's *Decrease of Certain Birds, and Its Causes* (State of Massachusetts, 1908); and *Frank M. Chapman in Florida,* edited by Elizabeth S. Austin (University of Florida Press, Gainesville, 1967). The quotation from Will Cuppy appeared in his book, *The Great Bustard and Other People* (Rinehart and Company, New York, 1941). The quotation from Ludlow Griscom appeared in his book, *Modern Bird Study* (Harvard University Press, Cambridge, 1951).

CHAPTER 6: Here I relied most heavily on Pearson, the AOU supplement referred to above, and various issues of *The Auk* and *Bird-Lore*.

CHAPTER 7: Besides various issues of *The Auk* and *Bird-Lore,* sources for this chapter included Robert Porter Allen's *The Roseate Spoonbill* * (National Audubon Society, 1942); Herbert K. Job's *Wild Wings* (New York, 1905); Charlton W. Tebeau's *Man in the Everglades* * (University of Miami Press, Coral Gables, 1968); and Chapman's *Camps and Cruises,* etc., (see above).

PART II: THE PRESIDENT AND THE FORESTER

As general background for this section of my book I consulted a number of historical works dealing with the closing decade of the nineteenth century and the opening decade of the twentieth century, as well as autobiographies and biographies of the leading figures in my story. I also consulted the following books: Matthiessen, Smith, Trefethen, and Udall; *Conservation and the Gospel of Efficiency: The Progressive Conservation Movement, 1890–1920,* by Samuel P. Hays (Harvard University Press, Cambridge, 1959); *Our Landed Heritage: The Public Domain, 1776–1936,* by Roy M. Robbins (Princeton University Press, Princeton, 1942); *The Closing of the Public Domain* by E. Louise Peffer (Stanford University Press, Stanford, 1951); *Whose Woods These Are: The Story of the National Forests* by Michael Frome (Doubleday, Garden City, N.Y., 1962); *Forest and Range Policy* by Samuel Trask Dana (McGraw-Hill, New York, 1956); *Breaking New Ground* by Gifford Pinchot (Harcourt, Brace and World, New York, 1947); *Gifford Pinchot: Forester-Politician* by M. Nelson McGeary (Princeton University Press, Princeton, 1960); *Remembered Yesterdays* by Robert Underwood Johnson (Little, Brown, Boston, 1923); and *Our Times* by Mark Sullivan (Scribner, New York, 6 vols. 1926–35).

CHAPTER 8: Sources for this chapter included "Johnny Appleseed: A Pioneer Hero" by W. D. Hailey (*Harper's,* November 1871); *Man and Nature* by George Perkins Marsh (Scribner, New York, 1864); and *Report on the Lands of the Arid Regions of the United States* (U. S. Government Printing Office, Washington, D.C., 1878).

CHAPTER 9: My chief sources were *Forest and Stream* (May 5, 1894) and the *Congressional Record* for various dates.

CHAPTER 10: S. A. D. Puter's *Looters of the Public Domain* (Portland Printing House, Portland, Oregon, 1908) is an exhaustive (and exhausting) account of skullduggery in the Western timberlands. I also consulted Gifford Pinchot's *A Primer of Forestry,* Parts I and II, Bulletin 24 (Bureau of Forestry, U. S. Department of Agriculture, Washington, D.C., 1900, 1905).

CHAPTERS 11–13: In dealing with the Roosevelt era I consulted (in addition to works listed above): *The Life and Times of Theodore Roosevelt* by Stefan Lorant (Doubleday, Garden City, N.Y., 1959); *My Brother, Theodore Roosevelt* by Corinne R. Robinson (Scribner, New York, 1921); *Theodore Roosevelt the Naturalist* by Paul Russell Cartright, Harper, New York, 1956); *Forests and Men* by William B. Greeley (Doubleday, Garden City, N.Y., 1951); and *From Roosevelt to Roosevelt,* unpublished manuscript by Harry A. Slattery (copy in the U. S. Department of the Interior Library, Washington, D.C.). In dealing with the "nature fakers" incident I also consulted various issues of *The Outlook, Everybody's Magazine* and the *North American Review* for the years 1903 and 1907.

PART III: FIGHT FOR THE LAND

Samuel P. Hays (see above) is invaluable on this era. Udall, Smith, and Pinchot (see above) furnish important background, as does John Ise in *Our National Park Policy: A Critical History* (Johns Hopkins Press, Baltimore, 1961).

CHAPTER 14: Slattery (see above) gives us a special glimpse of Pinchot's side of the Ballinger affair, while, in an extraordinary article, Harold L. Ickes supports Ballinger ("Not Guilty," *Saturday Evening Post*, May 25, 1940).

CHAPTER 15: Here John Muir's own voluminous writings are invaluable, as are Johnson (see above) and Linnie Marsh Wolfe's *Son of the Wilderness: The Life of John Muir* (Knopf, New York, 1945). A scholarly yet fascinating book is Holway R. Jones's *John Muir and the Sierra Club: The Battle for Yosemite* (Sierra Club, San Francisco, 1965). I also consulted the *Congressional Record* for the appropriate years, as well as various issues of the *Sierra Club Bulletin*.

CHAPTER 16: Robert Shankland's *Steve Mather of the National Parks* (Knopf, New York, 1951) and Ise (see above) were the chief sources for this chapter.

PART IV: FIGHT FOR WILDLIFE

I could not have written this section without the generous cooperation of John Ripley Forbes of New Canaan, Connecticut, in whose possession I found the complete works, published and unpublished, of William T. Hornaday, in addition to considerable correspondence and other papers. I am also indebted to James A. Dolph for his assistance in going over this collection of books and papers with me. Hornaday's most important writings include *Our Vanishing Wildlife* (New York Zoological Society, 1914) and *Thirty Years' War for Wildlife* (Scribner, New York, 1931).

CHAPTER 17: Sources for this chapter included Forbush (see above), in addition to various issues of the New York *Zoological Society Bulletin*.

CHAPTER 18: Pearson and Trefethen were sources for this chapter, as well as Hornaday's writings, *Bird-Lore* for the appropriate years, and various other publications of the Audubon Society.

CHAPTER 19: Again I drew heavily on Pearson, Trefethen, and Hornaday's own publications and correspondence.

CHAPTER 20: In writing this chapter I found Pearson, Trefethen, and Matthiessen helpful, as well as A. C. Bent's *Life Histories of North American Wild Fowl* * (U. C. National Museum *Bulletin Nos. 126, 130;* 1923, 1925). I also consulted *Forest and Stream* and the *Congressional Record* for various dates.

PART V: GOD'S PLENTY, AND WHAT BECAME OF IT

CHAPTER 21:   Here I relied mainly on two contrasting yet excellent accounts of the great scandal: *Teapot Dome: Oil and Politics in the 1920's* by Burl Noggle (Louisiana State University Press, Baton Rouge, 1962) and *Teapot Dome* by M. R. Werner and John Starr (Viking, New York, 1959); as well as on the *Congressional Record* for the appropriate years. There was an interesting contemporary portrait of Fall, "A Cabinet Minister Whose Life Story Reads Like a Dime Novel," in *Current Opinion* (LXXI, July 1921). Slattery and Greeley (for both, see above) were helpful, as were *The Wallaces of Iowa* by Russell Lord (Houghton Mifflin, Boston, 1947) and *The Empire of Oil* by Harvey O'Connor (Monthly Review Press, New York, 1955).

CHAPTER 22:   Smith was a prime source for this chapter, as were the following books: *The Conservation Fight* by Judson King (Public Affairs Press, Washington, D.C., 1959); *Ford: Expansion and Challenge: 1915–1933* by Allan Nevins and Frank Ernest Hill (Scribner, New York, 1957); *Integrity: The Life of George W. Norris* by Richard L. Neuberger and Stephen B. Kahn (Vanguard Press, New York, 1937); *Fighting Liberal: The Autobiography of George W. Norris* (Macmillan, New York, 1945); and *The Tennessee* by Donald Davidson (Holt, Rinehart and Winston, New York, 1948). I am grateful to *Ford Times* for permission to quote from its issue, dated IX February 1916, a portion of Edgar A. Guest's verse, "A Tribute to Henry Ford."

CHAPTER 23:   Leopold, Smith, and Udall give much of the background for this phase of conservation, as do Frome and Slattery (for both, see above). Hugh Bennett's biographer is Wellington Brink in *Big Hugh: The Father of Soil Conservation* (Macmillan, New York, 1951). Other sources for this chapter included *The Coming of the New Deal* by Arthur Schlesinger, Jr. (Houghton Mifflin, Boston, 1959); *Fire and Water: Scientific Heresy in the Forest Service* by Ashley L. Schiff (Harvard University Press, Cambridge, 1962); *Road to Survival* by William Vogt (William Sloane Associates, New York, 1948); *The Civilian Conservation Corps Program of the U.S. Department of the Interior* by Conrad L. Wirth (U. S. Department of the Interior, Washington, D.C., 1945); and *The CCC Through the Eyes of 272 Boys* by Helen M. Walker (Western Reserve University Press, Cleveland, 1938). I am grateful to Oxford University Press for permission to quote passages from Leopold's *A Sand County Almanac*.

CHAPTER 24:   I based section *i* on interviews with officials and members of the National Audubon Society, and on a profile of Rosalie Barrow Edge by Robert Lewis Taylor in *The New Yorker* (April 17, 1948). A chief source for section *ii* was Cameron (see above). Other sources included Leopold, Matthiessen, Trefethen, Hornaday (*Thirty Years War for Wildlife,* see above), and *Our Wildlife Legacy* by Durward L. Allen (Funk and Wagnalls, New York, 1954). I based section *iii* chiefly on my interview with Roger Peterson.

PART VI: THE SPIRIT AND THE FLESH

CHAPTER 25: My chief sources for this chapter were Leopold, Nash, and the *Sierra Club Bulletin, Living Wilderness* (the publication of the Wilderness Society), and the *Congressional Record* for the appropriate years. Also invaluable were the transcripts of hearings held on the Wilderness Bill between 1957 and 1964 by the Senate Committee on Interior and Insular Affairs.

CHAPTER 26: Sources for this chapter included *Silent Spring* * by Rachel Carson (Houghton Mifflin, Boston, 1962), *Killer Smog* * by William Wise (Rand McNally, Chicago, 1968), and two of my own books, *Disaster By Default: Politics and Water Pollution* * (M. Evans, New York, 1966) and *Since Silent Spring* * (Houghton Mifflin, Boston, 1970). I also consulted transcripts of the various hearings held during the 1960s by the Senate Subcommittee on Air and Water Pollution of the Committee on Public Works.

Certain portions of this book spring from magazine stories written for *Sports Illustrated*. I would like to thank| *SI* for permission to draw on them.

Index

Abbott Lyman, 121
Acadian owls, 47
Adirondack Mountains, 86-87, 111, 293
Afognak Island, 115
Agee, James, 282
Agriculture (farming), 73, 264-67. *See also* Irrigation; Soil; specific places
Agriculture, Department of, 106ff., 123, 221, 230-31, 261, 267 (*See also* specific agencies, personnel); and Wilderness Bill, 303
Agriculture Appropriations Bill of 1913, 198
Air pollution, 315-18
Alabama, 240, 241
Alaska, 185, 202-6, 229-30, 275; Cunningham claims, 145-50; "Great Duck Egg Fake," 212-16; Roosevelt's wildlife refuge, 135; salmon reservation, 114-15
Alaskan Railway, 205
Albany, N.Y., 190-91
Albright, Horace, 173
Alert (ship), 32
Allegheny River, 26
Allen, Durward L., 272, 295
Allen, J. A., 20, 23, 30, 32
Allen, Robert Porter, 55, 282
Alligators, 4-7, 17-18
Allott, Gordon, 307
American Bison Society, 184
American Forestry Association, 71, 303, 304
American Forests, 304

American Game Protective Association, 217, 218, 220, 221
American Museum of Natural History, 32, 50, 269
American National Livestock Association, 274
American Ornithologists' Union (AOU), 29-32, 33-38, 41-44, 181 (*See also* specific members); Model Law of (*See* Model Law); and passenger pigeons, 184; and Pelican Island, 115; and plume birds, 46ff.
American Ornithology (Wilson), 15, 16
Amherst, Mass., 30
Anaconda Company, 306
Anderson, George S., 82, 84
Andresen, August H., 224
Antelope, 19
Antiquities Act, 112, 128-31, 163
AOU. *See* American Ornithologists' Union
Appalachian Trail, 290
"Appleseed, Johnny," 66
Arbor Day, 71
Archaeology. *See* Antiquities Act
Arctic Wild (Crisler), 300
Arctic three-toed woodpeckers, 285
Arizona. *See* specific places
Arkansas. *See* specific places
Arms. *See* Guns
Armstrong Fire-Arms Law, 183
Army, U.S., 81ff., 88; Corps of Engineers, 129, 131, 132-33, 144, 163, 240-41ff., 248

Arnold, Matthew, 71
Aspinwall, Wayne N., 307, 308, 309
Audubon, John (son), 42
Audubon, John James, 16-17, 31, 60, 131; and Bachman's warbler, 42; on passenger pigeons, 25-26, 28
Audubon, Victor, 42
Audubon Plumage Bill, 189
Audubon Societies. See National Audubon Society
Automobiles, 174, 315-17

Bachman, John, 42, 60
Bachman's warbler, 42
Bad Lands, 102, 109
Baird, Spencer F., 37
Bald eagles, 4, 275
Baleen whales, 17
Ballinger, Richard Achilles, 139-50, 162, 172, 229, 262
Ballinger, Mrs. Richard Achilles, 149
Barnum, Phineas T., 78
Barred owls, 273
Baruch, Bernard, 244
Baseball, 234
Basocca (gunman), 233
Batty, J. H., 55
Bayne, Howard R., 192
Bayne Bill, 191-93
Bears, 19, 274; Alaskan Brown, 206; black, 4
Beavers, 17, 81
Beecher, Henry Ward, 41
Belgium, 201
Bell, Fred W., 92
Bennett, Hugh Hammond, 252, 264-67
Bering Sea, 185-89
Bern, Switzerland, 97
Bible, the, 65-66
Big Lake, Ark., 210
Big Trees, 157, 174
Bighorn sheep, 19, 102
Biltmore (estate), 95
Biological Survey, Bureau of the, 38, 270, 273-75, 278; meat dealers' attempt to abolish, 129; and Migratory Bird Act, 195, 198, 199, 218-19ff.; and Sulzer Bill, 202

"Biota," 255, 258
Birds, 4, 15-16, 19-62, 114-15, 181-84, 189-99, 268-72, 273. See also Birdwatching; Game birds; Plume birds; Shorebirds; Song birds; Waterfowl; specific species
Birds of Washington and Vicinity (Maynard), 115
Birdwatching, 269, 280-86; Christmas Bird Census, 184; Henry Ford and, 197, 245; Theodore Roosevelt and, 115
Birmingham, Ala., 248
Bison. See Buffalo
Black bears, 4
Black ducks, 193
Blackbirds, 23; rusty, 281
Blaine, James G., 74, 103
Bliss, Cornelius N., 98
Blue geese, 270, 272
Bluebirds, 30, 34, 47
Bobcats, 4, 274
Bobolinks, 23, 30
Boca Ciega Bay, 9
Bonneville Dam, 144
Bonton (sloop), 8-10
Boone, Daniel, 17
Boone and Crockett Club, 103, 124, 184, 217
Bootlegging, 222-23
Borax, 168
Borland, Hal, 300
Bortree, M. R., 214
Boston, Mass., 15, 34
Boston Herald-Traveler, 249
Boulder Dam, 144, 250
Bounties, 275
Bradley, E. R. (father of Guy), 56
Bradley, Mrs. E. R. (mother of Guy), 56
Bradley, Guy, 7, 8-13, 56-58, 60-62, 189
Bradley, Louis, 8, 10, 13, 56
Brandeis, Louis D., 146, 149
Brant, 195
Breaking New Ground (Pinchot), 99
Brewster, William, 30-32, 40, 49, 62; on Model Law, 42
Bridgehampton, Long Island, 20
British Humanitarian League, 121

Bridger, Joe, 76
Bromfield, Louis, 267
Bronx County Bird Club, 282, 283
Bronx Zoo. *See* New York Zoological Park
Brooks Range, 229
Brower, David R., 256, 294-95, 297, 301, 308
Brown bears, 206
Browning, Robert and Elizabeth Barrett, 71
Bryan, William Jennings, 94, 228
Bryant, William Cullen, 74
Bryce Canyon, 170-71
Buck, Glenn, 198
Budget, Bureau of the, 308-9
Buffalo, 38-39, 78ff., 102, 113-14, 181, 184, 208; Daniel Boone on, 17; and pacification of Indians, 18-19, 103n
Bull, John, 285
Buntings, snow, 192
Bureau of the Biological Survey; etc. See Biological Survey, Bureau of the; etc.
Burgess, Felix, 82, 83-85
Burlington, N.C., 51
Burnham, John B., 217, 220, 222, 224
Burroughs, John, 117, 118, 155; Henry Ford and, 197, 245-46; and "Nature Fakers," 119, 121; and Theodore Roosevelt, 117, 118, 119, 121
Bush River, 208
Butcherbirds, 47
Butterfish, 312
Butterflies, 4

California, 91-92, 93, 129-31, 169 (*See also* specific parks, places); and auto pollution, 317; game-bird law, 193; gold mining, 253; naval oil reserves, 231, 233, 234; Okies flee to, 266; sea otters, 188; skiing, 298; waterfowl hunting described, 210-11
California gulls, 38
California Redwood Company, 91-92
Callison, Charles H., 307-8
Cambridge, Mass., 30-32

Campfire Club, 186
Canada and Canadians, 197, 198, 212, 219 (*see also* specific places); and sealing, 185
Canadian Pacific Railroad, 212, 215
Cannon, "Uncle Joe," 109, 112, 148, 247
Canvasback ducks, 210
Cape Cod, Mass., 182
Cape Sable, Fla., 56-57
Caraway, Thaddeus H., 236
Carey Act of 1894, 111
Caribou, 202, 205
Carnegie, Andrew, 136, 218
Carson, Rachel, 312-15
"Cattalo," 113
Cattle (cows), 111, 129, 173, 200, 302, 306 (*See also* Grazing); and "cattalo," 113; and destruction of land, 258-59; and Taylor Grazing Act, 277
CCC, 262-64
Census Bureau, U.S., 285
Central Park (NYC), 74-75
Century Magazine, The, 157, 158
Chapman, Frank M.: and Bachman's warbler, 42; and Christmas Bird Census, 184; and Guy Bradley, 60, 62; and millinery, 47; and Pelican Island, 114, 115; on prairie chickens, 23-24
Chapman, John, 66
Chevalier (bird hunter), 9, 10, 13, 55, 56
Chickens, 39
Chile, 244
Chimney swifts, 51
Christmas Bird Census, 184
Chugach National Forest, 146
Cincinnati Zoo, 28, 115, 184
Civilian Conservation Corps (CCC), 262-64
Clark, Edward B., 119
Clarke-McNary Act, 257
Clement, Roland C., 285
Cleveland, Grover, 85, 93, 94
Cleveland *Plain-Dealer,* 249
Cliff Palace, 128
Coal, 144-50, 173

Coal Lands Act, 144
Cody, Buffalo Bill, 19
Colby, William E., 159
Collier's, 62, 122, 147, 149
Colorado, 44, 87, 129
Colorado River, 72-73; Boulder Dam, 144, 250; Storage Project, 296-97
Columbia River, 278
Commerce, Department of, 278
Commerce and Labor, Department of, 187
Commercial Fisheries, Bureau of, 188
Congress, 37, 123, 129, 133, 242 (See also Senate; specific legislation, members); attitude toward national parks, 169-70, 174-75; and Cunningham claims, 147-50
Connecticut, 43-44, 220
Conness, John, 157
Conservation and the Gospel of Efficiency, 109n
Consolidated Oil Co., 237
Constitution, U.S., 65-66
Cooke, Jay, 78
Cooke City, Mont, 79, 80, 81
Coolidge, Calvin, 235, 237-38, 247-48, 250
Cooper's hawks, 273
Coots, 41
Cormorants, 10
Corps of Engineers. See under Army, U.S.
Corpus Christi, Tex., 272
Cotingas, Pompadour, 46
Cottam, Clarence M., 295
Coues, Elliott, 30, 32
Cougars, 272, 274
Council of Conservationists. 297
Cowbirds, 285
Cox, Samuel S.. 80
Coyotes, 259, 273, 274, 276, 277
Cramton, Louis C., 176
Cranes, whooping, 20
Crisler, Lois, 300
Crisp, Charles F., 80-81
Crocodiles, 4
Crows, 16, 273; fish, 59
Cruickshank, Allan, 282, 284

Cruise of the Bonton (Pierce). See Pierce, Charles William
Crusade for Wildlife (Trefethen), 87
Cuckoos, 39
Cunningham, Clarence, 145
"Cunningham claims," 145-50
Cuppy, Will, 42-43
Curlews: Eskimo, 24-25; pink (See Roseate spoonbills); white (See Ibises)
Custer, George A., 19
Cuthbert (bird hunter), 59-60
Cuthbert Lake, Fla., 58-60
Cutright, Paul Russell, 115
Cutter, Robert K., 166-67
Czolgosz, Leon, 104

Dams, 129, 144, 242-43, 278. See also specific dams, projects
Dana, Henry, 32
Darling, J. N. ("Ding"), 278
Daugherty, Harry M., 237, 238
Day, Alfred M., 295
DDT, 310-15
Deadwood, S. Dak., 94
Decoys, hunting with, 209-10, 211
Deer, 17, 173; in Adirondacks, 86, 87; European, 193; in Everglades, 4; wolves and, 276-77
Democratic Party. See specific members
Denby, Edwin, 229, 232, 237, 238, 239
Derby, Ethel Roosevelt, 102
Desert Land Act, 70
De Voto, Bernard, 295, 300
Dickinson, Emily, 30
Dies, Martin, 170
Dilg, Will H., 221
Dingell-Johnson Act, 279
Dinosaur National Monument, 294
District of Columbia. 51. See also Washington, D.C.
Division of Entomology; etc. See Entomology, Division of; etc.
Doane, G. C., 76
Dobie, J. Frank, 272-73, 289
Dogs (hounds), 86, 87, 209, 274
Doheny, Edward M., 234, 236, 239

Dolliver, Jonathan P., 139, 148, 149
Doughbirds, 24-25
Douglas, Paul H., 297, 301
Doves: mourning, 52; rock (See Pigeons)
Downing, Andrew Jackson, 74, 75
Ducks, 4, 192, 193, 207-24; and Migratory Bird Act, 195, 196, 198, 207, 216ff.
Dutcher, William, 46, 47, 51-52, 60, 62

Earth Day, vii
Eagles: bald, 4, 275; golden, 273
Eastman, George, 218
Echo Park Dam, 295-97
Economic Ornithology and Mammalogy, Division of, 37-39
Edge, Rosalie Barrow, 268-72, 296
Edison, Thomas A., 245
Edwards, George, 46
Eggs, 20-23, 43, 212-16, 273
Egrets, 47, 48-49, 55, 56, 58ff., 191 (See also Herons); as pests, 194
Eider ducks, 207-8
Eisenhower, Dwight D., 294, 297, 307
Electricity. See Power
Elk, 19, 81, 102, 173, 200
Elk Hills, Calif., 233, 234
Elliott, Henry Wood, 185-86
Empire of Oil, The (O'Connor), 238
England. See Great Britain
English sparrows, 33-37, 39, 41, 53, 115
Entomology, Division of, 37
Erie Canal, 87
Erosion, 264-67
Eskimo curlews, 24-25
Eureka, Calif., 91-92
Evangeline (Longfellow), 26-27
Everglades, vii-ix, 3-7, 10-13, 54ff., 279-80; reddish egret in, 49
Everybody's Magazine, 119

Falcons, peregrine, 273
Fall, Albert Bacon, 227-39
Farming. See Agriculture
Faulkner, William, 299
Feathers. See Plume birds

Federal Migratory Bird Act. See Migratory Bird Treaty Act
Federal Power Commission, 249
Federal Power and Duck Bag Limit Facts, 219
Federal Tariff Act of 1913, 193-95
Federal Trade Commission, 249
Federal Water Power Act of 1920, 249
Fernow, Bernard E., 93, 133
Field Guide to the Birds, A (Peterson), 283-84
Field and Stream, 308
Fire and Water (Schiff), 257
Fires, 70, 254, 257
Firestone, Harvey, 245
Fish and fishing, 278-79, 312. See also specific fish
Fish crows, 59
Fish and Fisheries, Commissioner of, 37
Fish hawks, 47
Fish and Wildlife Service, U.S., 278, 295, 312
Fisheries, Bureau of, 187, 278. See also Commercial Fisheries, Bureau of; Sport Fisheries and Wildlife, Bureau of
Fisher, A. K., 42, 52, 53
Flamingo, Fla., 56-57, 60-61, 62
Flamingos, 10, 20, 49
Floods, 93, 130, 131, 242, 258, 265
Florida, 8-13, 16, 53-62, 201, 210 (See also specific places); Bachman's warblers in, 42; cost of electricity in, 248
Florida Wild Life (Simpson), 279
Folsum, David E., 76
Food Administration, 201. See also Hoover, Herbert
Forbush, E. H., 38-39, 182
Ford, Henry, 197-98, 218, 244-48
Ford Motor Company, 316, 317
Forest Management Act of 1897, 94
Forestry, Bureau of (later Forest Service), 106ff. (See also Pinchot, Gifford
Forestry, Division of (later Bureau of Forestry), 87-88, 99. (See also Pinchot, Gifford)

Forest Service, 124-28ff., 147-48, 149, 172, 228, 230, 253-56, 258, 290 *(See also* Greeley, William; Pinchot, Gifford); Ickes and, 261-62; and wilderness areas, 298-99, 301, 304, 307

Forest and Stream Weekly, 40, 41, 44, 113, 212; on Biltmore, 95; and "Great Duck Egg Fake," 213-14, 215-16; and Yellowstone, 80, 82-84

Forester, Frank, 208

Forests and forestry, 69-71, 74, 86-99, 105ff., 123-28ff., 134, 156-57ff., 253-58 *(See also* specific agencies, foresters, forests); CCC and, 262-64; reverence of Muir for, 156-57; and wilderness areas, 299ff.

Forestry (Pinchot), 97-98

Fork Railroad Company, 79-81

Foxes, 39, 275, 276

France, 45-46, 97-98

Free Rum on the Congo (Hornaday), 180-81

French Guiana, 46

Gabrielson, Ira N., 278, 304

Game and hunting, 112-15, 182-99, 200ff., 272-78 *(See also* specific species); birds, 20, 41, 43-44, 191-93, 195-99, 207-24, 276 *(See also* Shorebirds; Waterfowl; specific species); Lacey Law, 129, 190; plume *(See* Plume birds)

Garfield, James R., 143, 144, 146, 161, 162

Garibaldi, Giuseppe, 71

Geer v. Connecticut, 43-44

Geese, 195, 198, 208ff.; blue, 270, 272

Geigy, J. R., Aktien Gesellschaft, 310-11

General Dam Act of 1906, 129

General Grant National Park, 159

General Land Law Revision Act, 93

General Land Office, 69, 91, 94, 99, 106, 123; to Bureau of Land Management, 299n; and Cunningham claims, 145ff; and Pelican Island, 114; reserves withdrawn from, 124

General Motors (GM), 317

Geological Survey, 74, 112, 242, 309

George, Henry, 103

Germany, 97

Gilder, Richard Watson, 157

Gila Wilderness Area, 256

Gilpin, William, 69

Glavis, Louis R., 145, 146, 147, 149, 261

Glen Canyon, 297

Glenn County Club, 211

Gold, 253

Golden eagles, 273

Golden plovers, 24

Goldwater, Barry, 307

Gordon, John F., 317

Goshawks, 273

Grand Canyon: FDR and, 259; Hearst and, 175; Merriam and life zones, 39-40; Pinchot and Muir in, 96-97; Powell and, 72; Theodore Roosevelt and, 128, 135, 290

Grand Coulee Dam, 144

Grant, Ulysses S,, 72, 78

Grazing, 110-11, 127, 129, 159, 230, 258-59, 261. *See also* Cattle; Livestock; Sheep

Grazing Service, 261, 299n

Great Britain: British Humanitarian League, 121; English common law, 44; London, 187, 317-18; and sealing, 185

Great Bustard and Other People, The (Cuppy), 42-43

"Great Duck Egg Fake," 212-16

Great Falls, 248

Great Lakes, 70

Great white herons, 10

Greeley, Horace, 18, 157

Greeley, William, 127, 130, 230, 256-57

Greensboro, N.C., 51

Grinnell, George Bird, 40-41, 113, 191, 196, 202, 217; and Boone and Crockett Club, 103; and "Great Duck Egg Fake," 213-16; and lead poisoning of ducks, 212; and Yellowstone, 80-81

Griscom, Ludlow, 43, 282-83

Grosbeaks, pine, 47

Grouse, 39, 41, 44, 192; pinnated, 23-24; ruffed, 43

Gruening, Ernest, 249

Guest, Edgar A., 244-45

Guggenheim, Daniel, 145

Guide to Western Birds (Peterson), 284

Gulls, California, 38

Guns (arms; weapons), 183-84, 211-12, 216 *(See also* Game and hunting); manufacturers' American Game Protective Association, 217, 218, 220, 221; Remington rifle, 19

Hagenstein, W. D., 304-5

Hahn, Kenneth, 315-17

Hall, Redford, 302

Hall, Willie, 273

Hanna, Mark, 104

Harding, Warren G., 227, 229, 231ff., 237, 238, 244, 246; death, 235, 247

Harper's Magazine, 293

Harriman, Edward H., 159

Harrison, Benjamin, 93, 103, 115, 158

Hawk Mountain Sanctuary, 272

Hawks, 38, 39, 273, 275; fish, 47; red-shouldered, 58; sparrow, 115

Hayes, Rutherford B., 74

Hays, Samuel P., 109n, 145

Hearst, William R., 175

Heath hens, 15

Hedges, Cornelius, 77-78

Heflin, J. Thomas, 236-37

Heflin, Van, 282

Heliogabalus, 20

Herons, 9, 10, 30, 47, 48, 56, 59, 62, 190, 191 *(See also* Egrets); as food, 20; Job on, 58; as pests, 194

Herrin, William, 159-60

Hetch Hetchy, 151-67, 170, 172, 289, 296, 306

Hewitt, Abram S., 103

Hickey, Joseph J., 282

Hill, James J., 134

Hinckley, Minn., 70

Hitchcock, Ethan Allen, 124, 161

Hoar, George F., 59

Holmes, Oliver Wendell, 41

Homestead Act, 69, 73, 127

Hoover, Herbert, 173, 200-1, 238; and Fall, 235; FDR and, 260; and TVA, 250

Hornaday, William Temple, 179-88, 189, 192-94, 196, 198, 201-2ff., 217-18ff.; and crow shoots, 273; and Rosalie Edge, 270; on Theodore Roosevelt, 112; on William J. Long, 121; and World War I, 200, 201-2

Horned larks, 15

Horned owls, 273

Horse racing, 234

Horseflies, 57

Hotel Men's Association of New York, 192

Hough, Emerson, 82-85

Houghton Mifflin, 283

House of Representatives. *See* Congress; specific legislation, members

Howell, Ed, 81-85

Hudson River, 87

Hummingbirds, 30

Humphrey, Hubert H., 264, 297, 301, 303

Hunting. *See* Game and hunting

Ibises, 13, 55, 56, 58, 59

Ickes, Harold Le Claire, 106, 260-62, 266

Idaho, 76, 129, 254

Illinois, 23

Imperial Valley, 250

Indian River, 114

Indiana, 23, 44

Indians, 15, 17, 88, 274, 303-4; buffalo and pacification of, 18-19, 103n; and "Great Duck Egg Fake," 213, 214; vandalism of ruins, 128

Ingalls, John J., 79

Inland Waterways Commission, 131-33, 242

Insecticides, 310-15

Interior, Department of the, 69, 140-43ff., 168ff., 229ff., 261-62, 267 *(See also* specific agencies, secretaries); La Follette on, 229; opposition to Wilderness Bill, 303; and Yellowstone, 79

International Power and Paper, 249
Irrigation, 73, 93, 111, 112, 130, 140
Ise, John, 160
Italy, 182-83
Ivory-billed woodpeckers, 42-43

James River, 243
Jays, 30
Jefferson, Thomas, 14
Jews, 202
Job, Herbert K., 55-60, 62, 116, 117
John Muir and the Sierra Club
    (Jones), 159-60
Johns Hopkins University, 37
Johnson, Andrew, 78
Johnson, Lyndon B., 309
Johnson, Robert Underwood, 152, 155-
    66 *passim*
Jones, Charles J. ("Buffalo"), 113-14
Jones, Holway R., 159-60
Journal of Commerce, The, 74
Juneau *Empire*, 206

Kaibab Plateau, 276
Kennecott Copper, 306
Kennedy, J. F., 307, 308-9, 314
Kent, William, 163, 164, 166, 172
Kentucky, 17
Kentucky Derby, 234
Key West, Fla., 61-62
Kieran, John, 282
Kingbirds, 15
Kings Canyon National Park, 159
Kipling, Rudyard, 118
Kline, Horace A., 48
Krutch, Joseph Wood, 300

Labrador, 16-17
Lacey, John F., 53, 85, 124, 128
Lacey Act, 53, 129, 190
LaFollette, Robert M., 135, 229, 233,
    234
La Guardia, Fiorello H., 221
Lake Eleanor, 161
Lake Pontchartrain, 42
Lamar Valley, 114
Land, 3-7, 65-75, 139-76, 252-67. *See
    also* Forests and forestry

Land Management, Bureau of, 299
Land Office. *See* General Land Office
Lane, Franklin K., 168, 169, 172, 173,
    227; and Hetch Hetchy, 164; and naval
    oil reserves, 231
Langford, Nathaniel P., 78, 79
Larks: horned, 15; skylarks, 191
Lawyer, George A., 220
Lead poisoning in ducks, 212
Least terns, 10
Lee, Floyd W., 302
Lehman, Herbert H., 301
Leopold, Aldo, 254-56, 258, 290, 299-300,
    313; and passenger pigeons, 28; and
    predators, 275-77
Lesseps, Ferdinand de, 71
Lesser yellowlegs, 24
Lewis, Merriwether, 88
Life magazine, 121
"Life zones," 39-40
Lincoln, Abraham, 71, 157
Livestock, 298-99 (*See also* Cattle;
    Gazing; Sheep); and predator con-
    trol, 274ff.
Livingstone, Sir Richard, 259
Logging. *See* Forests and forestry
London, Jack, 120, 122
London, England, 187, 317-18
Long, William J., 117-22
Long Island, 192
Longfellow, Henry Wadsworth, 26-27,
    30
Longworth, Alice Roosevelt, 102, 227
Looters of the Public Domain, 92
Loring, Caleb G., 24
Los Angeles, Calif., 250
Louisiana, 18, 49, 213-14 (*See also* spe-
    cific places); Purchase, 66
Louisiana herons, 58
Lowell, James Russell, 30
Lower Klamath Lake, 222
Lumbering. *See* Forests and forestry

McAdoo, William Gibbs, 237-38
McCadden, Mary, 116
Mackerel, 312
McGee, W. J., 109, 131-32, 134, 241
McIlhenny, E. A., 49

McKay, Douglas, 295, 303
MacKaye, Benton, 290
Mackenzie, Alexander, 131, 132-33
McKinley, William, 98, 103, 104
McLean, Edward B., 236
McLean, George P., 196
McNary, Charles S., 222-23
Magpies, 273
Maine, 24, 69, 207, 249. *See also* specific places
Maine Birds (Palmer), 24
Malheur Lake, Ore., 210, 222
Mallards, 193, 210
Mammoth Oil Company, 232, 233
Man and Nature (Marsh), 71-72
Manatees, 4
Mangroves, 54, 114
Manson, Marsden, 161
Manual of the Ornithology of the United States and Canada (Nuttall), 32
Marine Biological Laboratory, 37
Mariposa Grove, 157
Marsh, George Perkins, 71-72
Marshall, Louis, 290-93
Marshall, Robert, 290-94
"Martha" (passenger pigeon), 28
Martha's Vineyard, 15
Maryland, 275
Massachusetts, 49, 182, 193, 210, 220 (*See also* specific places); protects robins and horned larks, 15
Mather, Cotton, 65
Mather, Stephen Tyng, 168-76
Mayas, 45
Maynard, Lucy W., 115
Meadowlarks, 23
Meek, Joe, 76
Mellon, Andrew, 246
Merriam, C. Hart, 38, 39-40, 119, 273; and Lacey Law, 129
Metcalf, Lee, 301
Mexico, 228
Miami, Fla., 55
Michigan, 23, 44, 70
Migratory Bird Refuge Commission, 220
Migratory Bird Treaty Act, 183, 195-99, 207, 216ff.

Milburn, G. R., 302
Milliners and millinery, 44, 45-48, 60, 190-91, 194-95. *See also* Plume birds
Millinery Trade Review, The, 53
Minelli, Vincente, 282
Miner, Jack, 221
Mineral Land Act, 71
Mineral Leasing Act of 1920, 253, 295
Mines, Bureau of, 309
Mining and minerals, 159, 253-54, 295, 302, 306, 309. *See also* specific minerals
Minks, 38, 270
Minnesota. *See* specific places
Mississippi River, 132, 242-43
Mitchell, John H., 212-13, 214, 215
Model Law, 41-42, 43, 50, 52, 53, 56
Mondell, Franklin W., 197
Montana, 76, 129
Moore, Marianne, 316
Moore, Myles C., 145
Moose, 202, 205
Morgan, Arthur E., 251
Morgan, J. P., 145
Morison, Samuel Eliot, 175
Morris, A. P., 302
Morse, Wayne, 298, 301
Morton, Sterling, 71
Mosquitoes, 4, 55, 57
Mount Desert Island, Maine, 175
Mountain lions, 117, 274, 275, 276. *See also* panthers
Mourning doves, 52
Mugwumps, 103
Muir, John, 96-97, 109, 133, 169, 289, 290; death, 166; and Hetch Hetchy, 151-57ff.; and sheep, 70, 104, 127, 156, 157; and Theodore Roosevelt, 117
Muir Woods National Monument, 163
Mule deer, 276
Mules, 38-39
Müller, Paul H., 310-11
Mundt, Karl E., 301
Murphy, Robert Cushman, 115
Murray, James E., 306-7
Muscle Shoals. *See* Tennessee River and Valley Authority
Muskrats, 270-72

Nabokov, Vladimir, 284
Nagel, Charles, 186, 187
Nashville, Tenn., 248
National Academy of Sciences, 95
National Audubon Society (formerly Audubon Societies; National Association of Audubon Societies), 41, 49-53, 56, 115n, 129, 191, 268-72, 278 (*See also* specific members); and alien gunners, 183; and bird feeding, 285; Christmas Bird Census, 184; and DDT, 312; and Echo Park Dam, 295; and Guy Bradley's death, 61, 62; and Migratory Bird Act, 216; and Pelican Island, 114; and Roger Tory Peterson, 284, 286; and Shooting Grounds Bill, 221; and Tariff Bill, 193
National Conservation Association, 147, 163-64, 229, 243, 253
National Conservation Commission, 134
National Forest Commission, 95-97
National Forest Wilderness Areas, 309
National forests, 124-27, 129-30, 134 (*See also* Forests and forestry; Forest Service; specific foresters, forest); wilderness areas in (*see* Wilderness areas)
National Game, Fish and Bird Protective Association, 213, 214
National Geographic, 171, 274
National Irrigation Congress, 111
National monuments, 128, 135, 297. *See also* specific places
National Park Act of 1916, 296
National Park Service, 147, 172-73, 175, 254, 298, 301
National parks, 106-9, 128, 147, 157-76 (*See also* specific parks); and wilderness areas, 297ff.
National Parks Association, 172
National Zoological Park, 103, 181
"Nature fakers" affair, 117-22
Navy, U.S., 135; oil reserves, 231-39
Nebraska, 24, 250
Nebraska Power Company, 250
Nelson, E. W., 218-19, 219-20, 222-23
Nevada, 112

Neuberger, Richard L., 297, 298, 301, 304-5
New Deal, 260. *See also* Roosevelt, Franklin D.
New England, 30-32. *See also* specific states
New Jersey, 52, 220
New London, Conn., 43
New Mexico, 228, 235, 256
New York City, 86-87, 145, 192, 196, 202 (*See also* specific groups, institutions, persons); albumen dealers, 215; Central Park, 74-75; millinery, 46-47, 50, 191; and passenger pigeons, 27; price for buffalo head in, 81
New York State, 50, 51, 86-87, 103, 189ff., 220, 259 (*See also* specific places); fire-arms law, 183; and heath hen, 15; and Model Law, 43
New York *Sun,* 103, 121
New York *World,* 228
New York Zoological Park (Bronx Zoo), 103, 113, 183, 184, 187, 217. *See also* Hornaday, William Temple
New Yorker, The, 268-69
Newark *Evening News,* 150
Newell, Frederick H., 109, 111-12, 131, 140, 144
Newlands, Francis G., 111, 112, 131, 242
Nitrates, 244, 246, 248-49, 251
Noble, John W., 93, 133, 158
Norbeck, Peter, 224
Norbeck-Andresen Bill, 224
Norris, George W., 148, 163, 165-66; and TVA, 246-47ff., 260
Norris, P. W., 79
North American Commercial Company, 186
North Carolina, 50-51, 208
North Cascades, 307
North Dakota, Bad Lands of, 102, 111
Northern Pacific Railroad, 79, 215
Northern shrikes, 47
Nuttall, Thomas, 32
Nuttall Ornithological Club, 32, 34

Oakland, Calif., 114
O'Connor, Harry, 238

Ohio, 27, 87, 220
Oil (petroleum), 231-39, 295, 306, 309
Okeechobee, 54
Oklahoma, 169, 184
Olmsted, Frederick Law, 75, 157-59, 230
Olmsted, Frederick Law, Jr., 172-73
Olson, Sigurd, 300
Olympic National Park, 272, 297
Ontario, Canada, 248
Ontario Power Authority, 249
Opossums, 270
Oregon, 92, 129. *See also* specific places
Ornithological Biography (Audubon), 16, 31
Ornithology and Mammalogy, Division of, 39-40
Ospreys, 47
Ostriches, 46, 52
Otters, 4; sea, 17, 188
Our Vanishing Wild Life (Hornaday), 179, 196
Outlook, The, 120, 121
Owls, 38, 39, 273; Acadian, 47
Oyster Key, 61

Pacific Gas and Electric Company, 166
Page, J. Wallace, 184
"Page Wildlife Fence," 184
Palmer, Ralph S., 24
Panama Canal, 132, 135
Pan-American Petroleum and Transport Company, 233, 234
Panthers, 4
Park Protection Act of 1894, 85, 113
Parker, Alton B., 123
Parrots, 20
Passenger pigeons, 25-28, 115, 184
Pearson, T. Gilbert, 50ff., 190-91, 193, 194, 196, 197; on advisory board for Biological Survey, 218, 222; and pelicans, 201; and Rosalie Edge, 269-70; and Winchester Repeating Arms Company, 216
Pelican Island, 114-15
Pelican Valley, 82, 83-84
Pelicans, 10, 16, 23, 118-19, 201
Pennsylvania, 26, 43, 49 (*See also* specific places); scalp act, 38-40

Pepper, George Wharton, 148-49
Peregrine falcons, 273
Permanent Wild Life Protection Fund, 217-18
Peshtigo, Wisc., 70
Pesticides, 310-15
Peterson, Roger Tory, 280-86
Petrified Forest, 135
Petroleum. *See* Oil
Pheasants, 41, 193
Pheasants Unlimited, 275
Phelan, James D., 161, 163
Phelps Dodge Corporation, 306
Pierce, Charles William, 7, 8-13, 47
Pierce, H. D. (father of Charles William Pierce), 9
Pigeons, 25-28, 195; passenger, 25-28, 115, 184
Pileated woodpeckers, 47
Pilgrims, 14
Pinchot, Gifford, 99, 100, 105-11, 116, 123-28, 130, 135, 243, 253ff., 260, 289; and Corps of Engineers, 242-43; and Fall, 229ff.; and Hetch Hetchy controversy, 159ff., 170, 172; and Ickes, 262; and Taft Administration, 139-43; and Washington conservation conference, 133-34; Wilderness Bill Controversy and, 304, 305
Pinchot, James M., 94
Pinchot, Mrs. James M. (mother of Gifford), 127-28, 149
Pine grosbeaks, 47
Pink curlews. *See* Roseate spoonbills
Pinnated grouse, 23-24
Pittman-Robertson Act, 278
Platt, Thomas C., 103
Platt National Park, 169
Platte River, 18
Plovers, 24, 192, 195, 198
Plume birds, 4, 8-13, 45-62, 207 (*See also* specific birds); and Audubon Plumage Bill, 189-91; and Tariff Act, 193-95
Politics of Conservation, The (Smith), 306n
Pollution, 310-18
Pompadour, Mme. de, 45, 46

Pompadour cotingas, 46
Portland *News,* 249
Portsmouth, N.H., 30
Powell, John Wesley, 71, 72-74, 88, 111, 131
Power, 127, 144, 230, 240-51. *See also* specific projects
Prairie chickens, 23-24
Predators, 272-80
Pribilof Islands, 185-88
Price, Overton, 109
Princeton University, 37
Public Domain League, 129, 144
Public Shooting Grounds-Game Refuge Bill, 220-22
Puffins, 207
Pulaski (forest ranger), 254
Pulp industry, 110
Puter, S. A. D., 88-92

Quail, 41, 43, 44, 51, 192
Quetzal, 45

Racoons, 270
Railroads, 70, 79-81 (*See also* specific lines); land grants to, 69; and promotion of national parks, 158-60, 171; vs. water transportation, 87
Rails (birds), 41, 195
Rainey, Paul J., Wildlife Sanctuary, 270-72
Raker, John E., 164, 166, 172
Raker Bill, 164
Rattlesnakes, 4
Reagan, Ronald, 156
Reclamation, Bureau of, 112, 140, 144, 147, 171-72, 241-42, 296
Reclamation Act of 1902, 111, 112, 140, 241
Reclamation Act of 1914, 140
Reclamation Service, 112
Recreation Magazine, 113
Red foxes. *See* Foxes
Red-shouldered hawks, 58
Reddish egrets, 49
Redhead ducks, 210
Redington, Paul G., 224
Redwoods, 91-92, 163, 169

Reed, James A., 194, 237
Remington rifles, 19
Report on the Lands of the Arid Region of the United States, A (Powell), 73
Republican Party, 102-3, 104, 139, 147, 150. *See also* specific members
Rhode Island, 50, 220
Ricebirds (bobolinks), 23, 30
Riggs, Thomas W., 205
Right of Way Act of 1901, 160
Rivers. *See* Dams; Waterways; specific rivers
Robertson, William B., Jr., 4-7
Robins, 15, 20, 23, 183; and egg-collecting, 43
Robinson, Corinne Roosevelt, 115
Rock doves. *See* Pigeons
Rockefeller, John D., 231, 234
Rodents, 259
Roosevelt, Alice. *See* Longworth, Alice Roosevelt
Roosevelt, Archie, 237
Roosevelt, Corinne. *See* Robinson, Corinne Roosevelt
Roosevelt, Edith Carow (Mrs. Theodore), 62, 102
Roosevelt, Ethel. *See* Derby, Ethel Roosevelt
Roosevelt, Franklin D., 259-60ff.; on Dust Bowl, 266; on Everglades, 279; and oil lands, 231; and TVA, 250-52
Roosevelt, Theodore, 62, 99, 100-35, 139ff., 150, 184, 231; and Adirondacks, 86; on cougars, 272; and Grand Canyon, 128, 135, 290; and Hetch Hetchy, 162; and Muir, 159, 162, 164; and Muir Woods, National Monument, 163; and Muscle Shoals, 241, 243; in Nuttall Club, 34, 36; and Sulzer Bill, 202; and World War I food resources, 201; and Yellowstone, 80
Roosevelt, Theodore, Jr., 232
Roosevelt, Theodore, National Memorial Park, 102
Root, Elihu, 100, 197
Roseate Spoonbill, The (Allen), 55
Roseate spoonbills, 48-49, 58
Ruddy ducks, 210

Ruess, Henry R., 301
Ruffed grouse, 43
Rusk, Jeremiah M., 40
Russia (Soviet Union), 302; and seals, 185
Russo-Japanese War, 135
Rusty blackbirds, 281
Ryder, C. J., 120
Rye, N.Y., 269

Sage, Mrs. Russell, 217
Salmon, 114-15, 275
Salt Lake City, Utah, 38
San Francisco, Calif., 160ff.
Sand County Almanac, A (Leopold), 28
Sanders, James T., 61
Sandpipers, 4, 24, 192, 198
Sargent, Charles S., 90, 95, 97, 133
Saturday Evening Post, 171, 262
Sawgrass, 54
Saylor, John P., 301
"Scalp act," 38-39
Scarlet tanagers, 30
Schiff, Ashley L., 257
Schurz, Carl, 74
Scott, W. E. D., 49
Screech owls, 273
Scribner's, 78
Sea Around Us, The (Carson), 312
Sea cows, 4
Sea otters, 17, 188
Sea swallows, 10
Seals, 184-88
Seattle, Wash., 98, 143
Segregation Bill, 80-81
Senate, 233ff. (See also specific legislation, members); Committee on Agriculture, 246-47ff., 273; Committee on Agriculture and Forestry, 222-23; Committee on the Conservation of Natural Resources, 186; Committee on Interior Affairs, 306-7
Sequoia National Park, 159, 174
Sequoias, 93; See also Big Trees, Redwoods
Seton, Ernest Thompson, 119
Shankland, Robert T., 168, 170
Sharon, William, 111

Sharp-shinned hawks, 273
Sheep, 98, 127, 156-57, 173, 202, 228; bighorn, 19, 102
Sheldon, Charles, 205, 206, 218
Sheridan, Philip H., 19, 103n
Shields, G. O., 113
Shiras, George, III, 195, 196
Shorebirds, 24-25, 41, 198-99, 207. See also specific birds
Shrikes, northern, 47
Sierra Club, 159, 164, 169, 173, 295, 306
Sierra Club Bulletin, 156n, 166-67
Silent Spring (Carson), 312, 313-15
Silz, August, 192
Simpson, Charles T., 279
Sinclair, Harry Ford, 233-34, 236, 237, 239
Sinclair, Upton, 250
Skiing, 298
Skunks, 273
Skylarks, 191
Slattery, Harry, 229ff., 254, 260, 261; and Ballinger, 144, 147; and National Conservation Association, 164; at White House conservation conference, 134; on Wilson and World War I, 173
Slaughter of Useful Birds (Hornaday), 196
Smith, Alfred E., 190
Smith, Frank E., 306n
Smith, Herbert K., 131
Smith, Hoke, 85, 95
Smith, Walter, 60-62
Smithsonian Institution, 249
Snipe, 199
Snow buntings, 192
"Snowshoe Pete," 82
Snowy egrets, 47, 49
Snowy herons, 58
Society of American Foresters, 110, 230
Soil, 252-67
Soil Conservation Act, 266-67
Soil Conservation Service, 266-67
Soil Erosion Service, 266
Soils, Bureau of, 252
Song birds, 20, 23, 182-83, 190-91, 207. See also specific birds
South Africa, Union of, 265

Soviet Union. *See* Russia

Sparrow hawks, 115

Sparrows, 23, 115; English, 33-37, 39, 41, 53, 115

Spoonbills, 48-49, 55, 58

Sport Fisheries and Wildlife, Bureau of, 40

Spring Valley Water Company, 161, 163

Square Deal for the Fur Seal, A (Hornaday), 187

Stahr, Elvis J., foreword by, vii-ix

Standard Oil Company, 234

Starlings, 285

Stickeen (Muir), 96

Stinson, Roxy, 238

Story of Mount Desert Island, The (Morison), 175

Sulphur, Okla., 169

Sulzer, Charles A., 202

Sulzer Bill, 202-6

Sundry Civil Bill, 134

Supreme Court, 43-44, 127

Sutherland, Dan A., 206

Suwanee River, 42

Swamplands Act, 91, 174

Swans, 197; whistling, 20

Swifts, chimney, 51

Switzerland, 97

Taft, William Howard, 139ff., 149, 150, 162, 164, 207; and Migratory Bird Act, 198; and waterways, 133, 242

Tanagers, scarlet, 30

Tariff Act of 1913, 193-95

Tarpon, 4

Tawney Amendment, 134

Taxidermy, 20

Taylor, Zachary, 71

Taylor Grazing Act, 261

Teapot Dome, 232-39

Tennessee, 23

Tennessee River and Valley Authority (TVA), 240-51, 260

Tequesta, 7n

Terns, 48; least, 10

Texas, 23, 69

Theodore Roosevelt, the Naturalist (Cutright), 115

Thomas, Charles S., 243

Thoreau, Henry, 30, 34, 290

Three Sisters Wilderness Area, 298

Three-toed woodpeckers, 285

Thrushes, 23

Thurber, James, 101

Timber. *See* Forests and forestry

Timber Culture Act, 70

Timber and Stone Act, 70-71, 74, 91

Time magazine, 297

"Tolling," 209

Toronto, Canada, 248

Tourists, 302. *See also* specific places

Townsend, C. W., 207-8

Treasury Department, 213, 227

Trefethen, James B., 87

Troike (soldier), 83, 84

Truckee-Carson ditch, 112

Truman, Harry S., 280

Tueeulala Falls, 152

Tuolumne River, 152

Turkey vultures, 59

Turkeys, 41

TVA. *See* Tennessee River and Valley Authority

U. S. Forest Service; etc. *See* Forest Service; etc.

U. S. News and World Report, 297

Udall, Stewart L., 111, 161, 265

Union Pacific Railroad, 59-60

Vanderbilt, George W., 95

Van Dyck, T. S., 81

Vaux, Calvert, 75

Venezuela, 191

Vireos, 23

Vogt, William, 283

Volstead Act, 222-24

Vultures, turkey, 59

Wall Street Journal, 232

Wallace, Henry Agard, 220n, 261, 267

Wallace, Henry C., 220-21, 230, 231, 261

Walsh, Thomas J., 235-36, 237, 239

Walton, Izaak, League, 221

Wapiti. *See* Elk

War Department, 132-33

Warblers, 23; Bachman's, 42; Wilson's, 47

Washburn, Henry D., 76

Washington, George, 14

Washington, D.C., 115; cost of electricity in, 248; government in (See specific agencies, persons, etc); National Zoological Park, 103, 181; Rock Creek Park, 116

Washington, State of, 92, 129; Olympic National Park, 272, 297

Water, 264-65 (See also Dams; Irrigation; Floods; Watersheds; Waterways); pollution, 312ff.; power, 127, 144, 230, 240-51 (See also specific projects)

Waterfowl, 41, 198, 207-24, 270-72, 278 (See also specific species); Oakland, Calif., refuge, 114

Watersheds, 87, 93, 111, 253, 257-58

Waterways, 131-35, 241, 242. See also specific waterways

Weapons. See Guns

Weasels, 38

Weeks, John W., 196

Weeks, Wingate, 253

Weeks Law, 253

Weeks-McLean Bill, 196-99

Whalebone, 17

White, Lynn, 156

White Fang (London), 120

White herons. See Herons

White House, 173; conference on conservation, 133-34

White ibises, 58

Whistling swans, 20

Whittier, James Greenleaf, 41

Whooping cranes, 20

Wichita Mountains Wildlife Refuge, 184

Wickersham, George W., 149

Wilbur, Ray Lyman, 93

Wild Animals I have Known (Seton), 123

Wild Wings (Job). See Job, Herbert K.

Wilderness areas, 256, 292-94, 297-309

Wilderness Bill, 289, 300-9

Wilderness Society, 294

Wildlife, 177-224 (See also Game and hunting; specific species); and DDT, 312-15; refuges, 114-15, 135, 298, 303 (See also specific places)

Williams, Hezikiah, 201

Williams College, 37

Wilson, Alexander, 15-16

Wilson, James ("Tama Jim"), 99, 124

Wilson, Woodrow, 164, 207, 228-29, 231, 242; and Tariff Bill, 193, 194; and World War I, 173

Wilson Dam, 244, 246

Wilson's warblers, 47

Winchester Repeating Arms Company, 216

Winning of the West, The (Roosevelt), 103

Wirth, Conrad L., 263-65

Wisconsin, 23, 44. See also specific places

Wolves, 274, 276-77, 290

Woman's Magazine, 171

Wood ducks, 207

Woodcock, 43, 44, 192, 195, 199

Woodpeckers, 23; Arctic three-toed, 285; ivory-billed, 42-43; pileated, 47

Woods Hole, Mass., 37

World War I, 173-74, 198, 200ff., 231, 243-44

World War II, 264, 311, 317

Wrentits, 281

Wyoming, 76, 79, 129 (See also specific parks); coal land, 145; oil reserves, 231ff.

Yale University, 94

Yard, Robert Sterling, 171-72

Yellowlegs, 192; lesser, 24

Yellowstone National Park, 76-85, 109, 113-14, 128, 181; Boone and Crockett Club and, 103; coal mine in, 173; entrance fee for autos, 174; Theodore Roosevelt in, 117

Yellowstone River, 76-77

Yosemite Valley and Park, 117, 152-53ff., 166, 169, 172, 173

Zahniser, Howard C., 296, 300, 301, 306ff.

Zeidler, Othmar, 311

Zurich, 97

32985

S
930
G7

Graham, Frank,
1925-.

Man's dominion

DATE			
NOV 4 1983			
APR 5 90			

© THE BAKER & TAYLOR CO.